Praise for *Warbody*

"Together, Joshua Howe and Alexander Lemons have written a book with greater scope than any memoir and more emotional punch than any history. To grasp the true consequences of war for human bodies, human minds, and the living planet, read *Warbody*."

—**Michelle Nijhuis,** author of *Beloved Beasts*

"This is an environmental history of war and its consequences unlike any other. The captivating product of a dynamic partnership between a talented scholar and a veteran of war, this book offers an urgently needed history that exposes the hidden dangers of America's most deadly warfighting."

—**Bart Elmore,** professor of environmental history, Ohio State University

"By mixing memoir with historical anatomy, Joshua Howe and Alexander Lemons brilliantly show how the toxic residues of America's strategic interests have come to rest in the flesh and bones of American soldiers. *Warbody* is an astounding reconceptualization of the environmental history of warfare."

—**Paul S. Sutter,** University of Colorado Boulder

WARBODY

WARBODY

A Marine Sniper and the Hidden
Violence of Modern Warfare

JOSHUA HOWE AND
ALEXANDER LEMONS

W. W. NORTON & COMPANY
Independent Publishers Since 1923

For information about permission to reproduce selections from this book, write to
Permissions, W. W. Norton & Company, Inc., 500 Fifth Avenue, New York, NY 10110

For information about special discounts for bulk purchases, please contact
W. W. Norton Special Sales at specialsales@wwnorton.com or 800-233-4830

Manufacturing by Lake Book Manufacturing
Book design by Daniel Lagin
Production manager: Lauren Abbate

ISBN 978-1-324-06633-0

W. W. Norton & Company, Inc., 500 Fifth Avenue, New York, NY 10110
www.wwnorton.com

W. W. Norton & Company Ltd., 15 Carlisle Street, London W1D 3BS

1 2 3 4 5 6 7 8 9 0

CONTENTS

PART 1

START WITH A BULLET
The Hidden Dangers of Lead

PART 2

WHIRLWIND OF EXPOSURE
The Ecology of Modern Warfare

INTRODUCTION

Alexander Lemons knows a lot about bullets. He has fired tens of thousands of them. Alex is a former Marine Corps scout sniper—a "Hunter of Gunmen," or HOG, the name given to a graduate of the most elite field craft and marksmanship program in the US military—who served four tours in Iraq and Kuwait and then came home and became seriously and mysteriously ill. He is also my former student, my coauthor, and my friend. This is a book about Alex's service, his sickness, and his quest to get healthy. It is also a book about what it is like to be both sick and healthy in an increasingly toxic world.

The first thing I noticed about Alexander Lemons when I met him in the fall of 2012 was his San Francisco Giants hat. I am a Giants fan, which is one thing. More than that, a student unironically wearing a ball cap was something of a rarity at Reed College, where I work as an associate professor of history and environmental studies. The small Portland, Oregon, liberal arts school has no official sports teams, and it is proud of that distinction. It also has a student body that consists of 99 percent undergraduates, and Alex was the only master's student in the class. He was a military veteran to boot, a rare sight in this progressive academic habitat.

Alex made it four weeks in my American Diplomacy course, and then he disappeared. Ghosted. I learned from the director of graduate studies that he left for health reasons related to his military service. That was about all I knew.

In 2009, Alex had been honorably discharged from the United States Marine Corps. Alex served four tours during the Iraq War and then came home and suffered from mysterious ailments. He was diagnosed with post-traumatic stress disorder (PTSD) and treated with immersion therapy, antidepressants, anti-nightmare medication, and a combination of surgery and platelet-rich plasma injections for severe plantar fasciitis, but three years later, he still wasn't getting much better.

In fact, while he was still at Reed, he was falling apart. Alex was having gastrointestinal problems, his allergies were flaring, and he couldn't sleep. The sun was too bright even when he wore sunglasses, which he always did. Writing created brain fog and headaches, and reading was all but impossible. He'd always loved baseball, and at night he'd go to Portland's Lents Park to practice hitting off of a tee, but he slapped the rubber neck more often than he hit the ball. The doctors at the VA had no idea how to treat him, so Alex began searching for doctors who did, landing on a proponent of "integrative medicine" who on a hunch had Alex pee in a cup and send the sample off to a lab for heavy metals screening. The sample showed that Alex had mercury and lead poisoning. His new doctor advised him to drop out of grad school. He needed to minimize his responsibilities and conserve his finances because treatment was going to be intense and expensive. That's when I lost track of him.

Alex moved in with his parents back in Salt Lake City and began treatments, the beginning of an arduous medical journey that would consume his mental, emotional, and financial resources for all of his thirties. Doctor visits, sessions with the VA psychologists, chelation therapy, online forums, vitamin supplements, special diets, and untold hours of research had left him years behind in his transition to civilian life and only marginally healthy, with few answers. Even so, in 2017 he decided to re-enroll in graduate school. I finally saw Alex again in the spring of 2018, when he showed back up at Reed—wearing a camo Giants beanie—in one of my upper-level environmental history courses. He seemed focused and motivated, if still far from entirely healthy, determined to finish his master's degree in liberal studies. It wasn't long before we began to develop a friendship.

In the interim between Alex's mysterious departure and his sudden return, my own career matured. In 2014, I published a book about the political history of climate change, and by 2017, I had begun work on a project investigating the role of strategic minerals like manganese, tin, chromium, and cobalt in American foreign policymaking during the early Cold War period. At first, I was interested in the way the periodic table could serve as a tool for mapping American Cold War priorities abroad, a new twist on some old ideas about the roots of American diplomatic strategy. But it didn't take long before I realized that many of the metals I was looking at were not only strategically valuable, but also in some forms quite toxic. It turns out that the Cold War helped shape the geographical distribution of these toxic metals throughout the world during the twentieth century. Through these toxicants, the Cold War's material legacy is actually written onto people's bodies across the planet, American power built on the backs of everyday people at a molecular level.

It was amidst this research that I reconnected with Alex and started to learn about his health struggles and his heavy metals diagnosis. My academic research had led me to a five-volume Truman administration report from 1952 called *Resources for Freedom* that, among other things, listed the twenty-nine minerals most important for maintaining domestic prosperity and national security in a Cold War world. One day that spring, walking through a fluttering rain of cherry blossoms between our class in Vollum College Center and my office in Eliot Hall, Alex showed me a hair test he had submitted to a specialty lab in West Chicago to try to get a handle on his metals exposure. The lists of metals were almost the same.

Obviously, the Cold War didn't put heavy metals in Alex's body, or at least not in any kind of direct or recognizable way. But the association got both of us thinking more about Alex's health struggles and his toxic exposures in Iraq. Alex's doctor believed there was mercury and lead in Alex's blood and bones. How had it gotten there, and where had it come from? Did other Marines have heavy metals in their bodies? Why weren't they sick? Or were they? What else had Alex been exposed to? And what, if anything, should he do about it?

Alex's exposures seemed like a natural enough conversation given the topics of my course. That spring we took deep dives into pesticide exposures among California farm workers and radiation exposure in the Hanford Reach alongside classics like Rachel Carson's *Silent Spring*. In the fall, Alex signed up for my methods course, where I try to coach students through the nuts and bolts of the craft of historical research and writing in a long-form research paper. Alex wanted to write about Vietnam veterans. I convinced him to write about baseball instead. It was a good paper that charted the complex relationships between patriotism and professionalization in Major League Baseball during the 1960s and '70s, and it included good material on baseball and the Vietnam War. But from the beginning I could tell that Alex didn't really want to write about baseball, or even Vietnam. He was scratching at another itch, a more personal one, and I later learned that one reason he signed up for my methods class was that he wanted help. I was being vetted. If Alex was going to write the story of his service, his sickness, and his quest to get better, he was going to need a partner. I was the guy. For once, I was a step ahead of him. While Alex was writing about baseball, I was thinking more and more about Alex's exposures. In October of 2018, before Alex got the chance to ask me if I was interested, I proposed the project myself.

In November and December of 2018, Alex sat down with me for a series of marathon oral history interviews, every time bringing stacks and stacks of medical records, journal entries, books, research papers, and printouts of the online resources that had guided his quest to get better. The interviews were meant to be about the war, but ultimately they were as much about Alex's postwar experiences as a sick veteran as they were about his time as a Marine. Each week, I would prop up two cameras, a four-track recorder, and a backup recorder on tripods and precarious stacks of books in my tiny office in Eliot, all trained on the hard wooden chair where Alex would sit, always in leather coat and camo beanie. Usually, I would hand Alex a piece of paper from his own personal medical archive—a set of records he "borrowed" and copied from the Marine Corps—and ask a question, and then sit back and monitor the recording as Alex's story flowed out into the room until the batteries in the recorders ran out.

Eventually, the process of unpacking those two stories—of Alex's exposures and of his decade-long battle with mysterious illness—became part of the process of recovery itself. At first, the process was like hydraulic mining. During the interviews, we began making lists of potential toxic exposures, and Alex would use those lists like a set of screens, passing a decade and a half of lived experience through each one to see what came out of the slurry. The writing came in cascading, comma-less torrents as Alex lifted the headgates on each set of stored memories. Then we would turn to the screens and try to figure out what, if anything, we had. Initially, most of Alex's stories and memories revolved around other people. Fellow Marines, family members, doctors, other sick people. The stories were atmospheric and allusive. Eventually, though, Alex began to write in earnest about himself, and the story of his service, his sickness, and his health began to take shape, not just for me, but also for him.

As I chased Alex through his evolving memories, I tried to use my own research to put together a plausible explanation for how he got sick and what his sickness might mean for how we treat other veterans with similar, often mysterious, ailments. Some of that work looked a lot like what I do as a historian, finding other primary sources to corroborate Alex's memories and his Post-Deployment Health Assessment forms (PDHAs), and putting them in a larger context. But I also spent a lot of time working synthetically, trying to bring together a variety of research by other scholars from a wide array of disciplines on questions related to Alex's story in a way that makes some sense of Alex's experiences in Iraq and afterward. The vast majority of these studies have been peer-reviewed and published in journals, or incorporated into reports published by the National Academy of Medicine or the Department of Defense.

If I were a medical research scientist, my approach to Alex's body would be a methodological disaster. Most medicine relies on a hierarchy of research, privileging large datasets, rigorous meta-analyses, systematic reviews, and randomized controlled trials. Not so here. My sample size is one: Alexander Lemons. There are no controls. His testimonial—that is, his memoir of his service, his sickness, and his quest to get better—not only counts as important evidence; despite my occasional questions about its reliability, it has structured much of my research from start to finish. I have synthesized plenty of rigorous statistical research here, but I have done no statistical analysis of my own. I don't even have a lab. The way I put information together from other scholars' research leaves my conclusions mired in uncertainty.

Uncertainty is not the same as ignorance, however. It certainly doesn't mean that any answer is as good as any other. And there is, in fact, a method.

I call the approach "historical anatomy." Historical anatomy is a way of making sense of an individual body—Alex's body—in the context of a unique collection of events and processes that shape modern bodies more generally. It is like the medical history you might find in a doctor's office if that medical history asked not just about, say, whether you smoked, but about the constellation of forces that would lead a person like you to smoke the kinds of tobacco you smoke, and what kinds of soils and pesticides and production chemicals that particular tobacco brings with it to your cigarettes. It is a medical history on steroids. Like any other anatomist, I am concerned with Alex's body and its structures. As a historical anatomist, I am interested in thinking about Alex's body and its structures in the particular times and places—Iraq in the early 2000s, for example—that have helped to shape them.

The term "historical anatomy" is mine, but the impulse to practice historical anatomy is not, especially among my colleagues in environmental history. Many of Alex's exposures have been discrete—lead from bullets and primers, mercury from tainted fish in the Tigris River and burning trash on forward operating bases (FOBs) all over Iraq, and a host of direct, repeated exposures to pesticides and other chemicals associated with military life. But those discrete exposures are difficult to distinguish through a simple hair sample or blood test from the assemblages of other potential exposures in both his civilian and military past. Bullets are an entry point, but they constitute only one chapter in a much longer, messier story. As Michelle Murphy suggests in her work on illnesses among modern office workers, historical anatomy is not an exact science.[1] It's not really a science at all. Rather, in the case of this project, it is a way of combining science, history, and memoir to make plausible sense out of Alexander Lemons's experience, in the process shedding light on the modern military experience more generally.

Alex and I worked on every part of this book together, talking, writing, editing, and revising back and forth for nearly five years. Even so, we tell Alex's story here as two distinct narrators, our approaches reflecting each of our expertise and experiences. Alex narrates his part of the story as a memoir, a mixture of wartime vignettes and personal reflections that paints an intimate and sometimes graphic portrait of his experiences of the war in Iraq and its aftermath in his brain, mind, and body. As Alex's stories unfold, I try to make sense of Alex's personal experiences, launching deep dives into substances like lead, mercury, pesticides, and particulate matter that made Alex and other Marines sick. Together, we use Alex's story to rethink the violence we associate with war, as well as the way we help our veterans recover from that violence in the months and years after war's end.

In Part 1, we deconstruct a bullet and focus on the lead it contains and Alex's exposures to it as a way of rethinking war's violence to include long-term chemical exposures, a variation on what scholar Rob Nixon calls "slow violence." For Nixon, slow violence describes "violence that occurs gradually and out of sight; a delayed destruction often dispersed across time and space."[2] It is typically associated with poverty and marginalization, but as we explore in following the toxic pathways of bullets, it is also helpful and important for understanding war's less visible impacts on both Marine and civilian bodies. In Part 2, we demonstrate how the reductionist, compartmentalized thinking that causes us to ignore that slow violence also blinds us to the relationships between the toxic things Alex and his fellow Marines were exposed to in Iraq and the long-term human relationships that underpin a functional civil society. American military planners revealed a startling myopia on both of these fronts, and the result was a war that can be described in multiple ways as toxic. In Part 3, we consider two non-chemical types of exposures common among Iraq War veterans, PTSD and traumatic brain injury (TBI), that overlap with, mimic, and exacerbate chemical exposures. These chapters present an argument for holistic thinking about both the violence of war and the health conditions that arise from it, advocating a "both/and" approach to veterans' health that takes combined exposures and traumas seriously. Finally, in Part 4 we pick up the same kind of myopic reductionism in the way we treat veterans and other citizens with difficult-to-diagnose illnesses, suggesting how mainstream medicine often both fails to accommodate and even alienates patients like Alex— patients who then often have to navigate a shadow system of alternative medicine and healers with the compromised faculties that come with exposure to toxic chemicals.

Ultimately, Alex and I argue that America's collective understanding of war is wrongheaded on both ends. On the front end, rather than focusing solely on the acute violence of bullets and bombs, we should also expand our understanding of war's violence to include the slow violence of toxic exposures and lasting trauma. On the back end, that same acknowledgment of the hidden violence of warfare should also inform our approach to veterans and civilians struggling to lead healthy, meaningful lives in the aftermath of war.

Joshua Howe

PART 1

START WITH A BULLET

The Hidden Dangers of Lead

"WHAT THE FUCK, RECRUIT?"

I began my Marine life in the summer of 2002 on the yellow thermoplastic footprints of Marine Corps Recruit Depot (MCRD), San Diego, just like any other boot ass motherfucker. Recruits painted boot outlines on the pavement beginning in the 1960s. In pursuit of more training, precious minutes of it, the Marine Corps glued polymer tracks to the deck at the end of the last century to outlast repainting. The footprints serve a double duty, the kind of two-in-one mindset Marines love. Standing on them teleports a recruit to a new world, leaving the old life behind forever. They correct the body and put it in a place it will stand for hundreds of hours on active duty and decades later in civilian life.

I enlisted because I grew up in a family of caretakers. No stinging patriotism. No rage for payback. Emotionally, the death of my homesteader grandmother less than a year before ranked higher than the deaths of the 9/11 victims. Three Mormon farmwomen raised me, and I learned early that life was nothing but endless sacrifice to the land, our families, and future generations. We gave to everyone else because we didn't know we were allowed to give to ourselves. We threw our shoulders under handcart wheels and pushed. I had little faith in my country's response to the attacks and expected that we would lash out blindly and dumbly, both at home and abroad. But sitting by and letting these failures be somebody else's problem seemed wrong to me, like hiding out when there was work to be done.

After boot camp I planned to pour through infantry school to become a grunt. I caught shit for that from day one.

""Recruuuitttt Lemons!" a voice shrieked from our squad bay office. That was my senior drill instructor, or DI, Staff Sergeant Vizcaíno. Years of yelling had permanently fried his vocal cords.

"Recruit Lemons!" all sixty recruits of Platoon 3097 called in unison.

This recruit is fucked. I wanted to remain anonymous. At least they pronounced my name right. Like the fruit. I pounded on the office hatch three times and another DI, Sergeant Martinez, shouted, "Get in my duty hut, right now, shithead." His voice always sounded like Joe Buck shouting a Vicente Fernández record.

I swung the door open and planted myself in front of a desk on a strip of tape in my still-inept drill steps. Martinez stood near the desk and Vizcaíno sat behind it.

Martinez spoke first. "Do you have a degree, Lemons?"

Discovered. "Yes, sir!"

Dumbfounded silence. Vizcaíno scratched the back of his shaved head and looked at my Service Record Book. He frogged, "What the fuck, recruit?" My peers had the same question. Recruits with college degrees went the officer route. But a degree didn't entitle me to anything. I could hear the farmwomen in my ear.

"Sir, this recruit was taught to start at the bottom and work their way up, sir."

A typical recruit body begins as a young, American body. It's a recruit at this stage, not a Marine. A macroinvertebrate, fungus, and nasty civilian. "It" carries eighteen years of bad food, an uncanny knowledge of pop culture, an eighth-grade reading level, a sense of progress rooted in technology, a mountain of teenage hormones, and a drive to prove the self against a challenge most will never face. The recruit body undergoes extensive medical screenings. It has drank underage and smoked weed. It has attended the churches of grownups and worked awful service jobs or hoed beet fields. Maybe it's been laid. Maybe it's picked up an STD. More than 75 percent of the time, it is a white body like mine. If not white, it is likely Latino (15–20 percent), and if not Latino, then black (10–12 percent), then Asian (2–3 percent), then American Indian (~1 percent), then Pacific Islander (~1 percent), and sometimes "unknown" (3–10 percent). In San Diego, it always identified as male until 2021, though at Parris Island, women also trained to become Marines.[1]

The DIs don't care. All recruits are green. No matter its outward appearance, the recruit will put this body at risk for a sleazy grand per month and the hope of a better future through a life of discipline and coveted veteran's benefits. It's rarely a good trade.

MCRD San Diego is the first landscape the recruit body encounters. That landscape has a peculiar environmental history. We train right on top of San Diego International Airport. Locals once called the area Dutch Flats, and for as long as we know—likely centuries—it lapped up the floods from San Diego Bay. That changed on March 2, 1919, when engineers flattened and smoothed the area with hydraulic fill. Recruits began indoctrination at the site in 1923. Other bases have experienced a cyclone of contamination events, but at MCRD San Diego these were confined primarily to the transportation pool. On the Depot, recruits and Marines dumped excess oil, paint, and pesticides, from DDT to 2,4-dichlorophenoxyacetic acid (2,4-D), into dumpsters headed for the desert or washed them into the bay through the late 1970s.[2] The Navy and the Environmental Protection Agency cleaned up the contaminated soil, underground petroleum tanks, and landfill junk by 1997.[3]

Nearly every inch of the 388 acres of Depot contains pavement or buildings. There are no alligators or birds. If insects lived in San Diego, I never saw them. The camp persists in a cauldron of city, airport, and shipping. My DIs told us stories about barely dressed sunbathers catching rays just minutes away at the beach. You could look over the fence and into the windows of taxiing planes where faces ignored or pitied you during three-mile runs. The air constantly smelled of kerosene and burnt rubber. We had to compete with traffic and jet engines. We learned to yell louder.

Once in boot camp, the recruit acquires a specific physiology that grows over the coming years. It experiences unknown stressors and first-time exposures. It prepares for war by exercising, getting gassed, shooting, enduring necessary mental pressure, and going without sleep. Then the recruit graduates, no longer an "It," and leaves the Depot to specialize in a trade. The newly minted computer programmer, water treatment specialist, or mortarman deals with loving comrades and cruel management. We live on spartan bases and ships all over the world. A Marine's body soaks up discarded trash and toxic molds in leaky buildings. We guzzle 24 packs of bad beer the night before a ten-mile hike and grow unique flavors of athlete's foot. We live in crashed landscapes and wear test dummy equipment. Bugs bite us and chemical formulations shower us over the course of an enlistment.

In my case, I stayed in California and checked into First Battalion, Fourth Marines, 1/4, or "one-four," as a rifleman in December 2002 and loaded onto a ship headed for the invasion of Iraq. I deployed to Iraq with my battalion again in 2004 as a scout sniper. Another deployment as the senior sniper, known as the "chief scout," at 1/4 had me running training exercises as we floated the Pacific and then stood as the operational reserve in Kuwait during 2006 while Iraq tore itself apart in civil war. My final pump came during the surge in the late spring of 2007. The yearlong orders listed my billet as "Driver" for the Commanding General of Multi-National Force-Iraq. I wasn't a driver at all. As part of the brain trust under David Petraeus, I worked in the field with two other Marines as advisors to a Polish Army division, several Iraqi Army battalions, and spent time convincing tribal leaders to turn on insurgents.

The recruit body is a site of germ warfare, too. Boot camp helps it build a safety net. It loses its hair not only to eliminate its identity and save time, but also to decrease its susceptibility to lice and other pathogens. An immune system strengthens with shared spit and gut microbes from the Mariana Islands to the Navajo Nation. It has its dental cavities filled with mercury-based amalgams, and has its blood drawn and tested for antibodies. It gets poked with needles, vaccinations for varicella, influenza, MMR, meningococcus, hepatitis A and B, polio, tuberculosis, and yellow fever. It is not, however, routinely tested for lead, mercury, cadmium, thallium, herbicides, or any number of other things that might be useful as a baseline down the road.

Later, a jarhead (Marine) gets vaccinations against anthrax and a million other theater-specific threats. We ingest drugs to protect against malaria and chemical weapons, and those drugs mix with pesticides meant to keep us safe from even more pathogens and jet fuel meant to help keep us safe from stagnating waste. Our bodies absorb fire retardants and lead paint from the decks of ships, and inhale lead aerosols from weapons and aerosolized metals from explosions and partially combusted bits of everything you can imagine from burning trash and all the dust you could possibly fill your nose and mouth and eyes and lungs with.

If the Marine Corps were a civilian job, you would immediately quit and report conditions to your state department of environmental quality.

Recruits also carry their own pollutants to the Depot, the baggage of industrialized civilization. Pesticides from low-cost foods and fertilized lawns, lead from old pipes and old paint in postwar homes or from fuel additives, other heavy metals like mercury in the blood or radioactive isotopes in soft tissues from power plants. Fresh off the farm, from the hood, reservation-raised, or deep in suburbia, every recruit transports bits of those places into their new life. Poverty also leaves chemical markers, and the enlisted ranks fill up with the children of working people and the disappearing middle class. More lead in the water and other heavy metals mix with bad food and poisons from train derailments. In the chemical game of chance that is a Marine enlistment, most recruits come with loaded dice.

And yet, not all of us get sick. When we do, the pieces of home we carry with us to MCRD combine with a whole host of genetic predispositions, childhood abuse or sexual assault, lifestyle choices, further exposures, and contingent events that make it all but impossible to say why.

Why did I get sick for a decade after my tours of duty? Maybe I'm just lucky.

2

THE VIOLENCE OF EXPOSURE

L et's begin with a bullet. You have seen movies; you pretty much know what a bullet can do. Maybe you are a hunter and have seen its impact up close, a hole in an elk's lung or a grouse's broken neck. A heavy projectile traveling at speed, the lead tears skin, rips apart muscle, explodes soft tissue, and breaks bones. The living target bleeds. Feels pain. Dies. This is violence. Dramatic violence. Fast violence. We think of this as the violence of war. And it is. It is a violence that a sniper visits upon the human enemy, body and weapon working seamlessly together as a coordinated precision instrument to do the job of causing death at a distance. It is the same kind of violence Alexander Lemons spent hours, days, weeks, and months working to avoid, for himself and for the Marines under his command.

If you are on the wrong end of one, this is really all you need to know about the violence of bullets. When the bullet strikes home, the moment marks a major inflection point in a Marine's life. You are one thing before, and another thing after.

But put a bullet back in its cartridge, take the cartridge out of the gun, and then take that cartridge apart, and you will see that a bullet can contain another kind of violence. This violence does not have a specific, identifiable inflection point, a discernable moment when it changes a grunt's or a civilian's life. It is a violence of exposure. A violence of practice. The violence of firing ten thousand bullets, visited not on the target but on the shooter, and not via the acute trauma so often associated with war, but rather by the long-term erosion of the body's core functions by the constant incorporation of toxic molecules into the shooter's body.

Bullets are not the only things that have inflicted violence on Alex's body. In fact, in the grand scheme of things, they may not even be among the most important of Alex's toxic exposures as a US Marine. But if we are looking for an entry point into Alex's military exposures, it seems appropriate to begin with a sniper's tool.

If you're like me, when you hear "bullet," you think about a few things at the same time. You probably think about a projectile—the thing that does the damage—but you also probably think about a pointed metal contraption, wrapped in brass, that might fit in a bandolier. Technically, the first thing is right—the projectile that comes out of a gun and kills or maims things is the bullet. The contraption as a whole, which us lay people often call a "bullet," is more accurately called a cartridge, or a round. A round consists of the bullet, the casing, the rim, and the assortment of primers, powders, and propellants inside the casing that make the bullet go.

For people in Alex's world, this explanation is elementary, a bit like explaining the component parts of an ice cream cone, an object so familiar in its entirety that you forget that the cone is actually only a part of the whole. But for many, a bullet is the least familiar object in the world, a strange and terrifying symbol of a threatening part of our culture that has normalized not only bullets, but also guns and acute violence of all kinds.

The word "bullet" comes from the French *boulet*, and early in the development of gunpowder projectiles, a "little ball" of just about anything heavy would do. Early modern European cannons shot stones, iron (sometimes iron balls heated to as hot as 800 degrees that doubled as incendiary devices), lead, chains, and just about anything else soldiers could jam into a barrel. (When times were truly desperate, you could always fire the silverware.) As gunsmiths began to experiment with more sophisticated bullet shapes and more accurate and agile small arms in the nineteenth century, lead emerged as the material of choice.

Lead is dense, malleable, easy to mine, common, and relatively cheap. It also tends to resist corrosion. And because it's heavy, it flies straight. Since it was first smelted almost nine thousand years ago in what is now Turkey, the substance has been a sort of jack-of-all-trades for the world's metallurgists, showing up in everything from currency to writing implements in the ancient world. More recently, lead has found employments as an anti-knock agent in gasoline, a base for paint, and a component in lead-acid batteries, which today account for more than 85 percent of US lead consumption.[1] It has also persisted in bullets, the standard substance for delivering quick death at a distance.

Of course, lead's big liability is that it is toxic. Really toxic. Long before it became the standard for bullets, lead was identified as a poison that caused a neurological condition called *plumbism*. Marked Pb on the periodic table for the suggestive Latin *plumbum*, lead was the primary material for pipes in the Roman world, a use that persisted until the mid-twentieth century. Rome's plumbing system yielded lead levels more than a hundred times higher than those in surrounding spring water. Perhaps more troublingly, wealthy Romans were also known to boil fruit and make wine in lead vessels, sweetening their libations with a form of salt called lead acetate that may have contributed to widespread gout and other ailments in the Roman Empire. (Europeans continued the practice of sweetening wine with lead acetate into the eighteenth century.) As early as the second century BCE, Greek scholars described lead-poisoned subjects suffering from paralysis and other ailments. The Roman physician Dioscorides, interested in the psychological effects of lead poisoning, noted astutely the way that lead could make the "mind give way." Some historians and classicists go so far as to point to lead as a major cause of the fall of the Roman Empire.[2]

We now know that lead is a neurotoxicant that can attack nearly every major system of the human body, most severely and alarmingly among them the central nervous system. By the late nineteenth century,

European and American doctors were already encouraging regulations on lead, particularly in household consumer goods. And indeed, for most of its major applications (except batteries), lead has been supplanted by safer, more effective materials in the last fifty years. Most European countries banned interior lead paint as early as the 1930s, for example, and even the United States—which has been laboriously slow to regulate lead—began a comprehensive effort to reduce the lead in America's air and homes in the 1970s, culminating in a full ban on lead in gasoline in the Clean Air Act of 1990.

For bullets, however, lead still rules. And it rules in a big way. According to the United States Geological Survey, in 2014 alone the United States used more than 85,000 metric tons of lead in military and civilian ammunition.[3] A metric ton weighs a thousand kilograms, or about 2,200 pounds—a little bit more than the original Type 1 Volkswagen Beetle. Imagine 85,000 Volkswagens made of lead. That is how much lead Americans put into bullets and other ammunitions in a single year.

Since September 11, 2001, Americans have put roughly enough *plumbum* in munitions to rebuild both of the World Trade Center's towers entirely out of lead.

IN 2012, RIGHT AROUND THE TIME I FIRST MET HIM, ALEX SENT TWO vials of urine to a firm in North Carolina. The samples were the first in a series of "challenge tests" meant to measure the quantity of heavy metals relative to a substance called creatinine in Alex's urine before and after the administration of a chelating agent called 2,3-dimercapto-1-propanesul fonic acid (DMPS). A chelating agent is a chemical compound that binds with certain metal ions, making those ions unavailable to other charged compounds that occur naturally in the body. Once bound to a chelator, metals become water soluble, enabling you to pee them out. If you take a chelating agent and then you pee lead, the idea goes, you can reasonably assume that you have some lead hiding out somewhere in your body.

Alex and I now know that post-chelation challenge tests are, to paraphrase the American College of Medical Toxicology on the subject, mostly crap.[4] But for Alex, they represented an inexpensive starting point for a sick veteran concerned about his body's burden of lead, and he didn't have a lot of other options. Perhaps not surprisingly, in 2012, the piss that Alex had sent in tested positive.

Regardless of the method you use, there are a few problems in testing for lead exposure. One of them is that a vanishingly small amount of the stuff can cause serious problems. The most common way to test for lead exposure, measuring a person's blood lead level, underscores the point.[5] Blood lead levels (BLLs) are typically measured in micrograms per deciliter, abbreviated μg/dL. One microgram, or 1 μg—the same unit typically used to measure doses of LSD (often 100 μg)—is about one-millionth of a gram. For reference, a dollar bill has a mass of about a million μg.

Meanwhile, a deciliter of liquid comes out to just less than 3.5 ounces—enough, in booze, to mix a pretty stiff drink. As a measure of just how toxic lead can be, the Occupational Safety and Health Administration (OSHA) uses 50 μg/dL as the red-flag BLL for industrial workers—a standard that the Centers for Disease Control and Prevention (CDC) and the National Institute for Occupational Safety and Health (NIOSH) and many scientists consider lenient and outdated. For its part, the CDC uses 5 μg/dL—that is, five millionths of a gram of lead per three and a half ounces of whole blood—as the reference level for public health actions to prevent lead poisoning. That's five one-millionths of a dollar bill dissolved in a snifter of brandy. Below that, however, they still allow for the possibility of real problems from lead.

Absorbed in human flesh, the quantity of lead the United States puts into munitions every year would be enough to poison every person who has ever lived on planet Earth with double the OSHA-allowable BLL. And there would be plenty left over for the same level of exposure in many generations down the road.[6]

Testing lead in whole blood is a good way to measure short-term lead exposure, and from a public health standpoint, BLL is the best way to tell you if you have a problem right now. It's also typically a good indicator that you have recently been exposed to high doses of lead—probably in air, water, or food, and maybe because you have just spent a bunch of time somewhere like a shooting range where there is a lot of lead from bullets floating around.

But the half-life of lead in your blood is only about two weeks, that is, every two weeks after an exposure incident, your BLL should go down by about half. Some of the lead in your blood "clears," or comes out through your kidneys in the form of urine, as would all kinds of other natural and artificial toxins. But not all of it. Some of it also gets stored in the body's soft tissues, where it can do damage to cells and prevent or alter the production of important enzymes. The half-life of lead in soft tissues is significantly longer, on the order of ninety days. Meanwhile, some of that lead stays with you even longer, residing semipermanently in bone. Lead thus has the maddening capacity to operate both as a short-term toxicant, delivered straight to the nervous system by the blood in the days and weeks after exposure, and as a cumulative toxic burden, residing in your bones, with the potential to be released back into your blood down the road.

Measuring truly long-term accumulations of lead requires doctors to focus not on blood lead levels, but rather on *bone* lead levels. If you're a six-year-old, they can do this pretty easily. Doctors concerned about populations of children exposed to lead take samples of the bone material inside of discarded baby teeth, and from that they can get a direct measurement of lead in those children's bones.[7]

In adults, however, similarly direct measurements would require an invasive and expensive bone biopsy (or some harsh dental work). To measure bones in most of the population, scientists use X-rays to dislodge electrons from lead atoms, and then measure those electrons to determine the relative quantity of lead in bones. The technique is called X-ray fluorescence, or XRF, and the measurements are referred to as K-line or K-shell measurements and L-line or L-shell measurements, depending on which type of electron the XRF targets.[8]

But that's getting into the weeds. The short version is that for adults, bone lead levels provide the best measurement of a person's cumulative exposure to lead. And if you have a lot of lead in your bones, you have probably at some point had a lot of lead in your blood, which means you have also probably had lead in your brain and other important organs. And maybe still do. For women—and particularly pregnant women—the lead in your bones does more than tell you about your exposure history. It also has a pretty good chance of making it back into your bloodstream. Expecting mothers with high bone lead levels can expect to endure a second blood lead surge from their own bodies while they pass some of that blood-borne lead on to the fetus. (Doctors use placental lead measurements to figure out maternal and prenatal lead exposures in vulnerable populations.) For men, the extent of the return of lead from bone to blood is less clear . . . unless, of course, you damage a bone, in which case the lead stored in your bones is fair game. You don't want to break a leg if you work at a lead smelter. Or a firing range.

IF YOU WANT TO ACTUALLY TRACE THE LEAD FROM A BULLET INTO A body, you can start with the skin. According to OSHA, you can't actually absorb standard lead through the skin itself, so it's probably not a big deal to simply pick up a bullet, even with bare hands.[9] But let's think about what happens when you pick up lots of bullets. Marine Corps snipers like Alex handle literally thousands of rounds over the years, without gloves. They load and unload rounds in weapons and magazines over and over again, every day of their training and every day of their deployment. They pull lead bullet fragments out of targets and backstops at firing ranges. They collect spent casing containing lead residues from the bullets they once contained. On their own time at home, most of them pack their own rounds, working in garages or basements or living rooms to physically assemble lead and brass and primer and powder into hundreds of perfect rounds. Your skin provides a pretty good barrier against most kinds of lead, but if you touch bullets all day and then touch your eyes, nose, or mouth, suddenly you introduce particles of lead to porous tissue that makes a much poorer barrier between the inside of your body and the outside world.

Bullets are mostly solid lead, which, in the grand scheme of things, is actually not that easy to absorb, even if you handle bullets all day long. But the solid lead in a bullet—especially as you follow it through its use—is almost always accompanied by another form of lead: lead dust. Every time a bullet leaves the barrel of a gun, small pieces of metal enter the air, settling over surfaces, equipment, hair, and skin. Theoretically, Marines would wear gloves every time they handle ammunition or weapons. They would wash their hands after every session at the firing range and every batch of rounds they pack. They would lay sheets over shooting areas for practicing kneeling and prone shots near the ground, where lead dust collects. And they would wash their hands before meals.

In reality, however, Marines don't often take these precautions. As a result, lead dust from bullets finds its way into bodies. It enters mouths directly when Marines bite their nails or lick their fingers, and it finds its way into digestive systems via contaminated food, water, containers, and cigarettes.

It also comes back with them to their barracks in what some researchers refer to as "take-home lead."

In 1991, NIOSH took a tour of the facilities and dormitories at the FBI Academy training center in Quantico, Virginia. "Fuzz Central," as Alex calls it. The FBI training center at Quantico actually sits within a massive Marine Corps training facility—a civilian training center within a military training center. Agents take basic field training courses at Quantico, but the agency also holds executive leadership sessions there, and it uses its facilities—which are, again, *inside* a Marine Corps facility—to train other law enforcement agents. There is an FBI driving school there. And, of course, there is a shooting range.

The outdoor shooting ranges at Quantico highlighted some growing concerns about lead at ranges more generally that echoed similar studies in the late 1980s and early 1990s. At law enforcement firing ranges and private gun clubs around the country at that time, airborne lead was becoming a potential occupational hazard, in part because of increased firearms training and practice associated with increasing violence from Ronald Reagan's "War on Drugs." Though few subjects hit the OSHA limit of 50 µg/dL, shooting instructors, trainees, range employees, and recreational shooters showed a consistent pattern of increased BLLs associated with shooting, first at indoor ranges, and then at outdoor ranges.

NIOSH didn't believe the ranges were the whole story, however, and at Quantico, administrators wanted to get a fuller picture of lead exposures across the FBI training program. In addition to measuring lead in the air and soil at indoor and outdoor firing ranges, NIOSH analyzed the dust in the carpets of dorm rooms used by FBI firearms-training students and compared them to the rooms used by visiting law enforcement officials not using the firearms site. The carpets of the FBI trainees contained three and a half times the lead found in the non-trainee rooms.[10] Lead dust on clothes and in trainees' hair collected and accumulated because trainees lived together in common housing during firearms training. Students at the FBI's training academy—where firearms training constitutes one of many student activities—were living in lead dust.

And that is the FBI range at Quantico, where agents were also learning how to drive dangerously and develop leadership skills and do trust falls. Imagine what a military base looks like. Or a barracks at a Marine Corps Scout Sniper School, where shooting is king.

3

"CONSISTENCY IS ACCURACY"

S nipers have a phrase that defines their preparation for and execution of combat: "Consistency is accuracy." The meditation will calm the nervous system in any clime or place, lock the shooter into an unemotional state, and deliver the scientific calculus needed to murder the target.

All great shooting begins and ends with observation. We notice things no one else does, and the information gathered by our senses converts into gold dust. In sniper platoons, we play observation games to retrain the senses. One involves an instructor hiding ten military items—plastic G.I. Joes, dog tags, brass casings—in a wall of vegetation or along the sides of a green shipping container or on a sand dune. Start the timer, and Marines with binoculars and spotting scopes twenty-five yards away have thirty minutes to find and draw every item, along with the entire backdrop in which they are hidden.

Another game is KIM: Keep In Memory. An instructor claps, "Time starts now," and you gather around a group of ten items. A boot band, Staff Sergeant Schmuckatelli's identification, a lance corporal chevron, a 9mm brass casing, and so on. "Time's up." You go away and carry on. Hours later a voice commands, "Time starts now." You must draw and write down all ten items from memory: size, shape, color, condition, and what you think it is. If you aren't entirely sure, then you must annotate "ATB": appears to be.

The longest observation game is "the sketch." I would run Marines to decrepit buildings or up a hill near Camp Horno, at Camp Pendleton in Southern California where we were stationed, and then set out the perimeters of an area I wanted drawn in under an hour. You must measure distances correctly—after all, this could become your range card. A range card is a hand-drawn map of important buildings, roads, or terrain features along with distances staked out in a half-circle measured in hundred-yard increments. Distances on the card let you adjust the elevation of your sniper rifle or set up for artillery strikes. The sketches are more elaborate than a simple range card. You add in more details on weather and terrain. You analyze potential entryways and ambush sites. You identify where you might land a medevac helicopter. When I graded sketches, I looked for more than what a Marine drew. What did they see and smell, taste, hear, and touch? What didn't they see and smell, taste, hear, or touch? One lesson bestowed in all observation games is that information, the kind most untrained minds blankly miss, is worth more than a kill. Computers, drones, and satellites can't perform the artwork found in human reconnaissance. A tiny, seemingly useless observation could change an operation in ways no one would predict.

THE BEST EXAMPLE I CAN SHARE HAPPENED WITH MY BATTALION, 1/4, ON AUGUST 20, 2004, during one of the hottest days I remember living through in Iraq.

Charlie Company planned an assault near the Grand Mosque in Kufa, east of Najaf. Charlie was one of the four companies in our battalion; each company was composed of 175 grunts of different specialties. Opposing us was the Jaysh al-Mahdi Army, a Shia militia created by the cleric and politician Muqtada al-Sadr, which moved several hundred troops from Baghdad into a technical college near the mosque. They could quickly reinforce the fighters we had battled for days in one of the world's oldest and largest cemeteries. The satellite imagery and footage from our hand-thrown aerial vehicle, the Raven, didn't offer answers on how to reach them, and our intelligence sources provided nothing. My chief scout, Randy Revert, and I volunteered to get eyes on in a recon by vehicle with four Humvees from the anti-armor team in Weapons Company.

We had not left early enough to avoid the heat, and it was over 100 degrees when I piled into the front seat of the lead truck, Chaos 1. Revert snuggled into Chaos 2. The armored doors only covered half our bodies, and the truck had no air-conditioning. The four vehicles started up, dragged themselves out of the compound and onto Route Miami heading south to the farms outside Najaf. We crept along a dirt road separating suburbs from farms, and then we cranked a turn pointing north and drove towards the Kufa Mosque. It kept getting hotter and I avoided touching any of the metal in the truck. The gold plating from the 1,300-year-old structure flashed back at us in the morning light. We crawled another mile through the city before we hit an open field in full view of the towers and domes on our right.

We stopped.

I saw three men through our windshield working over a table behind the open trunk of an orange-and-white paneled sedan. They threw everything in the trunk and slammed it shut before tearing away on balding tires. Not an IED crew, I told myself. A couple of dads working on some awful home improvement project. School children darted into the alleyways on my left.

"This is it," the driver said, "we're not going any closer."

Rounds slammed into our doors and our machine gunner in the turret cussed. Fast. Accurate. I knew those were 7.62×54mm rounds from Mahdi snipers. They were just as good as the guys in my platoon. Calls to identify the direction of fire came over the net. I swung the metal door open and used it for what cover it could offer. The .50cal machine gun spat above me. Then the Mahdi started plunking our trucks with AK-47s and light machine guns. We couldn't fire back into the mosque.

Our recon mission quickly became a high-stress memorization game. We kept taking single shots from the high walls of the mosque across the field to the east. My rifle never left the inside of the truck. I plugged my binoculars into my eyes for a closer look at the field and the buildings surrounding it. I looked and memorized. Revert did the same, his truck herringboned behind ours. Gunny Collins, the platoon sergeant for the patrol, had a digital camera somewhere near the back and we let him snap away.

Three 120mm mortars crunched into the earth around our trucks. The dust splashed thirty feet from us, and I felt the ground shake standing behind the door. The next set of rounds would probably dunk us. That gave us anywhere from thirty seconds to a minute. If they were slow.

The white walls of the mosque looked thick and strong over the walls of the houses nearby. The field wasn't like anything I saw on maps or imagery. It wasn't flat. It sat high on our side and sloped down towards the mosque with ruts, holes, and thick brush. Some tentative plans expected Charlie Marines to dismount in the field to secure the mosque before moving into the tighter streets around the tech college. Only one dirt road crisscrossed the field to the gate of the mosque. Parts of the tech college stood another five to eight blocks east by the map and across the river, but I couldn't see it from where we stood.

My binos moved from east to north. An Iraqi police station guarded the asphalt road leading past the mosque. Alpha Company had hit it the morning before, where the gunfight ended in flames eating the building. Was anyone still in there? Past the smoke-streaked walls of the station and other apartment buildings, I ran into a different blue dome with two towers standing alongside it. I learned years later that this was the burial tomb of Maytham al-Tammar, an enslaved date seller freed by Ali Hussain in the seventh century who later became an Islamic scholar. The number of students and shoppers crossing the pavement and running errands near the tomb made it hard to believe Najaf was being fought over by two armies.

Boooom. A small roadside bomb erupted behind me. I ignored it.

At the intersection directly in front of us, I stopped scanning. A white box sat underneath a tree and backed up against a house. Whatever I was looking at didn't look like a truck filled with shovels and an excavator. Four barrels stacked neatly together pointed away from us in the pickup bed. It appeared to be a ZPU-4 anti-aircraft gun. It let the gunner fire 14.5mm rounds down any approach. No one sat in the turret seat or behind the wheel of the truck. Two lazy guards protected it and still hadn't seen us.

"Time to fucking go!" Sergeant Ashley, the convoy team leader, shouted from the second truck. "Lemons!"

I jumped inside and the door bumped against my pistol as I slammed it. Each driver yanked a three-point turn in sequence. The small arms fire remained consistent and another mortar strike bit us in the ass as we broke contact.

As we drove back to Forward Operating Base (FOB) Hotel, our walled-off compound in the desert, I scrolled through the recording in my head. The Mahdi attacked us again with small arms from a small building, near an industrial quad in the center of the city. This time, the grunts could fire back, and our column came to a halt as the grunts ripped into the insurgents and the building exploded in flames. I let them do their jobs and went through my recording.

Inside our FOB, the convoy stopped. The grunts laughed like children as they unloaded. They slapped each other and joked in the joy that comes from a near-death experience with no wounded or dead. The heat crippled us as it climbed towards 110 degrees. Revert and I pulled the company commander, charged with the raid against the technical college, around the engine of my gun truck. He was one of the rare officers who earned his Marines' respect. I was half his size. I spread out my map on the hot hood and we gave him what we observed.

The heavy mortars told me that any entrance from the south was already expected. The ZPU-4 gun truck had to be vaporized before any insertion, and its mobility meant they could hide it. The open field with its single road, potentially being loaded with more IEDs as we spoke, and high-story buildings with Mahdi snipers looking down on it would slow any advance. The cemetery had no civilians within it and now we had to tread carefully as we chased the Mahdi Army. Wrecking the mosque or the tomb to reach the college would violate our rules of engagement and make everyone in the city hate us.

We answered his questions. We told him where we thought the mortars were coming from. I didn't give the number of Marines I thought would get maimed or killed, let alone Iraqis, but I didn't see the payoff. The current plan was a suicide mission.

"It's fucked," I told him. "We have to find a different route, sir."

He moved his dip around his bottom lip and nodded. He took the information back with him to the command post. Revert and I humped back to our tent, wired and drained, hoping we had observed enough. The daytime high eventually spiked at 120.

One quarter carried out the strike on the militia fighters in the technical college the next night using our intel. They moved in from the east on the other side of the river to avoid the Grand Mosque and the ZPU-4 altogether. With blocking positions by other companies set up in the north and south, Bravo company struck the target. No Marines were killed. We reportedly killed 300 fighters and the Mahdi abandoned the college for good.

Observation is our main objective. We also train to shoot. But not right away. In a Marine sniper platoon, it might take weeks or months before you're permitted to fire the weapon. First you will dry fire. Then you will dry fire some more. Then you will dry fire again. The HOG sets up the gun and the PIG, "Professional Instructor of Gunmen," crawls behind it, the same way, hundreds of times to master correct eye relief, the distance between eye and scope that yields the clearest, most accurate picture of the target. An instructor might attach a one-inch black sticker to a wall or have the Marine aim in on the "m" of a Domino's pizza box at a hundred yards. The list grows: bone support, muscular relaxation, natural point of aim. Consistency is accuracy.

In a perfect world, a shooter would engage from the prone in every shot. Lying on your stomach, the body absorbs as much of the recoil as possible and you remain the smallest target. At all times, embracing pain, the shooter must not break position. When aiming, the shooter concentrates on the reticle (the black lines inside the scope), not the target. The target should move from clear to blurry as the shooter's eye locks onto the reticle.

To aid in trigger control, shooters master breath control. Again, a consistent and accurate shot will build on taking the same amount of air into the lungs every time and does not let the rise and fall of the lungs move the rifle. I had a fifteen-second cycle, breathing in and then out. Sometimes, I might need to speed this up. The ideal trigger control and breath control produce a shock of surprise when the trigger is slowly squeezed, and in the strange world of a respiratory pause, the round explodes out of the barrel.

Before intensive trigger time begins, however, you must learn internal, external, and terminal ballistics. In the science of internal ballistics, a sniper tries to re-create the exact same explosion with every shot. The shooter learns about the primer, cartridge, barrel pressure, cleaning procedures, rifling twists, seating their round, and ammunition. Cataloging Lake City M118 long-range, 175 grain, 7.62×51mm ammunition makes up a large component of this process. The boxes of twenty rounds are stamped with a unique code such as "LC-03H271-018 Sublot B." Tiny variations in pressure of the primers or the burn rate of the gunpowder adjust the behavior of the round inside the rifle. Shooting LC-04L280-019 Sublot C rounds instead of LC-03H271-018 Sublot B might move the flight path of the round an inch over a hundred yards or several inches over five hundred yards. Thus, under ideal conditions, a shooter would stockpile as much of the same batch as possible, physically shoot every round the same way, and clean the weapon the exact same way after firing and during daily care.

Consistency is accuracy. It's our calling card.

The moment the bullet launches from the muzzle and hits the target defines external ballistics. You cannot control gravity, drag, wind, temperature, altitude, barometric pressure, humidity, or mirage, but you can learn the effects and then compensate through calculations and turret adjustments in your scope.

Calling wind is the most important skill in shooting, yet the hardest to learn. A PIG learns to examine the ways invisible wind impacts the natural world with visible consequences. A 3–5 mph breeze feels light on the face, 5–8 mph causes tree leaves to rustle and makes a distinct sound, 8–12 mph raises loose paper and dust and 12–15 mph causes small trees to sway. Without trash or plant life, you can still measure wind through mirage. As the sun heats the surface of the earth, rising warm air collides with denser, cooler air above it. The result is a shimmering air mass everyone has seen across an asphalt road on a summer day. Once you've identified the direction and speed of the wind, you can break the wind into sections: wind at the shooter, wind at the target, and wind in between. Two of those zones will usually agree with each other. From there, you check your charts on paper or whatever you've memorized and make an adjustment. Wind reading is all a guess, but an extremely educated guess.

Finally, the spotter and shooter must compute and imagine what the round will do when it strikes the target. Terminal ballistics is all about the type of wound you want to inflict and obstructions you might have to shoot through—glass or body armor, for instance—that would affect that wounding. Head shots immediately incapacitate the target. Hitting the tiny triangle between the eyes and nose or blasting through the ear canal ends a life in the most humane way. Yet, heads sit minutely on large bodies. Often, you'll find a head shot too distant or obscured and now center mass hydraulic shots to the heart or lungs become the priority.

Concentration rests on only one shot, not past or future rounds. Shooting collapses into a Zen experience. You have to relax in an activity that oozes continuous stress. All the hours and days of dry firing, body adjustment, breathing, trigger control, and observation games replicate range performance. Range performance should ultimately simulate combat. I did this for so many hours and years that it became a part of my autonomic nervous system. Even now, I'm more at ease holding a bolt action rifle than a baby or a Louisville Slugger.

Consistency. Is. Accuracy.

ON AUGUST 5, 2004, TWO WEEKS BEFORE THE RECON MISSION IN KUFA, BURNY AND I faced westward on our stomachs. We scanned windows, nooks, and rooftops, relaxing our eyes and ignoring the grunts and Iraqi police shooting and screaming beneath us. Our bodies worked from muscle memory built during untold hours laying behind glass in training. Burny moved the spotting scope. With our teammates Revert and Thomas squeezed in behind us and searching, we all felt wind on our faces from our fourth-story perch. We waited and watched under our helmets and in our flak jackets.

You discover a target in the natural world by finding something straight next to something crooked or a color or shine out of place. A black, vertical radio antenna next to a crooked, gray scrub oak or the sheen on a new sand-bag. Here, I saw a black stick poking out from behind a brown pillar. The black line moved in tandem with the person holding it. An AK-47 rifle. The shooter held a narrow brick, a squad radio, in another hand. More danger-ous than the AK. He stood behind a thick steel beam, bobbing out, moving the radio to his lips, and then moving back behind the beam. An observer.

I called the readout in the range finder: "One thousand, one hundred yards." A 7.62mm round gets wobbly after reaching one thousand yards; eleven hundred yards was probably beyond the limits of the rifle. We didn't have the time to make a range card, double-check the math, or guide the machine gunners to him. We weren't going to drop mortars on a building where there might be families inside. A cold bore shot, the first round out of a clean barrel. What is current temp versus the temp we'd zeroed at? I grabbed the barrel of my M40 sniper rifle. Definitely warm, but not hot. Ammo cool. I had never taken a shot beyond a grand with 7.62mm. My rifle had a new scope with limited data. I hadn't fired it beyond 750 yards in Kuwait. Fateh, Iranian 60mm mortars, continued falling on us and would keep dropping on the police station until we killed the observers. What is my firing solution? Make a decision.

Calm down. Breathe.

Grunts beneath us fired back and some lay pinned down behind ripped-up sandbags. The wind picked up to full value, blowing 8–12 mph from the left of us and streaming right. "Eight to twelve raises dust and loose paper," I chanted from memory. We saw plastic bags on the roof drift and wrappers hundreds of yards away follow the same path. Fuck, it was getting hot. It might be 1400 or 1500 in the afternoon now. The insurgent was wrapped in mirage. He vibrated inside my scope and looked no bigger than a watch face number. He stood on the same floor as us. No angles to worry about. Aim center mass.

I cranked the elevation and windage knobs before telling Burny, "On target."

More shots and mortars fell into and onto our building.

"On scope. Fire when ready. Same wind."

Be in the bubble. Safety off. How's your breathing? Deep breath in and start exhaling. Target a blur, slow steady squeeze, focus on the reticle, blur, squeeze, blur, reticle, air nearly out. My heart beat slowly, but I felt the pulse in my neck. Squeeze.

The shot took me by surprise, just like it's supposed to. I worked the bolt as I waited for the call.

"Where's the target?" No fucking way I missed.

During known-distance qualification in sniper school, I shot the class high of thirty-one of thirty-five rounds. Five for five at the 900-yard line and four for five at the grand. At each of the four shots I dropped during known distance, my marksmanship instructor Sergeant Mulder cursed, "Miss!!! Blahhh!!! That's a fucking combatant you let walk, Lemons." Then he berated my spotter, the more important Marine in a sniper team. We both knew it was a paper target, but we also understood the real meaning of Mulder's statement.

"You're a hunter," another instructor, Sergeant Hamblin, would quip when we got lazy and stopped imagining the training as the real thing. "But you are always being hunted."

I kept my face glued to the cheekpiece and turned my eyes to Burny.

"I can't see him." Burny looked through his scope, fiercely, as if willing it to show him the observer again. I peered back at the beam, trying to come down from the high of pulling the trigger. Light, nothing. Shadows, nothing. It was the first time I shot at someone as a sniper. That was Burny's first taste of combat. Maybe he was nervous calling wind. Maybe the heat raised the trajectory of the round and we failed to make the adjustment. I've analyzed how we missed the observer for years and have no excuses.

"Down or fucking what?" I kept my face on the gun.

We didn't see him again.

Several hours later we packed up. We had helped the grunts stop the Jayesh al-Mahdi attack on the police station. We hadn't lost anyone. I looked up to the pool-table-sized roof the four of us laid on before crossing back through the doorway. I saw where a round smashed into the wall, twelve inches below my helmeted face. We had sky-lined ourselves in the worst possible way, our silhouettes clear targets against the blue backdrop. I never heard the shot. But there it was, a bullet's history written in fractured cement. Sargent Hamblin's words played back silently in my ear. You're always being hunted.

AFTER ENLISTMENT, THE CHOICE THAT MOST PEOPLE WANT ME TO QUESTION IS THE choice to become a sniper. There is little ambiguity about the job, and in civilian logic, this choice should mark a watershed moment at least as important as my decision to enlist. But it doesn't. In the logic of the Marine Corps, becoming a sniper was hardly a choice at all. The highest and best use of a Marine's skills is the job that benefits other Marines the most, and for me, that meant sniper school, where I learned the one combat job that keeps more Marines safer than any other.

In 2005, I took up the chief scout position at the 1/4 and instituted the most range time for the platoon anyone remembered. I didn't want my crew to learn shooting mistakes in the painful ways I did in Iraq. I raised the amount of shooting to twice per week if we were not running recon and surveillance training missions. When we shot, I forced us all to binge. I made close friends with everyone I needed to on Camp Pendleton, from other sniper platoons to grumpy warrant officers who ran rifle ranges to the base military police. If I could plug some of my shooters in with anyone else, I'd drive them there in my Tacoma with their weapons (breaking military law) and leave them with a can of ammunition from the stockpile I kept in my barracks (also breaking the law). On weekends, I took the platoon to the base pistol range with boxes and boxes of 9mm I had bought.

In Kuwait, we could train in ways we couldn't anywhere else. The desert ate grenades, anti-tank missiles, small arms, and .50cal. It contained endless expanses for 7.62mm. During a three-day shoot of sniper rifles at steel targets, each shooter blasted 150 rounds per day. For twenty-four shooters total when I finally called the line cold, that tallied 10,800 rounds. We shot twice that with small arms, often letting the sands do our work for us and devour the brass. I suspect ocean liners of American brass cover much of Kuwait.

Kuwait contained other debris. Underneath the blades of springtime grass and shifting sands, you could see the detritus from 1991. An old Soviet cupola sticking out of nowhere, abandoned trucks burnt and warped with each subsequent year as they were shot again in training. Shattered rounds and shavings from derelict T-72 tanks all mixed with the dust and gently powdered our faces, rifles, and uniforms. If you slept outside without an eye mask, then you would awake to glued eyelids collecting the gray-brown flour.

Ranges in Iraq contained many of the same freedoms of Kuwait. The old Iraqi military bases we inhabited contained wrecked buildings and ranges we could smash with 40mm grenades, .50cal, and small arms, often training the Iraqi Army. Even on small FOBs and outposts, we found ways of carving out the hundred yards necessary to continue practicing and to check zeros. What little practice we squeezed in between operations kept us sharp. We lived walking distance or short drives to all those ranges.

Working parties and weapons ranges go hand in hand. Snipers must account for every spent 7.62mm casing. Losing just one cartridge out of the boxes you fired means you left a target indicator for the enemy to find, alerting them of a sniper presence. Since boot camp, we learned that the best way to police call—that is, pick up your trash—after firing requires a line of Marines to pick up expended brass and dump it in their covers. (There are no "hats" in our Marine Corps.) You stand shoulder to shoulder and pick up casings until told to stop. Then you dump the brass into an ammo can or wooden crate and put your cover back on.

"Any complaints, bitches, or saved rounds?" I'd call as the range safety officer at the end of firing.

In sniper school, we shared ranges with the SEALs, and, in exchange for who knows what, the piglets of my class had the pleasure of cleaning out their team shooting house, a cinder block building where they live-fired weapons during room clearing drills, every week. No doubt they pounded beers in flip-flops off base and laughed at the stupid jarheads cleaning up their mess. We pushed brooms as brass rattled behind the bristles. The piles grew and grew. Then we deployed shovels and dustpans to shove it all into wooden cases. Clouds of black and gray lead dust floated upwards with each sweep and scoop. As we all mastered our own urban shooting, we cleaned up similar rounds indoors across Camp Pendleton and Twentynine

Palms. Even when we weren't shooting, we were never far in time or distance from the wrong end of a firing range.

Sniper platoons primarily engage two practice targets: paper and steel. At a range like 117A, a million sniper rounds have left barrels and found themselves piercing cellulose or ricocheting off metal and landing in the coastal desert soils. As you moved the steel targets on the range or raced from one yard line back to the next, you found disintegrated pieces of lead cores with every footfall. Some looked like tiny pancakes and others like minute broken bottle shards. Every one of them had fragmented in some way upon impact.

The one activity where cleaning made sense, even when taken to typical Marine Corps extremes, was weapons maintenance. Cleaning a weapon doesn't merely happen after firing. Weapons live in the environments we carry them through, and we guard them against water, dust, and heat. In the case of an M40 sniper rifle, I learned a universal cleaning method. Bolts and the chamber were cleaned with the military issue MIL-L-63460 Break Free CLP (cleaner, lubricant, and preservative). I cleaned the barrel with bore and powder solvents to remove lead and powder fouling the same way hundreds of times. We cleaned at the armory. We used the same CLP or similar products to clean pistols, small arms rifles, and machine guns. It broke up carbon, kept the bolt lubed, and resisted rust. With the addition of forced air, even more carbon could be broken off and dust blown from the rifles all over the armory. We predicted that those solvents would kill us by cancer based on the gallons and gallons each of us had dutifully bathed in. We never considered lead.

We only eat after cleaning weapons. Consequently, we'd head from the armory directly to chow. Most of the carbon, dust, and cleaning materials clung to our skin and faces. During boot camp and my first two tours, I never wore latex gloves or a mask and I sometimes left the armory looking like an apprentice coal miner. In the field, we rubbed our skin furiously with the ethylene oxide and 1,4-dioxane of baby wipes. Back in the rear, we might rush to the office sink and scrub with GOJO Natural Orange Pumice Hand Cleaner, covering ourselves in a citrus stink. Or we pumped hand sanitizer all over and went inside the chow hall. Only during my longest periods of leave—up to three weeks—would I notice that I didn't smell like a gun range.

Machine gunners had it worse. Marine machine gunners, also known as 0331s, notoriously carry a zero-fucks-given attitude. Some were known to walk around the barracks at Camp Horno naked and in shades, with a 24 pack over their shoulder and sandals flip-flopping beneath their feet. Big, dumb, and lovable, the gunner and a-gunner, who hauls the spare barrel and extra ammo, save lives when you get stuck in a brawl. They rush wildly to set up guns under fire. They take it and they give it back.

When air cools a smoking barrel after a cease-fire call, gunners act like belt-fed weirdos. The ones who passed the screener to get into our sniper platoon had intense strength and stamina. They also seemed universally slow-minded. Machine gunners appeared to stumble into higher amounts of non-judicial punishment than other infantry jobs, too. Anecdotal, I know, but that's how I saw it.

Any 0331 rips tens of thousands of 7.62mm and .50cal rounds during a four-year enlistment. There are 250 rounds in one can of 7.62mm linked machine gun ammo. Josh ran a rough estimate of my firing range exposures based on an Israel Defense Forces study of troops firing 135 or 170 rounds a day. In sniper school and after, we were shooting more like 400. 0331s were in a different universe. A day at the range with three to five guns could easily burn twenty cans to reach 5,000 rounds. That doesn't include 40mm. They probably all have hearing loss and slipped disks. I never thought about all that lead.

4

LEAD POISONING

When most people think of lead poisoning, they think of paint chips and lead pipes. Like lead dust from bullets, both are vectors for ingesting lead. And eating and drinking lead is indeed a way to give yourself lead poisoning. Of the lead you ingest, the vast majority gets flushed out of your body through your liver and kidneys within twelve to twenty-four hours. For adults, somewhere in the neighborhood of 3–10 percent of ingested lead ends up in your bloodstream. For young kids, that number can go up to as high as 50 percent. In a lead-dust-rich environment—like a shooting range or an FBI trainee dorm room or a sniper school barracks—that can lead to a significant rise in blood lead levels.[1]

But the lead dust you pick up from bullets at firing ranges also affects the amount of lead in the air, and the impacts of ingested lead pale in comparison to the impacts of inhaled lead. Human lungs are remarkably good at transferring lead from the air into your body. They are, in that sense, the opposite of skin. When you breathe lead in, your lungs can absorb a full 100 percent of the lead you inhale directly into the bloodstream. According to NIOSH, if you're a construction worker and the air you're breathing averages anything over 30 µg of lead per cubic meter of air over an eight-hour workday, you have a lead problem. Background airborne lead at most gun ranges is well below 30 μg/m³, but specific jobs at gun ranges—like sweeping—and particular locations at those ranges entail short-term exposures to much higher concentrations of lead. And for Marines and FBI agents living in take-home lead, the eight-hour workday doesn't mark the end of the day's lead exposure.

Perhaps surprisingly, airborne lead at firing ranges doesn't just come from bullets. In fact, because inhaling lead is so much worse than ingesting it, bullets themselves may not be the most immediately dangerous part of a cartridge from a toxicity perspective. When the hammer or firing pin of a gun strikes the center of a cartridge, it compresses an internal cap full of a compound called "primer," releasing heat and gas that ignites the powder or propellant that forces the bullet out of its casing and down the barrel of the gun towards the shooter's target. Both primers and propellants contain lead, and most primers are composed of around 35 percent lead styphnate and lead peroxide. The lead that shooters inhale during target practice comes mostly from primers. That lead tends to be emitted at right angles from the barrel of the gun in aerosol form, often remaining airborne and enveloping the shooting area for much of the shooting session.[2] Even if you fire bullets made from other alloys—copper, tungsten, depleted uranium—you may still be using lead primers.

There are also some insidious ways that airborne lead comes from bullets themselves. When bullets hit targets or the earthen barriers behind them, they tend to fragment, sending large and small particles of lead scattering into the surrounding soil. Shooting at hard metal targets like steel plates or other discarded equipment increases this type of fragmentation. Lead particulates from fragmentation form loose bonds with other soil compounds, which can then be transported on the wind as dust literally years down the road. In some places, the half-life of lead in soil has been measured at 700 years.[3] Any time the wind blows at an outdoor shooting range—or any time that space or soil gets put to a different use that kicks up dust, which is a frequent occurrence both on military bases and elsewhere—you have an active source of short-term lead exposure. The gift of lead bullets keeps on giving.

It is difficult to get a handle on just how much lead Marines like Alex picked up in their blood preparing for combat in Iraq. In 2012, the Department of Defense commissioned the National Academy of Sciences to investigate the potential lead exposure of DoD personnel at government firing ranges, suggesting that the military is at least aware of the issue. One active Navy SEAL I interviewed reported frequent lead testing during his training evolutions. But results of these tests are not publicly available, and they still don't have to report whom they test or what the results are to NIOSH or other public health agencies.[4] They certainly weren't testing Alex in the early 2000s.

One way to get a sense of the kind of exposure Alex and his fellow Marines had in the early 2000s is to look at another sophisticated military organization: the Israel Defense Forces. In 2006 and 2007, a team of scientists was allowed to test airborne lead and take BLLs for four IDF infantry combat units as they passed through basic and advanced training for fifteen weeks. Scientists took BLLs from each participant before and after basic training and again before and after advanced training. They also took air samples from about 30 cm away from the faces of both trainees and instructors during a variety of firearm-related activities, wet and dry, day and night.

The results were perhaps predictable: IDF trainees and instructors were exposed to lead during basic and advanced training. The team found it very likely that about 5 percent of the trainees and 25 percent of the instructors of basic training were exposed above Israel's actionable level of airborne lead.[5] They found it likely that more like 10 percent of advanced trainees were exposed above the actionable lead level. And they noted rather dryly that "military personnel participating in automatic weapon marksmanship training can be exposed to considerable levels of airborne lead during outdoor firing range training."[6] Probably not the foremost issue on the minds of IDF soldiers likely destined for hot patrols and live fire scenarios within the next six months.

But more generally, before the tests, 174 of the 175 soldiers tested had so little lead in their blood it was essentially undetectable. After basic training, 25 percent of the soldiers registered a BLL over the detectable amount—and after advanced training, 89 percent of the study group did. No amount of lead in the blood is actually safe. And unlike Alex and his Marines, these cadets received specific information at the outset of the study on the dangers of lead exposure; were in fact wearing protective gear and washing their hands; and abided by strict prohibitions against eating or drinking at the range. And they *still* saw BLLs increase by a factor of ten.

IDF trainees were also shooting fewer bullets than a PIG or HOG like Alex Lemons. It may seem like common sense: the more you shoot, the more lead you're exposed to. In the IDF, basic training recruits could expect to shoot an average of 135 rounds in a day of arms training. Soldiers in advanced training shot an average of 171 rounds per day.[7] Alex's shooting logs reveal for PIGS and HOGS, shooting 175 rounds was common practice—on a light day. When they were really practicing or training, they shot more than 400 rounds per day. Their training included both small arms rounds like those used in the IDF study and rounds from much bigger guns, which tend to put off more airborne lead per round. If IDF trainees saw their BLLs increase by an order of magnitude with good hygiene in a controlled shooting environment where they spent 170 rounds per day, how should we assess a Marine Corps truck driver's exposure? A sniper's exposure? And what about a Marine Corps machine gunner?

The IDF study is one of many studies that show a correlation between firearms practice and lead exposures. As early as 1989, a series of blood lead level tests of Virginia State Police Academy cadets going through firearms training revealed mean BLLs that rose above the CDC's actionable level for adults.[8] In 2000, a study of US Special Forces troops engaged in shooting activities showed the same.[9] And a 2009 study in New York State revealed that more than half of the participants in a study of frequent target shooters had BLLs significantly higher than the CDC's actionable level.[10] Based on the rounds he fired and the conditions under which he fired them, it is almost certain that Alex's shooting activities would have yielded the same, perhaps for months at a time.

That there was lead in Alex's urine is hardly a surprise.

BETWEEN 2012 AND 2019, THIRTY-EIGHT AMERICAN SERVICEMEN, mostly from Special Forces units, were tested for chronic lead poisoning at Mount Sinai Hospital on Fifth Avenue in New York City. The *New York Times* carried a story on them.[11] They were confusing medical cases. Many of the soldiers demonstrated symptoms of post-traumatic stress disorder and the long-term effects of traumatic brain injuries—and, in fact, many of them likely did suffer from PTSD and TBI. Some had difficulty maintaining their concentration, or became angry and irritable for no apparent reason. Some had high blood pressure or diminished sex drive. Others had trouble with their peripheral vision and hearing. Few had solid explanations of their continuing and worsening symptoms after their tours of duty in Iraq or Afghanistan, and their referrals to Mount Sinai followed months if not years of tests, therapy, and medications prescribed by their primary physicians at home, at VA hospitals, at specialists' offices, or at Walter Reed National Military Medical Center in Maryland. Given a K X-ray fluorescence bone lead test—the test I described earlier that can reveal a person's cumulative exposure to lead over time—a dozen of them tested positive for elevated levels of lead in their bones.

There is no good reason for there to be lead in your body. Unlike other elements, it has no known physiological value for humans or any other animals. Once in your body, it is really good at messing you up. Lead molecules interfere with DNA transcription—a key step in cell reproduction—and with the function of enzymes that help to maintain the integrity of cell membranes. Weakened cell membranes, in turn, can result in anemia as red blood cells become more fragile. Meanwhile, lead can also disrupt the metabolism of bones and teeth; inhibit the synthesis of vitamin D; cause the production of the excess inflammatory proteins associated with a variety of autoimmune symptoms, including asthma; and suppress the activity of other important immune cells. It can cause unwanted buildups of calcium in cells, and create reactive radicals that further destroy cell structures.[12]

At acute exposure levels, lead poisoning looks like a lot of other types of poisoning. Its special neurological talents are that it causes pain, weak-ness, numbness, and tingling, and sometimes the litany of neurological symptoms (headache, stiff neck, brain fog, vomiting, hallucinations, fever, and memory and hearing problems, for starters) associated with inflammation of the brain. As a more plebian poison, it causes abdominal pain, nausea, vomiting, diarrhea, constipation, kidney damage, and even shock. Some lead-poisoned people pee blood; others hardly pee at all. Acute lead poisoning is often not that difficult to diagnose—it's pretty bad, and it tends to come from relatively obvious acute sources.

Chronic lead poisoning is a different beast. In the short term, lead in your blood makes you obviously sick; in the long term, lead stored in organs and soft tissue, along with lead leaching slowly back into your bloodstream from your bones, makes you sick in subtler, more nefarious ways. Cumulative lead exposure tends to show up in more than one of the body's systems at once, and the symptoms are common enough that unless there is an obvious vector for lead, even a good primary care physi-cian wouldn't necessarily associate them with lead poisoning.

Even in relatively low doses, long-term lead exposure tends to pres-ent in gastrointestinal trouble—abdominal pain, diarrhea, reduced appetite, and sometimes vomiting. These may sound obvious, but the symptoms are often intermittent, and who doesn't have a bad stomach some days? Moreover, Marines like Alex have long histories of gastro-intestinal discomfort—including some protracted "shitting their brains out" episodes—dating back to their exposure to "Saddam's Revenge" and other water- and food-borne pathogens in Iraq. Veterans with loose bowels typically have other things to think about than lead primers.

Chronic lead poisoning also tends to show up in the nervous system—the material connection between mind and body that a Marine Corps scout sniper like Alex works so hard to train. Most of the litera-ture out there on the neuropsychiatric impacts of chronic lead poisoning focuses on lead exposure either in children or in adults who were exposed as children. And, in part, this makes sense. Adults exposed to lead have typically undergone most of the important stages of neurological devel-opment before exposure, and they store most of their lead burden in their bones, where it doesn't move around much or very quickly. Children, on the other hand, store much of their lead burden in soft tissues, making it available to their brains as they build the neurological structures that help make them who they are.

That said, old assumptions about the safety of lead stored in adult bones and about the impacts of both acute and chronic lead on adult brains have come under scrutiny in recent years. It turns out cumulative lead does bad things to adult brains, too.[13] Those bad things can be particularly cruel in the case of a Marine.

The reason that lead is so good at being bad is that it looks to our bodies a lot like things we need for important functions of the nervous and circulatory systems, particularly calcium, iron, and zinc. Because of its chemical structure, lead can imitate any of these three elements, but when enzymes bind to lead instead of, say, iron, the lead doesn't do the work the enzyme recruited iron to do. Rather than catalyzing a reaction that binds iron to other molecules to create the robust heme at the heart of hemoglobin—that is, blood—lead actually suppresses that reaction, creating weak blood cells. As a result, lead poisoning can cause anemia, with all of its frustrating and debilitating symptoms: a decreased ability to carry oxygen in the blood, weakness, general fatigue, shortness of breath, and a poor or decreased ability to exercise. A tough pill for anyone to swallow, but an especially tough blow when your job and your identity are wrapped up in your physical training.

Perhaps not surprisingly, lead does its most nefarious shape-shifting enzyme infiltration in the nervous system, where the brain lives. Of all the organs in the body, the brain is by far the most sensitive to lead.[14] Here again it's as if the element was perfectly designed to hunt Marines. Lead can pass into the cells of the brain because, to the gatekeeper cells that make up the barrier between the brain and the bloodstream, it looks a lot like calcium, which the brain needs. The nervous system needs calcium in order to make neurons grow, and it relies on enzymes to grab free calcium and put it to work.

Once inside the brain, lead binds to those same enzymes, taking calcium's place. But once bound, lead won't do the trick, and rather than growing more robust, the nervous system structures that help Marines concentrate, stay sharp, and coordinate their movements quickly begin to atrophy.[15]

There is one nervous system structure in particular that highlights the perversity of a Marine's lead exposure: the myelin sheath. As journalist and business advisor Daniel Coyle explains in *The Talent Code*, myelin is a fatty substance that coats the axons of nerve cells, helping them move more information across nerve structures faster. You can liken the myelin sheaths that coat your axons to insulation around a wire. As Coyle explains, our brains tend to build more myelin around the nerve structures we use most frequently—they are, in a way, what makes a learned action like shooting a basketball (or a rifle), with enough practice, second nature. Drawing on studies of ballerinas, tennis players, virtuoso musicians, and Brazilian soccer stars, Coyle identifies a form of conscious, attentive, repetitive learning he calls "deep practice" as the key to building more robust myelin sheaths faster—that is, they are the key to developing a thing we call "talent."[16]

When I read Coyle's description of deep practice and the myelin it builds, the first thing that came to my mind was Alex's sniper training. "Consistency is accuracy." Deep practice in a martial key. In most people, deep practice not only builds myelin; it also increases the brain's ability to build *more* myelin. In healthy adults, the efficiency with which we build myelin sheaths begins to fall off in middle age (hence the saying: "You can't teach an old dog new tricks"). Until then, though, the more people work to master and acquire a particular skill, the more they increase their ability to acquire and master skills in general. You don't just build stronger myelin sheaths around the axons responsible for shooting a basketball; you get better at making myelin. In neuroscience jargon, the building of myelin sheaths is a type of "long-term potentiation," the ongoing strengthening of synapses based on activity. Good practice begets more effective practice.

And Marines are good at practice.

At the cellular level, however, lead turns the Marine Corps' great strength against itself. By interfering with the way our brains build the physical structures that support synapses, lead decreases long-term potentiation. And it gets worse. Lead facilitates something called "long-term depression," a reduction in the efficiency of our synapses in response to an activity. This is the opposite of long-term potentiation. Long-term depression of nervous system structures is something like overtraining in muscles: it's what happens when practice no longer helps, and even sometimes starts to hurt.[17] Whereas calcium helps us build myelin, organize ion channels, and develop more robust synapses, the lead that sneaks into our brains under the chemical guise of calcium ions does exactly the opposite, eroding the structures we build to think and react more efficiently and effectively.

Thus does chronic lead poisoning target the very deep practice that Marines rely on for efficacy and survival.

THE NEUROPSYCHIATRIC IMPACTS OF LEAD POISONING GO WAY beyond the suppression of myelin. That one strikes me as particularly perverse, but the symptoms are myriad and diverse. For adults, short-term memory loss is probably the biggest red flag in this category, though it also includes a number of other symptoms a well-trained Marine would notice: loss of concentration, loss of coordination, numbness or tingling in the extremities, tremor, fatigue, headaches. Whereas stomach problems tend to be associated with a slow drip of lead exposure, these neuropsychiatric symptoms are typically the legacies of some more intense, short-term exposure event. But as with the GIs' gastrointestinal-tract issues, these neuropsychiatric symptoms are also common enough among veterans for other reasons that a family doctor—even a military doctor—is unlikely to connect them to lead exposure. Getting from symptoms to a confirmed lead poisoning diagnosis is rarely a sure thing, in part because a Marine with a tremor, headaches, and memory problems rarely ends up in a toxicologist's office. The veterans who showed up at Mount Sinai for lead testing were the exception rather than the rule.

And there is a good reason for that. Alex's postwar symptoms track symptoms of lead exposure really well, and we know from his shooting logs, from the monitoring of FBI recruits at Quantico, and from the IDF study that it is exceedingly likely that Alex was exposed to significant amounts of lead, lead dust, and lead aerosols.

But lead is not a slam dunk, because it turns out that the symptoms of lead exposure—and of heavy metals poisoning more generally—are not unique to lead. The physical symptoms of lead poisoning can also arise from a variety of pathogens and autoimmune disorders, as well as from other forms of exposure—like, for example, exposure to mercury. So too do the neuropsychiatric symptoms of lead poisoning mimic other biological and psychiatric conditions altogether, many of them associated with other aspects of warfare. Perhaps most importantly, the symptoms of lead poisoning tend to overlap with or mimic symptoms of two other conditions that both the family clinic and the VA hospital are currently keenly attuned to: PTSD and TBI. Long before we think exposure, we think trauma.

ALEX AND I HAVE FOCUSED ON LEAD BECAUSE IT SERVES AS A CASE IN point about the slow violence and uncertainty of toxic exposure in the context of the violence of war. The bullet we started with may kill the target in the near term, but a deep dive on lead reveals the way that bullets in their numbers ultimately do violence to the shooter as well.

Between 2003 and 2008, Alex checked the boxes on his Post-Deployment Health Assessment forms marked "often" for exposure to DEET, smoke from oil fires, smoke from burning trash or feces, vehicle exhaust fumes, JP-8 fuel, fog oils from smoke screens, lasers, loud noises, excessive vibration, industrial pollution, sand/dust, medical waste, pesticide strips, tent heater smoke, animal bodies, insect bites, and human body parts/fluids. He also checked the boxes marked "sometimes" for pesticide-treated uniforms, environmental pesticides, flea or tick collars, and paint.

During that time, Alex also reported a variety of symptoms potentially but not necessarily related to a variety of toxic exposures: chronic cough, runny nose, skin and eye irritation, headaches, fatigue, chest pain, ringing in the ears, difficulty remembering things, and pain and stiffness in his joints.

Bullets, it turns out, do not travel alone in warfare. In truth, modern warfare entails a multitude of toxicants, each with their own histories and epidemiological complexities. Those toxic substances interact, both directly with each other and indirectly through the ways they impact the various systems of a human body. As Alex discovered in Iraq, war does not introduce these toxicants one at a time in the kind of controlled experiment a scientist might appreciate. Rather, they come alongside the more traditional trials of warfare in a whirlwind of exposures that can take years to sort out. To understand what might have made Marines like Alex sick during and after their service in the Global War on Terror, we have to go back to the beginning and follow Alex into the whirlwind.

PART 2

WHIRLWIND OF EXPOSURE

The Ecology of Modern Warfare

5

"GAS! GAS! GAS!"

The amphibious transport dock, USS *Dubuque* LPD-8, that steamed us towards Iraq in January 2003 was not a cruise ship. It launched August 6, 1966, and carried itself to a mothball decommission on June 30, 2011. Named after the French-Canadian explorer and overleveraged dandy Julien Dubuque, the ship could haul 840 Marines stuffed into coffin-sized racks along with all the junk grunts carry, a few shipping containers, and several helicopters and trucks. The Navy crew running the floating village peaked at 400 sailors. They gave the workhorse a motto: "Our Country, Heritage, and Future."

The ship was full of asbestos, pathogens, and shit water.

On board, the crew scrambled to wire together and bolt down equipment. The power turned off and the ship drifted for hours. Damage control crews ran through our berthing, cursing the hulk, as they raced to steam turbines feeding on jet propellant kerosene, JP-5. The crew duct-taped, hammered, swore, and then sweetly caressed the boat to start again. Pipes rattled and hatch handles broke. The hot water never worked. We imagined the rust on shower pipes was no different than the rust on the hull. I woke up almost every night to check the compartment for flooding.

The at-sea experience felt like forty days in a living museum. Old logbooks and graffiti contained memories of the "Mighty 8" during the American War in Vietnam: ferrying jarheads off and on in I Corps, mine-sweeping in North Vietnam, probably transporting Agent Orange barrels, and evacuating refugees as Saigon fell. Who knows how many coats of lead paint sailors had applied since 1966. Hundreds of beautifully made American parts and diodes had been caked in asbestos, a practice the Navy wouldn't abandon until the mid-1980s. Sailors doubted all of it had been or could be removed.

As we moved closer to the equator, the air-conditioning failed. Our berthing of twenty-three in Second Platoon, Alpha Company smelled like a moldy sock stuffed inside an unwashed jockstrap. Those without sea legs barfed into gallon-sized ziplock bags. Moving outside for a jog on the flight deck or hanging out on the catwalk got you fresh air mixed with jet fumes or cigarette smoke in the same heat. The *Dubuque* quickly took on the nickname *Dubpuke*. As we worked out, served and ate chow, sweated, and trained, the ship appeared to crumble above and underneath us.

Navy ships use an epoxy coating called Chemsol Non-Skid, MIL-PRF-24667 to wick away water and give you grip on deck. The dead gray held sharp ripples making ship life safe. During live-fire training on the helo pad, I discovered that Non-Skid also shreds flesh. Knees, elbows, faces. My torn skin was bad enough that our company commander put the drills on the shelf until we got to Kuwait.

Non-Skid collected everything like a lint trap. It soaked up leaks from fuel hoses, decades of crotch sweat, oil, chopper exhaust, and torn up tires. During hours of calisthenics, my face pressed into the chemical bouquet.

Non-Skid also housed the fire foams perfluorooctanoic acid (PFOA) and perfluorooctane sulfonate (PFOS). Fire at sea will always be more dangerous than on land. PFOA and PFOS, also known as "forever chemicals," tackled flames and saved lives since their introduction after 1967. The creamy bubbles smothered oxygen without drowning the crew or rusting out equipment. They also cause cancers and other health problems. Eventually, I learned from the firefighters in the chow line, they would scrub and hose the foam off with fresh water, dumping the remnants into the ocean. But they never flushed everything off. Puddles of foam formed tiny chain lakes that hung on for hours. We carried them all over the ship on our boots and uniforms and skin.

The hot, floating prison made the ideal petri dish. We picked up respiratory infections and diarrheal diseases as we interacted with the Navy squids. Since they wouldn't let Marines off the boat for the entire float, the only STDs we had to worry about came from each other. Athlete's foot lurked. When we weren't in boots or running shoes, we wore shower shoes to keep our feet from sweating. Marines scratch their genitals whenever possible. On ship, we scratched because athlete's foot had already spread to our junk. Topical fungicides went round and round. We sprayed cans or applied ointments or powders to itchy areas.

Pubic lice worried you the most on ship. They jumped from rack to rack and crotch to crotch with wildfire speed. The Navy and Marine Corps had answers. The pest killer permethrin knocks out mosquitos, lice, and ticks upon contact with treated clothing and sticks within the material over a half-life of 51–71 days. The wool blankets on our racks came soaked in it. On the battalion grinder at Camp Horno back in December, unmasked junior Marines pumped the insecticide onto our uniforms. Other than the rashes some had from wearing the doused blouses and trousers, the odorless chemical yielded no complaints.

Inside the petri dish, we received smallpox vaccinations in preparation for a supposed biological attack. The world had eradicated smallpox by the 1972 release of The Godfather; now, and in another century, our command told us the Iraqi military had weaponized it. Our platoon sergeant, Staff Sergeant McGuire, repeated the high command's talking points and said 30 percent of us would die if we contracted it. The injections were worth the discomfort compared to the lengthy, horrific death by fever, body aches, and oceans of pus-blowing blisters. No one could confirm or deny this inside our floating bubble any more than rumors of the death of Britney Spears or Ricky Martin's coming out. The grainy, built-in ship televisions gave us official Navy news and a few NFL playoff games. The interweb rarely functioned, mail came in two-week intervals, and nothing in the ship's library helped. Everyone in the Alpha Company assumed the worst and got ready to be slimed.

Hospital Corpsman DJ Moreno checked my record and prepped my smallpox shot in the sick bay one morning somewhere between Pearl Harbor and the Marshall Islands. Born in our ex-colony of the Philippines at Subic Bay, Moreno bounced around the globe as a Navy brat before ending up in Gering, Nebraska, an unexpected eddy of the Filipino diaspora. But Moreno behaved and sounded as corn-fed as every other Marine from the Great Plains. He had imagined being a medic or nurse since childhood and delivered a bedside manner no one else mustered.

"You ready, Alex?"

"Not like I can refuse, Doc." What he held looked like a pitchfork, not a hypodermic needle. Moreno smiled. Jab-jab-jab. Fifteen smallpox jabs in my left tricep. His wingman, Doc Aaron Newton, slapped a Band-Aid over the poked holes and told me, "Don't pick it and keep the band-aid on."

We tried not touch our arms as a red, itchy bump developed. It was impossible. It morphed into a quarter-sized blister that secreted pus. Shower floors contained strange puddles of scab ooze or juicy bandages. When we trained in martial arts or room clearing, you bumped up against someone's bandage or tore it off. With the intermittent air-conditioning, healing slowed down, and bandage funk levitated in the chow hall and berthing.

Vomiting and dysentery followed closely behind the injections. That was bad for the head.

The head was the only place outside your dreams where anyone had privacy. During my fourth week on board, PFC Alcantar, Sergeant Mattmiller, and I entered our head in unison after noon chow and sat on the toilets to escape the worsening cabin fever. Through the cracks in between the door and stall walls, I eyeballed the brown paper bags covering the urinals. The urinals, like everything else on the ship, constantly broke. They flooded, dumping piss, dip spit, and pubic hair onto the deck. Sometimes the supposedly fresh water that flooded the cabin from the toilets had become contaminated by jet fuel. With the pissers closed, we had even more privacy.

I took a moment to stare at the squares and rectangles and 1960s space-age starbursts on the blue laminate floor. My thoughts looped through the same reel every time I was alone on ship. They took me home and back to my little brother. I imagined how worried and sleepless my father was and how many ski runs my mom had taken to escape his anxiety. Then they took me back to the decision to be here and how disappointed I was with the Corps. My leaders in Alpha Company, from the corporals to the captain, had a robotic faith in all things Marine and believed humiliation and personal threats would get us ready in weeks for the war against Iraq. I thought they would get us killed.

A toilet flushed above us and brought me back to the ship we were trapped inside. Peering through the crack, I watched the paper bags turn from light brown to black. Water spilled over the sides. They began to vibrate, and hissing sounds pushed up from the pipes below. *Drunnng.* Pounding noises. *Drunnng.* More pounding noises. *Drunngggggg.* The leftmost bag burst, and water sprayed into the ceiling and slammed the stall walls.

Alcantar swore through his stall, "*Joder!* Ahhh, fuck no." We grabbed our trousers and jumped up onto the toilet lids as piss water swelled below our feet. We looked at each other. On ship, nearly every room had raised doors to contain incursions of seawater. The flood rose by two inches. Noises started coming from other shitters. Mattmiller made a run and splashed through the fluid as he yelled. I didn't want soaked boots. I looked at Alcantar and pointed up. The urinal geyser diminished, but the toilet bowls sounded like they would blow. I opened my door and swung along the pipes towards the door in a high-consequence session on the monkey bars. Alcantar followed. I opened the hatch with my feet and then swung out into the passageway and we stood on our feet laughing. "*Me cago en todo,*" Alcantar declared, as the toilets burped feces, toilet paper, and yellow fizz onto the deck.

CHEERS, SIGHS, AND MIDDLE FINGERS WENT OUT AS SECOND SQUAD CLIMBED into the ass of a CH-53 and left the *Dubuque* for good on the morning of day forty. We soared off the deck and circled the ship for an hour until we headed inland, past Kuwait City, and into the desert. I spotted isolated camps of trucks, tanks, and tents in the distance. We chopped towards the southernmost outpost, called Living Support Area (LSA) 1, or "Camp Inchon."

Thirty yards after disembarking the bird, we tossed rucks into the back of a truck parked on the cool, solid earth.

"Gas! Gas! Gas!"

Marines threw out dip wads and groped for our masks. We clamped eyelids shut and held our breath. We exhaled and tightened each of the six tiny straps around the backs of our heads. With each tug, I hoped my shave had been close enough to remove any gaps. I looked through a jumble of images. My outer lenses had been smashed during training and Supply had no replacements. My company gunny barked through his mask to hurry up with the packs and we only heard mumbling. Twenty minutes later someone screamed "All clear! All clear!" We ripped the masks off and gasped.

The chemical, biological, radiological, and nuclear training and equipment we received in preparation for the invasion formed part of the grand lie we told ourselves. We feared IG Farben nerve agents like soman, sarin, and tabun as the primary weapon of the Iraqi Army. In the gruesome lectures we sat through, a slimed Marine would flop and jerk in seizures. Eventually the brain stopped working and you fell into a poisoned coma lasting hours or days. Our only real or imaginary protection came from gas mask kits that never left our legs or hung from our racks when we slept in Kuwait. Inside the bulky OD-green case, you found an assembly of your mask, nerve agent shots, and pills.

M17 PROTECTIVE GAS MASK

Every recruit goes through an afternoon at the gas chamber in boot camp. On paper, a Fleet Marine should revisit and retest their ability to don and clear a gas mask every year. Visits to the gas chamber build confidence in the gear and training. In each session, we humped to a secluded, windowless building. We donned masks outside. Inside, an instructor cracked tablets of CS—2-chlorobenzylidenemalononitrile (tear gas)—and dumped them into ammo cans warming on a plug-in hot plate.

We entered the room and the door closed behind us. The instructor fanned clouds of gas around the room where it clung to skin and sweat. "Build a house, shitheads." We cracked the seal by pressing our fingers into the lenses and slid the mask above our foreheads. We locked eyelids and didn't exhale until the signal sounded. Then we reapplied the mask, blew to clear the remaining gas, and tightened straps.

You never cleared all the tear gas. You couldn't see it. All you could do was breathe slowly, like breathing through a garden hose, and hope the filters worked. The gap between a gas shell exploding and masking up—the Great War poet Wilfred Owen called this moment "an ecstasy of fumbling"—left no room for error. Just a pinch of CS could ruin your day. The same amount of chlorine gas or nerve agent would kill you.

The mask had several filters, facepieces, and outserts to protect the face, neck, and airway from exposure. The built-in voice emitter sounded like a man yelling into a 600 hp diesel engine. We often used fingers or a bayonet to point at things or carve letters in the sand. Radio communications became garbled, and we often tore the mask off to complete a transmission. Sometimes the drinking tube worked. Sometimes it didn't. Like everything else in the desert, the masks needed constant cleaning and checking.

Donning a gas mask assured other problems. You cannot accurately fire your weapon behind it and your night vision goggles will be nearly impossible to see through. The world inside the mask slowed life down. Months of exercising in or sitting with the mask on, I always felt suffocated. I forced myself to calm down and pretend the mask wasn't there at all. None of it worked.

MARK 1 INJECTORS

Each mask bag contained three sets of one 2 mg in 0.7 cc of atropine and one 600 mg in 2 cc of pralidoxime (2-PAM). A Marine could self-administer these nerve agent antidotes in the outer thigh, through their uniform. The drugs tell your fired up parasympathetic nervous system to calm down and open collapsing airways. The smaller atropine injector looked like a black magic marker with a yellow backstop. It would go in first followed by the tan-marked and larger 2-PAM injection. Side effects included dizziness and confusion, dilated pupils, dry mouth, and nausea. Each injector should've been labeled with an orange sticker: "Good Luck, Marine."

ONE DIAZEPAM INJECTOR (CANA-CONVULSANT ANTIDOTE FOR NERVE AGENT)

When the Mark 1 kit failed and you seized, another Marine should remove the gray tip of CANA and slam the black end of the injector into your outer thigh or buttock and hold for ten seconds. CANA is valium. It should disrupt the seizure. I imagined the drug's true purpose was to calm you down as you drifted into unconsciousness, so your friends didn't watch you flop like a dying fish.

PYRIDOSTIGMINE BROMIDE

Pyridostigmine bromide (PB) pills might fight sarin fired by Iraqi gunners. The nerve cells moving your eyes and making your fingers turn pages as you read this book release a neurotransmitter called acetylcholine to carry those signals to muscle cells. After getting the message, the body destroys the acetylcholine—the messages—through another material called acetylcholinesterase so the lines of communication don't get gunked up. Sarin wrecks acetylcholinesterase. PB binds to those enzymes, so nerve gas won't squeeze them. It's like a controlled burn in fire season. It also primes you for anticholinergic drugs like atropine.

We were told to chomp on a few pills per day to constantly stimulate cholinergic receptors in the body. The white, 30 mg tablets came in a silver, covered blister pack of twenty-one. The battalion had no standing order on the use of PB pills. No waivers. Use at your own discretion seemed to be the word of the day. I recall trying them once or twice out of terror. The medical literature says PB makes you constipated, but the pills gave some of us the shits. Others had headaches. But with all the other medications, I couldn't differentiate. The pills also worked under a three-hour half-life. Could any-one contact Iraqi gunners a few hours before they fired nerve agents into

Second Platoon so we could take the pills on time? I chucked the blister pack by the time we crossed the Line of Departure from Kuwait into Iraq.

M291 SKIN DECONTAMINATION KIT

You might tear open these napkin-sized charcoal pads to brush off any blistering agent that hit your skin. The pads made me laugh. I added the "Feel Good Wipes" to this list of "protective gear."

MOPP SUIT

We invented another fictional armor with the "Mission Oriented Protective Posture," MOPP, suit. The designers created a two-piece second skin, made of a nylon inner and a cotton shell, lined with charcoal, to protect from chemical and biological agents, along with radioactive material. Lightweight but not at all breathable, it looked like a set of ice-climber bibs and a zip up parka.

The suits began tearing before we crossed the Line of Departure into Iraq. We sealed holes with black and green duct tape. The jacket zipper—couldn't a nerve agent glide through the tiny gaps in the zipper teeth or up your ankles or around your waist?—often broke. Then you relied on the Velcro to keep the jacket together. The Marine Corps, as an extra special slap on the back, sent us into the desert with woodland patterned MOPPs. We stuck out like sore thumbs.

As the levels of contamination rose, you donned the hood, added lace-up booties, and pulled on oversized kitchen gloves. The black rubber boots and gloves made you look like a slaughterhouse janitor. Sweat pooled in the bottom of your mask lenses and at your toes and fingertips.

If you took a round or piece of shrapnel in a chem environment through the MOPP, then you were truly fucked. Opening the jacket, trousers, gloves, boots, or mask would expose more skin to blistering agents or bacteria. Even Doc Moreno concluded that it seemed better to let you die slowly inside the suit after attempting to seal wounds with duct tape than trying to offer treatment in a cloud of gas. Either way, they would eventually have to transport your body to a decontamination tent in the rear.

ANTHRAX VACCINE

Weeks after 9/11, letters packed with anthrax arrived in the offices of American senators and journalists. The spores delicately sealed in those letters murdered five and infected seventeen. Anthrax grows naturally in dirt, and the noncontagious spore-formed bacteria cause disease in farm animals. Unless you work with livestock, the only way to get infected comes through breathing or touching spores cultivated in a lab. Inhaled anthrax causes a sore throat, coughing, then pulmonary edema, shock, and final coma. Anthrax can also enter cuts or abrasions causing a rash, developing into a blister, swelling, and ending with headaches, vomiting, and final coma.

Rank-and-file Americans scanned their junk mail more closely and stockpiled the antibiotic ciprofloxacin to fight the bacteria as real and imaginary stories sizzled across the country. Some officials blamed al-Qaeda and then tied the attacks to Iraq. No one aboard the *Dubpuke* observed Secretary of State Colin Powell shaking a vial of pretend anthrax in front of the UN Security Council. In my daydreams, Powell's vial was full of the Meal Ready to Eat "Vanilla Dairy Shake Powder" because the FDA recalled the delicious shakes in 2009 due to years of *Salmonella* contamination. In the end, the evidence pointed back to the United States. Federal investigators and prosecutors would suspect but never confirm Bruce E. Ivins, a defense microbiologist at Fort Detrick, Maryland, as the sole attacker on August 6, 2008.[1]

In our world, we accepted the threat. The DoD had already initiated the Anthrax Vaccine Immunization Program against potential bioterrorism in 1998, but the latest attacks stoked the project. Full immunity required six vaccinations over eighteen months. The sole provider, BioPort Corporation, built the vaccine in the 1970s for animal-based anthrax exposure, but not for weaponized forms. Despite the shortcomings and unlicensed status by the FDA, the DoD used the vaccine to inoculate 150,000 Americans against Iraqi artillery with at least one dose in 1990 during the First Gulf War.

Doc Moreno plugged me with the first, mandatory shot on December 18, 2002, at Camp Horno. "You ready, Alex?" Same as on the ship.

I never got another anthrax vaccine. I later learned that a federal judge stopped the mandatory anthrax vaccine program in district court.

WAR CANARIES

The only chemical-detecting devices I trusted were the homing pigeons we put in cages bolted onto the front of our company Humvees. Millions of dollars in detection kits like the Improved Chemical Agent Monitor and mobile labs failed or delivered an official "MAYBE" to contaminated air. The birds had no gas masks. If we got hit, then we would wait and watch our avian comrades. If they passed out, flopped, or died, then we would keep the masks on no matter what the chemical experts and devices thought.

I walked by the company headquarters tent every day and after guard duty in Kuwait to check on the newest boots. The Marine Corps ordered 200 chickens as the first detectors, but they all died from dust asphyxiation upon reaching our camps. Marines who will remain nameless plucked and roasted some of the chickens. Our parent unit, Regimental Combat Team 1 (RCT-1), replaced the chickens with pigeons. Nobody had a clue how to care for them. Each bird cost $55.00. By D-Day, the regiment had forty pigeons on watch. Few survived past the fall of Baghdad as they died from heatstroke and dust. They were completely forgotten.

The birds deserve a memorial.

6

CHEMICAL WEAPONS

O
f all the buzzwords and catch phrases of the Second American War
in Iraq, none encapsulates the public ambivalence about the war
better than "weapons of mass destruction." According to the Bush
administration, WMDs stood at the heart of the United States' invasion
of Iraq in 2003, and their subsequent absence has since provided critics
of the war with their most powerful rhetorical tool in attacking the credibility of the president and the morality of his project. As it did in the First
American War in Iraq in the early 1990s, the threat of WMDs also shaped
the material conditions for US troops on the ground in 2003. For troops,
military planners, and the public alike, in 2003 it was difficult to avoid
looking at the situation in Iraq through the distorted lens of a gas mask.[1]

In its broadest sense, the phrase "weapon of mass destruction" refers
to any weapon capable of killing large numbers of people indiscrimi-
nately. In military parlance, the acronym for this group has evolved from
ABC (atomic, biological, and chemical) in the immediate post-WWII
period to NBC (nuclear, biological, and chemical) after the advent of
the hydrogen bomb to CBRN (chemical, biological, radiological, and
nuclear) in the post–Cold War period. When the Bush administration
presented intelligence on WMDs in Iraq to Congress, it emphasized the

possible presence of all three of the main Cold War categories: chemical, biological, and nuclear.[2] And in fact, at various times Saddam had sought to develop all three. When Lance Corporal Lemons landed in Kuwait in 2003, however, Iraqi WMDs, if they existed, were most likely to be chemical.

The dark and often ironic history of modern chemical weapons is oddly wrapped up with an equally ironic, if not unequivocally dark, history of modern agriculture. The "father" of modern chemical weapons was a German-Jewish chemist named Fritz Haber.[3] Before the outbreak of the war, Haber and Carl Bosch famously devised a method for synthesizing ammonia from hydrogen gas and nitrogen gas—that is, a method of "fixing" nitrogen at an industrial scale for use in things like fertilizer. As a key limiting factor in agricultural production, nitrogen fertilizer was one of the world's most important commodities in the late nineteenth and early twentieth centuries—so much so that nations were ready to go to war over tiny, bird-shit-spattered "guano islands" across the seas to protect their store of ready bird dung for their crops. The Haber-Bosch process suddenly made a whole lot of good fertilizer available for farmers across a hungry world, and for cheap. At the end of the twentieth century, the Haber-Bosch process underpinned more than half the world's agricultural production. In 1918, Haber received a Nobel Prize in Chemistry for his work.

But ammonia is not just good for crops; it's also good for blowing stuff up. Almost immediately upon its advent, nitrogen fixation began to feed the German war machine not just with crops, but also with explosives. Meanwhile, Haber put his considerable talents as a chemist to further use in the service of Germany's war effort, working to synthesize and militarize chemicals like chlorine gas and later mustard gas to complement more traditional explosives as head of the Chemistry section of the Ministry of War. He insisted on personally overseeing the release of chlorine gas at the Second Battle of Ypres in May 1915, when the weapon was first deployed by German soldiers who simply opened canisters of the stuff and let it drift across the battlefield towards the French trenches in the wind.[4]

The chlorine gas at Ypres was one of the more notorious episodes of the Great War. French soldiers recall the mysterious horror of watching the gray-green cloud, heavier than air, waft low and menacing over the battlefield and flow into their trenches, leaving their comrades suddenly gasping, clutching at their throats and eyes in panic as they fled down the lines. The initial discharge of gas—168 long tons of it—caused more than 6,000 allied casualties, and opened a four-mile-wide gap in the French front. Eventually, chlorine and a related but more deadly gas, phosgene, would account for more than 85 percent of the chemical warfare casualties of the Great War.[5] Many of the gas victims recovered physically, but the attacks created a new psychological dimension to the war that soldiers often found even more difficult to grapple with than war's physical injuries. The gas attack came to define the terror of the new trench warfare on both sides.

In the interwar period, German scientists continued to dominate the field of chemistry. Some continued to work on problems of war, but by the 1930s, many had returned to the agricultural problems that had originally motivated Haber. With the nitrogen fertilizer problem largely solved thanks to the Haber-Bosch process, the next generation of agriculturally minded chemists began to focus on pest control. Their results—and particularly those of Gerhard Schrader—echoed Haber's in eerily familiar ways.

Schrader worked for the German chemical giant IG Farben synthesizing new pesticides, and in the mid-1930s he began to experiment with a variety of chemicals called organophosphates that promised to kill insects by interfering with their nervous systems. What he found in 1936, however, was something called tabun, a tasteless, colorless substance with a faintly fruity odor that may in fact kill insects, but that most definitely kills humans. Immediately "recruited" to classified War Ministry work, Shrader soon produced the deadlier and thus more popular sarin gas in 1938, and later soman in 1944. He was also responsible for the synthesis of the most toxic nerve agent in this category—again, originally a pesticide—cyclosarin. Together, tabun, sarin, soman, and cyclosarin constitute the "G-series" anticholinesterase organophosphate nerve agents, so labeled for their German origins.[6]

Allied chemists responded with organophosphate nerve agents of their own: the V-series, the most familiar of which was called "Venomous Agent X," or VX gas. All of the organophosphate nerve agents bear striking chemical resemblances to their pesticide counterparts, and since the 1940s the pesticide industry in the United States has enjoyed a cozy relationship with the Department of Defense. Technical information has flowed in both directions. Sometimes, the science of killing people has informed the science of killing pests; sometimes, the science of killing pests has paved the way for new ways to kill people.[7]

For many veterans exposed to organophosphates during America's wars in Iraq and Afghanistan, the distinction between them is little more than a painful irony.

THE BEST WAY TO UNDERSTAND WHAT HAPPENED WITH THE WEAPons of mass destruction at the heart of the George W. Bush administration's justification for war in Iraq is to turn to the final 2004 report of the Iraq Survey Group. After a year of study, the group concluded that the WMDs Bush had waved before Congress and the American people simply didn't exist.[8] As David Kay said flatly upon his resignation as the head of the group in January 2004 before the Senate Armed Services Committee, "it turns out that we were all wrong."[9] Kay's successor, Charles A. Duelfer, later confirmed that the chances of finding WMD in Iraq were "close to nil."

More specifically, the Iraq Survey Group found that the intelligence community was wrong to believe that Saddam Hussein had developed weapons of mass destruction after the end of the First American War in Iraq in 1992. Addenda to the Iraq Survey Group Report in 2005 confirmed that it was unlikely that he had destroyed or exported chemical or biological weapons equipment before the American invasion. He simply never had them.

That is not to say that there were no chemical or biological weapons in the country when the US invaded in 2003. Nor is it to suggest that Alex and his fellow Marines were running around in MOPP suits and gas masks for nothing. Saddam's Iraq had a long history with chemical weapons.

But by the time Alex arrived in Iraq in 2003, most of what was left of Saddam's chemical arsenal after the Iran-Iraq War was gone, targeted and destroyed during the first hundred hours of Operation Desert Storm in 1991. According to the Iraq Survey Group, Saddam hoped to maintain the capacity to produce WMDs once the United Nations lifted sanctions on the country in the late 1990s, but the lifting of the sanctions themselves was his immediate goal throughout the decade. Even as he gave UN weapons inspectors the runaround in the mid and late 1990s and continued to bluff Iran with the possibility that he still had an active chemical weapons program, only small numbers of chemical munitions persisted, often poorly marked, in munitions facilities throughout the country. There is some evidence that Saddam himself didn't know where parts of his chemical weapons arsenal from the late 1980s and early 1990s were, and that he feared that weapons inspectors might find them before he had a chance to destroy them.[10]

All the more reason for Alex to keep an eye on the company pigeon.

7

"ECCENTRIC"

Life in Northern Kuwait required constant battles with dirt and disease. On our first day, Second Platoon swept out the tent. Push brooms and hand brushes assembled a five-pound bag of all-purpose flour at one end of the tent. Someone dumped it outside. The next morning a jarhead called reveille and the fluorescent lights popped on. I shook my sleeping bag. Brown flour floated above me. I put my feet into my shower shoes. Soft powder rubbed against my soles. We all coughed brown and black mucus from our lungs in unison. Everyone had bloodshot eyes. My fireteam looked like someone applied makeup to their cheeks and foreheads plus a fresh coat of dandruff. The sweeping began again.

During firewatch, training, and chow, I cataloged the varieties of soil and sand.

Kuwait Rock: The camp and training areas housed basketball-court-sized fields of gray-pink feldspar and black carbonates. Sometimes these rocks showed up elsewhere as lone individuals. The camp and training areas housed basketball-court-sized fields of gray-pink feldspar and black carbonates. The rocks cut through uniforms and skin. But they might protect plant life and plant life might tell you where to find water.

Hardpan: This was the last place to dig a ranger grave, a deep pit to sleep in and protect you from getting shelled. Your entrenching tool bounced off this concrete clay-sand with the first whacks. You needed a pickax to cut it.

Gunny Sand: Sharp stuff that always flew under your uncomfortable helmet sideways and slammed into your eyeball or turned wiping your ass into the application of premium grit sandpaper.

Fluff: The softest material in most of the sand, colored gray and light brown. Since we tasted the bitter stuff at chow, in training, and sleep, I knew it was gypsum.

Weapons maintenance became continuous. Marines kept painter's brushes at the ready in the same pocket that held dip and cigarettes. The tight rifle tolerances in our weapons demanded removal of every grain of sand or puff of dust. Swish. Swish. Swish. The rifle looked clean. Minutes later, sometimes seconds, dust re-blanketed it. Everyone tracked down muzzle covers, preventing Kuwait from drifting into the barrel. Adding the necessary lubricant to the bolt required caution. If you dunked the bolt, then grit magnetized to it and racking the bolt slowed or stopped.

None of our room clearing, foot patrols, and shooting prepared us for the dangers of desert warfare. Second Platoon crawled towards full strength with forced extensions for senior Marines and last-minute graduates of infantry school flown directly from the States. Thirty of us made a night movement in our new seven-ton trucks during our second week on the ground with the rest of the Alpha. Occasional raindrops splattered on the vinyl roof, and I held my rifle with its M203 grenade launcher tightly. Lightning cracked near one of the vehicles. Instead of heading back to Camp Inchon, we took a long security halt. The staff had our radio operator, LCpl Tommy Aguero, stand in the darkness with his PRC-119 backpack radio and six-foot whip antenna extended. He was hit by the next flash.

"Yeah, that was me bud," Aguero reminded me years later in a string of messages we typed to each other. He was Chamorro, a fisherman's son, and grew up on the empire's edge in Guam. "That was one of the worst nights. I had black shit coming out my ears and nose. Doc Van Houten was the one that tackled me to the ground after my radio blew up in my pack."

The operation should have stopped after Tommy got hit. It didn't. One of the trucks drove over hardpan and took a nosedive into a pile of fluff, landing on its side. Calls of "Corpsmen up! Corpsmen up!" echoed in the darkness. Our docs leapt from the truck and struggled to cross the sinking fluff to reach the pile of Marines. Our company commander had us line the truck beds with sandbags hoping it would protect us from future tank mines. He hadn't considered this altered driving physics and crushed humans during a rollover. He might have asked the drivers what they thought. Two Dustoff birds landed and the rest of the injured piled into a medevac truck before we drove, even slower, back to Camp Inchon.

<hr/>

OUR CAMP FOUGHT A LOSING WAR AGAINST THE ENVIRONMENT. DIVISION ENGI- neers along with contractors and subcontractors built tent neighborhoods like Camp Inchon inside the giant Tactical Assembly Area Coyote a month before we landed. They bulldozed twenty-foot berms of rock and sand around the camp. The berms slowly crumbled under constant winds. They dropped gravel mixed with getch, a clay that bonds rocks together, from the United Arab Emirates, as temporary roads. To minimize erosion of those million-dollar roads, a truck sprayed a polymer tar oil once a week. Wind blew the tar oil onto the tents, or the heat evaporated the fluid. Marines surrounded diesel generators in tall cement walls, only to have sand crawl through cracks or over the top and fall into the machines.

Division kept the camp Spartan so we wouldn't get comfy. The white-yellow tents trucked in from outside Kuwait contained kerosene coating as waterproofing. The engineers and contractors wired mercury fluorescent lights and zip-tied them vertically on the golden tent masts. There was no firefighting equipment and no plan for fire escape. At least on ship, every berthing had fire extinguishers and "forever chemical" foams. In Kuwait, you would probably burn alive inside your sleeping bag before you heard the alarm. Whatever the tent material had been soaked in, tent burnings happened multiple times after we left and into the summer of 2003.

Daily and nightly winds coasted into Camp Inchon from the surrounding deserts. Two sides of Second Platoon's tent looked more worn out and sand-caked than the others. The worst sand blasts came from northwesterly *shamals*. A cold front blew through Inchon on March 1 and March 2. It rocked tents all night, and next day the platoon redirected stakes and tightened lanyards.

A larger megastorm hit on the night of March 12. It was a Wednesday. I remember the day only because McGuire updated me on the Elizabeth Smart case. Smart was abducted at knifepoint from her childhood home in Salt Lake City in June 2002. The captor, in true Utah fashion, was a man claiming to be a religious prophet. The relentless search went on for ten more months and McGuire and I followed the story obsessively, hoping she would fight her way to survival.

Staff Sergeant McGuire was undoubtedly the most interesting Marine I ever worked with. He served in the Navy and as a young squid he unloaded bodies of dead and wounded Marines after the Beirut bombing. Then he made an interservice transfer and started all over again. He didn't yell or scream except in the rare instances where he lost his temper and then exploded. (We had this in common.) He managed his duties coolly and quietly oversaw our training.

In its pursuit of automatons, the Marine Corps had a word for people like McGuire. It was the same word that popped into my mind when I thought of the commanding general of my division, James Mattis. *Eccentric*. Eccentric to me meant you were proficient at your job and still maintained your personality. Eccentric to the Marine Corps meant cowboy and dangerously independent.

McGuire was eccentric in a whole bunch of little ways that I appreciated. He washed his own clothes in a garbage bag instead of making one of the junior Marines clean them. He brought a survival radio that patched us into BBC transmissions—our source for Smart case updates—that he argued were more reliable than anything our command passed. He wore the lowest possible regulation haircut and paired it with a Tom

Selleck-meets-rodeo-rider mustache when the rest of us looked like the Adolf Hitler fan club. Instead of Vietnam-era birth control goggles, he rocked a pair of non-issue black frame glasses. Unlike the dimwitted and belt-fed company gunny, he treated us like adults. "This is the real show," he told all of us on our first week with Alpha in California that December. "Every training evolution is serious business. Forget the usual Marine Corps games. Listen, learn, and if you don't understand, ask questions." He and I talked about animals (he liked cats and birds), history, and his Navy time, but ultimately what interested him was my Mormon heritage.

"Geez Lemons, Mormons are fucking weird," he'd tell me endlessly on ship and in Kuwait. No argument from me. He had more questions. He couldn't believe I wasn't a polygamist. He pressed for more knowledge. "What exactly was Utah famous for other than Karl Malone and John Stockton? It's famous for beautiful deserts, religious zealots preying on young people, and Jell-O. And two out of three of those we can chalk up to the Mormons." These statements rang true, but I defended my state and my family's 1834 start in the faith.

He said all of this wearing black tight-fitting gloves and black polished boots, both of which he wore all the time in eighty-degree weather. Maybe he had a circulation problem. Or maybe he was just fucking weird.

McGuire dragged us through the March 12 storm, arm in arm, tying the tents back down and looking for a lost Marine before we came back empty-handed. Another squad found him full of valium injectors and suicidal in one of the port-o-shitters. "The next time one of you fuckers wants to take your own life," the braindead staff sergeant from the lost Marine's platoon lectured the next day, "please just go condition one [round in the chamber] and shoot yourself in the mouth." The rest of us were glad the Marine was alive and going home.

Despite the near-death thrill of walking through a dust blender, I admired the storm. It made the Marine Corps shut up for at least twelve hours as we quietly reassembled Camp Inchon and cleaned our equipment and bodies. We coughed and sneezed the desert back out.

Shamals—seasonal Iraqi dust storms like the one that struck us that night—made the desert look uninhabitable. No wetlands, no trees, hot days with sunshine slamming and frying microbes, and intensely cold nights. Colorado and Utah had millions of acres that tourists and locals considered barren, too. I knew this wasn't true. They didn't put their noses in the soil. Kuwait was similar. It rained in the winter. Cryptobiotic soil and other organic matter hung in safe micro-terrain, like Kuwait Rock, where *Rhanterium* shrubs and annuals like sea rockets grew.

Healthy soil and plants provided a home for insects, arachnids, and rodents that found hiding spots in our plywood-floored and canvas-cloth tents. Desert pathogens accompanied arthropods, reptiles, and other critters. Biting sandfleas enjoyed Marine bodies. They exchanged the tropical parasite *Leishmania tropica* for protein in our blood. The tents had probably been sprayed with d-phenothrin aerosol pesticide, or maybe chlorpyrifos, to deal with some of these critters. It left a sweet smell in an otherwise-gym-locker environment where we practiced weapons manipulation, boxed, and gobbled up every second of training we could stuff down. Pest strips of dichlorvos hung from the sagging tent roofs. DEET and OFF! bug juice were always available if you wanted them, and they never failed.

The corpsmen handed out other medications. We took mefloquine, trade name Lariam, as an anti-malaria drug. The VA has a webpage on it: "Neurologic or psychiatric side effects may occur at any time during drug use and may last for months to years after the drug is stopped." There's a number for a suicide hotline right on the page.[1] We took a pill from the blister packet once a day during our time in Kuwait. For anyone experiencing side effects like headaches, diarrhea, or a rash, it was hard to know if mefloquine caused it or one of dozens of other things we did or ate.

One way or another, malaria scared me more than any imagined WMD and I popped the meds. The corpsmen also ordered us to consume tiny blue pills before dinner called doxycycline. The tetracycline antibiotic "Doxy" could prevent malaria, kill infections caused by ticks or mites, and treat anthrax. It wrecked your GI tract and made you more susceptible to sunburns and heat injury. The whole thing seemed like antibiotic overuse. We snapped up the pills before evening chow and then hiked over to the dining hall.

We ate with our hands still covered with OFF!, more DEET, and rifle cleaner.

8

GULF WAR REDUX

From the American perspective, the First American War in Iraq—the Gulf War—was a smashing success in nearly every respect. American smart bombs paved the way for an overwhelming siege that liberated Kuwait, shattered the Iraqi Army, and chastened the belligerent Iraqi dictator. The fighting lasted one hundred hours. American casualties were few, and American Patriot missiles served to mitigate the threat to Israel, America's vulnerable ally in the region. A new twenty-four-hour news network, CNN, chronicled the bombing in vivid nighttime images for the American public. Perhaps unexpectedly, Saddam Hussein refrained from deploying chemical or biological weapons at a significant scale (though there were some reported attacks), and in a matter of days the American-led coalition forces dismantled the Iraqis' war-making machine for the foreseeable future. Plenty of critics called loudly for Saddam's ouster, and hawks in the military begged for permission to finish the job, but for most Americans, the view from the Persian Gulf in 1992 looked pretty good.

If the war had few traditional, immediate casualties, however, veterans of the First American War in Iraq soon began to feel its legacy in puzzling and persistent ways. Almost as soon as the conflict subsided,

American veterans began showing up at VA hospitals with a variety of similar, poorly defined symptoms. Of the more than 600,000 Persian Gulf veterans, 125,000 of them underwent VA health registry examinations. More than 50,000 of them complained of fatigue, skin rashes, headaches, joint or muscle pain, and loss of memory.[1] They were diagnosed variously with musculoskeletal diseases, mental disorders, and "ill-defined conditions," but VA doctors had no explanations for the onset of the veterans' conditions, nor could they say whether their conditions were service-related. Later, studies of Persian Gulf War veterans next to control groups of veterans who did not serve in the Gulf confirmed the association between service in the region and a predisposition towards these unexplained symptoms, and by 1998—around the same time the VA began to grapple in a real way with the long-term impacts of Agent Orange on its Vietnam War veterans—doctors had begun to describe the bundle of pathologies as "Gulf War syndrome."[2]

Even before it had a name, Gulf War syndrome inspired a multitude of hypotheses about its origins. The leading candidate was obvious: chemical and biological weapons. As Michigan's Democratic senator Don Riegle put it in 1994, "It does not take a Ph.D., knowing Saddam Hussein's record, knowing he had the production facilities, knowing that we went and bombed some of those production facilities . . . to understand that such exposure may—and I underline the word *may*—be causing the problems of a lot of our sick veterans that otherwise are defying explanation."[3] For Riegle, who held a set of high-profile hearings on the subject before the not-entirely-appropriate Senate Committee on Banking, Housing, and Urban Affairs, taking care of sick veterans was important. But so too was the fact that Iraq had received many of the materials necessary for synthesizing chemical and biological agents from the US Department of Commerce in the 1980s. Riegle's final report spelled out the connection explicitly, claiming that "coalition forces were exposed to mixed chemical agents as a result of coalition bombings of Iraqi nuclear, chemical, and biological facilities and that the fallout from these bombings may be contributing to the health problems currently being suffered by Gulf War veterans" following the

Gulf War.[4] For Democrats, this looked like Ronald Reagan's chickens coming home to roost.

In reality, however, the story of Gulf War syndrome wasn't so simple. First of all, just trying to determine who might have been exposed to what and how much turned out to be exceedingly difficult. This would become a pattern for veterans' exposures, and it is a pattern that persists today. For the first five years after the war, the Department of Defense maintained that no American soldiers had been exposed to chemical agents in Iraq. And to be fair, allied forces detected no obvious *offensive* uses of chemical agents by the Iraqi Army during the war. But alarms signifying low-level chemical agents in the air went off more than 18,000 times during the conflict, leading many observers to suggest that coalition bombs meant to destroy Iraqi chemical weapons facilities had inadvertently sent plumes of sarin and soman wafting over positions throughout the country.[5] Most famously, in March 1991, after the war's official end, a US demolition team blew up a weapons depot at Khamisiyah that contained sarin, setting off detectors throughout the coalition ranks. Eventually, the DoD relented and admitted that there may have been some low-level exposure among troops in the Gulf.[6] But even with sophisticated modeling techniques, it is impossible to determine exposures with the kind of specificity required for a definitive medical study.

Perhaps more importantly, even if US troops were exposed to sarin gas, it wasn't the only or even the worst thing they were exposed to. It's no surprise that veterans and doctors worried about the long-term impacts of nerve agents in the Gulf. The threat of CBRN warfare scared the shit out of soldiers in the field, and it's understandable that it continued to scare them after they returned home. Nerve gas is bad stuff, and the military had a pretty good handle on just how bad from a series of dangerous, semi-consensual experiments it had conducted on US army personnel at the Edgewood Arsenal in Maryland in the 1970s.[7] But again, with the gas mask on it's difficult to get an accurate picture of the terrain. The same troops who *might* have been exposed to nerve gas in amounts that *might* have long-term consequences were also *definitely* exposed to a wide variety of other potential toxins in the Persian Gulf theater. Ironically, two of those toxic substances—the two that researchers would most closely associate with the syndrome that the medical community came to call Gulf War illness—were directly related to chemical weapons. Indeed, the first and most likely contributor to Gulf War illness is actually a nerve gas prophylactic: pyridostigmine bromide, PB.

As Alex has explained, PB is a cholinergic drug that binds reversibly to the acetylcholinesterase enzymes that serve to neutralize a nerve impulse. The stuff is most commonly used in large doses as a treatment for an autoimmune neuromuscular disease called myasthenia gravis, but the FDA granted the Department of Defense a waiver to distribute PB to soldiers during the Gulf War as an "investigational product." During the Gulf War, troops were meant to take 30 mg PB pills every eight hours during periods when nerve gas exposure was likely, but unit commanders gave varying orders to troops on when and how much PB to take. All told, more than 250,000 troops self-administered more than 5 million doses of PB during the war. Many felt the drug's side effects—mostly headaches, diarrhea, and nausea that poked through the other background discomforts of deployment—but less than 1 percent of those troops required medical attention for acute side effects of PB.[8]

Even in 1991, nobody thought that PB was particularly good for you. After all, at a cellular level, it does some of the same things as the nerve gas it is meant to thwart. But it is certainly less bad in the short term than sarin gas, and there is little in the toxicological literature on PB outside of the Gulf War context to suggest one way or the other whether low-dose PB exposures over time might present long-term health risks. It was only later that PB emerged as a major exposure concern for Gulf War veterans.

In 1998, Congress charged the Department of Veterans Affairs with forming a Research Advisory Committee on Gulf War Veterans' Illnesses (often shortened to RAC) to help direct and coordinate studies of Gulf War veterans reporting multisymptom illnesses. In their 2008 report, the RAC found ten major studies of Gulf War exposure conducted since the end of the conflict that had considered PB. In nine of them, researchers had found a clear association between PB and Gulf War veterans' multisymptom illnesses. Moreover, in six of those studies, researchers had controlled for other, potentially confounding exposures, and in all six cases, the association between PB and these same symptoms still held strong.[9] Researchers even discovered what is called a "dose-response" effect. The more PB troops took during their tours in the Gulf, the more likely they were to present symptoms of Gulf War illness, and the more severe those symptoms were likely to be.[10] It is likely that low-level exposures to chemical weapons agents contributed to many Gulf War veterans' conditions.[11] The RAC found several studies that established such an association. Regardless of their exposure to chemical agents, however, it is *almost certain* that the pills they popped to try to mitigate the damage of those chemical agents helped make them sick down the road. The cure may not have been worse than the disease, but there are nevertheless a whole lot of veterans still suffering from the cure.

In the early 1990s, mask-toting soldiers and Marines took PB to protect them from organophosphate nerve agents used in chemical weapons. Even as they did so, however, they were also more or less bathing in a related set of organophosphates and similar compounds meant for a different, also deadly purpose: killing pests. (Thank you Gerhard Schrader.) According to the DoD, troops had access to sixty-seven different pesticides during the Gulf War, fifteen of which were either organophosphates, carbamates (which also act on AChE enzymes), or pyrethroids that the RAC called "pesticides of potential concern."[12] As with PB pills, these fifteen pesticides showed up as a group in ten major studies of Gulf War illness. This time, all ten studies found an association between pesticides and GWI. Of the six studies that controlled for other exposures, five still showed a significant correlation between pesticide exposure and Gulf War illness. Again, researchers found a "dose-response" relationship.[13]

As with other exposures, when it comes to pesticides it is difficult to know who was exposed to how much of what in the Gulf. Marines' primary concerns were biting sand fleas and the ubiquitous and aggressive flies of the region, but both Kuwait's desert and its cities housed a wide variety of small biting things. Pesticides consequently came in many forms. Crews sprayed organophosphates like malathion, diazinon, and chlorpyrifos in concentrated liquid form into corners and crevices,

and they "fogged" larger areas with a more diluted solution. Chlorpyrifos also showed up alongside the organophosphate dichlorvos in No-Pest
Strips in cantinas and latrines throughout Kuwait. Meanwhile, just as
Alex would a decade later, Gulf War service members frequently took
insect control into their own hands, most often using military-issue
DEET (75 percent concentration) alongside commercial repellents like
OFF! and various flea collars, which they put around bedposts and hung
from tent poles. Finally, troops treated their uniforms with a military-
issue pyrethroid called permethrin, often at a frequency and in quantities
that far exceeded the product's commercial recommendations.

Individual pesticides have the potential to be quite toxic, but in isolation and used as directed, most of the pesticides employed during the
Gulf War are considered relatively safe. They were certainly better than
many of the nasty pest-borne diseases they were deployed to mitigate.
But in Kuwait in the 1990s, pesticides were neither used in isolation nor
as directed. In retrospect, the synergistic effects of multiple pesticides
and other theater-specific substances—that is, the way these substances
mixed together in bodies to create bigger problems than they would
individually—seem willfully perverse. In their attempts to protect themselves from the country's critters, Americans exposed themselves to a
cocktail of chemicals that worked together to compromise their long-
term health in a variety of nefarious ways.

One key ingredient in this chemical cocktail was permethrin. Permethrin is not an organophosphate; rather, it is a pyrethroid, one in a
much safer family of synthetic chemicals meant to mimic the natural
bug-killing compound in the flowers of plants in the pyrethrum family.
Think chrysanthemums. Permethrin is a fast-acting neurotoxin primarily used to kill bugs on contact. The RAC lists it as a repellant, but from an
insect's perspective it is chiefly a poison. And like the chrysanthemums
it imitates, permethrin is remarkably effective. It is also cheap, easy to
make and distribute, and has been shown again and again to be safe for
topical human use, even for small children. The World Health Organization has listed it among the world's "essential medicines," and in addition to its efficacy in treating scabies and lice in individuals, it has been

used effectively in large-scale insect control and malaria prevention campaigns around the world.[14] It's bad for you if you eat it, it's a disaster for aquatic ecosystems, and it's highly toxic to cats (but not dogs), but short of excessive application, permethrin alone is a mostly harmless wonder substance. Which is why the military had troops wash their shirts in it.

So why are we worried about permethrin? The answer, it turns out, is that it is pretty safe . . . *unless* you happen to be exposed to a rarely used cholinergic drug called pyridostigmine bromide. PB was yet another key ingredient in the Gulf War's signature chemical cocktail, one more abiotic component of the combat ecosystem that helped make so many soldiers sick. PB makes permethrin way worse for you than it otherwise might be.

Typically, we don't readily absorb permethrin through our skin. Any permethrin that does get into our bloodstream soon meets glucuronidase enzymes that break the substance down, letting the remainder flush from our bodies.

But ingesting PB pills changes all that. In 1991, troops with PB in their system could absorb as much as six times the permethrin through their skin than they would without PB in their system. Marines taking PB pills could expect a similar spike in their absorption of DEET. To make matters worse, JP-8—the ubiquitous jet fuel used across the military in Kuwait for heavy equipment that has recently been associated with deficiencies in auditory processing—also increased the absorption and bioavailability of permethrin and DEET through the skin. Service members weren't just exposing themselves to high doses of permethrin by overtreating their uniforms; they were also opening themselves up to those extra doses of permethrin by taking PB as a measure against chemical attack, by using DEET to control bugs on their bodies, and simply by being around the variety of substances used in military maneuvers.

Inside their bodies, the situation for Gulf War veterans did not improve. Most vertebrates that aren't feline can metabolize permethrin rather quickly, but when researchers at Duke University put PB and permethrin in blood together in a test tube, they found that each managed to block the enzyme that metabolized the other. Take PB, and you won't metabolize permethrin. Expose yourself to permethrin, and you

won't metabolize PB. Meanwhile, both PB and permethrin also significantly inhibited the metabolism of DEET. And the organophosphate
chlorpyrifos—which teams sprayed all over camps and forward operating bases during the Gulf War—inhibits the metabolism of the whole lot.
In human blood, processing one type of neurotoxin tends to get in the
way of processing others, giving substances like permethrin and DEET
more time to damage the nervous system. In 2008, the RAC detailed
twenty different experiments designed to mimic Gulf War PB and pesticide exposures in mice, rats, and hens. Nearly all the experiments showed
that combinations of PB, DEET, permethrin, and chlorpyrifos "yielded
significantly greater neurotoxicity than single exposures." (Not surprisingly, the menagerie of nonhuman test subjects did not fare well in this
particular laboratory ecosystem.)[15]

There are two final perverse effects of the combination of PB, DEET,
and permethrin, both of which underscore the broader intractability of
Gulf War illness as a whole. First, the effects of PB, DEET, and permethrin together get worse when you add the one thing combat veterans
simply can't avoid: stress. The research here remains controversial, but
animal studies have shown that the combination of PB, DEET, permethrin, and a mild stressor lead to significant increases in the permeabil-
ity of the blood-brain barrier in four distinct regions of the brain. The
blood-brain barrier describes a collection of gatekeeper cells that determine what compounds get to move from a person's blood into their brain
and central nervous system. As I described earlier, lead manages to cross
this barrier by duping enzymes into thinking it is another element, calcium, that the nervous system needs. Together, PB, DEET, permethrin,
and stress may make lead's job—and mercury's, and cadmium's, and a
variety of other toxicants'—that much easier. Meanwhile, the same combination of PB, DEET, permethrin, and stress has also been correlated
with markers of injury to the same regions of the brain. Other animal
studies have described behavioral markers to match.[16] Gulf War veterans spent years convincing the VA and others that Gulf War illness was
a physical phenomenon rather than a purely psychological one, but the

emotional environment of war seems to have made the toxicants of the physical environment in the Gulf far worse.

By the time of the 2003 invasion, the Department of Defense had a good deal of evidence that suggested there had been problems with the military's distribution of pesticides in the Gulf War. And those problems did not get fixed before Alex deployed in 2003. A report by the Army Medical Research Institute of Chemical Defense at the outset of Alex's war sums up the situation up well:

> It seems prudent to recommend avoidance when possible of untoward levels of simultaneous exposure to incompletely studied combinations such as PB, permethrin, and DEET while at the same time realizing that currently available evidence is insufficient to warrant abandoning current doctrinal guidance concerning the military use of these compounds.[17]

Which is to say: we're not sure, so we're just going to keep doing the probably toxic thing we've been doing. In the gas mask logic that carried over from one war to the next, PB was reauthorized in 2003 under the condition that its use was strictly controlled and documented. Which it wasn't. The military kept dousing blouses and trousers in permethrin. And Marines kept writing home for care packages of DEET to keep the bugs off.

Thus did grunts like Alex in the Second American War in Iraq in 2003 repeat the two sets of exposures most strongly associated with Gulf War illness after the First American War in Iraq in 1991–92.

9

"SPEED, SPEED, SPEED"

On March 15, 2003, our sojourn in Kuwait ended. As usual, McGuire's radio transmissions from the BBC passed swifter word than our command. I traded in my grenade launcher for a light machine gun and was switched from assistant team leader (ATL) in Second Squad to a gunner in First Squad. We ditched the trucks in exchange for amphibious tractors—amtracs—without sandbags. Then we received our second shower of the month. The Marine Corps wouldn't let you scrub down unless it was about to send your ass downrange. Word passed from the company that we'd receive nonalcoholic beer that night. Finally, the division delivered Pizza Hut to our doorstep. Dirt and gypsum lightly salted the pizzas. It was cold and hard, for those who got a slice. We ate without complaint.

It never felt like an invasion, and it still doesn't. Nothing like what I saw at Utah Beach and Pointe du Hoc in France. Not at all like the Second Persian Invasion of Greece. This was more like a spring break road trip, periodically broken up by drive-by shootings, car crashes, and building clearings. Sometimes, the trip reminded me of a sleepless cattle drive. Lots of dust, strangers, assholes, and flies. We lived inside our amtrac, blindly driving from one pit stop to the next, fixated on the journey. If there was a strategy, we never saw it.

As the Pulitzer Prize–winning journalist Thomas E. Ricks wrote, "Strategy" goes like this: "Who are we, and what are we ultimately trying to do here? How will we do it, and what resources and means will we employ in doing it?"[1] Once you answer those questions, you have a blueprint that everyone from a general down to a private can hold and work from no matter what happens. Tactics is what you *do* from strategy. Most of us dumbly obsess over technology and skills, as if those things are more important than the ideas and ideals they are deployed to support. Training counts, but you can't do things in the wrong order.

Our obsession with gas masks underscored our wrongheaded approach. If I applied the mask in time and didn't have razor bumps breaking the seal, then the mask might protect me from the worst imagined threat. But what were the worst threats? With the mask on, I didn't see dust, bug spray, or things that would hurt us just as badly as shrapnel and anthrax. I didn't see how closed factories and a shortage of medical supplies from the United Nations sanctions in the '90s would help create disciplined insurgents in the '00s.

In 2003, this was all I knew: I was Lance Corporal Lemons, just an average grunt, and understood nothing other than my platoon's survival. My command, even a brighter-than-average general like Mattis, told me Saddam Hussein had abandoned regional ambitions in favor of nuclear weapons and a fanatical partnership with Osama bin Laden, Iran, and North Korea that was bent on attacking the rest of the planet. Killing Saddam, his army, and the Ba'ath administration would end this nightmare while germinating democracy in Iraq and in turn across the Greater Middle East without costing the United States and its allies anything.

More than twenty years later, I haven't met any American grown-ups willing to admit they believed this back then. But anyone who says they lived through the whirlwind and didn't hear or sometimes trust these messages is lying to you.

My battalion sat within Regimental Combat Team 1, and RCT-1 sat within First Marine Division, roughly 20,000 Marines and sailors from Southern California, traveling among 8,000 vehicles that ranged from water support trucks and tankers to vehicles transporting everyone from trauma surgeons to artillery gunners.

Amidst the excess of equipment, Second Platoon behaved compara-tively like ultralight backpackers. Rucks contained issued gear or meager personal belongings. The entrenching tool, known as an e-tool and used to dig both catholes to shit in and ranger graves to shoot from, became your best friend. Porn mags, Tapatío Hot Sauce, K-Y Lube, compact disc players, first-generation MP3s, pocket pussies (commercial and field expedient), dip, letters from home, extra Doxy, lucky rabbits' feet, batteries we bought at the post exchange, and wet wipes topped off the few inches of empty space. Division Logistics cut daily food rations to two and some days one MREs in exchange for more artillery shells. Each brick-sized meal contained 1,200 calories. MREs, as a rule, should only be consumed for twenty-one days. With no fiber, the rations produce gut-blocking constipation. Hence the blackjack limit. We also carried a limited amount of bottled water but had reverse osmosis and chlorination purification systems on hand. We shut off idling engines after ten minutes to save fuel. C-130 aircraft would land directly on freeways or temporary airfields to resupply us with fuel and some water. Mattis had summed up the backpacker model back in December of 2002. "The sooner we get it over with, the better. Our overriding principle will be speed, speed, speed."[2]

Alpha company traded the seven-ton trucks we trained in for amtracs, the Mark 7A1 AAV. On paper, the sweet 1970s swimmer fit three crew, one troop commander, and twenty-four Marines in the belly. With all our gear on and rucks strapped on the outside, we barely squeezed fifteen inside. Then we stashed more ammo and bottled water beneath the seats. We looked like the military edition of the Clampett family in *The Beverly Hillbillies*. I could barely wiggle my toes inside. The steel benches we sat on had a one-inch pad that flattened to nothing under the hundred pounds of gear.

Over the Line of Departure, we drove through smoke from the oil fires. Every one of our 8,000 vehicles left a wake of fine dust, which flooded our cabin. A packet of wet wipes couldn't remove a quarter of the dirt on your face. Uniformed enemy soldiers were scarce; gunfights against Fedayeen Saddam guerillas became the norm. Friendly fire became more frequent than the nonexistent Iraqi artillery as we rolled into the first large city on the Euphrates River, Nasiriyah.

We stopped outside the city and entrenched in the town dump. Mounds of plastic, diapers, glass, and paper waste surrounded us. The rot strained everyone's noses. "Don't worry, we won't be here long," McGuire advised. An hour passed and that meant fixed positions. My battery mate and fellow *Dubpuke* survivor Alcantar and I dug in and cleared away syringes and rotten food. We shoveled out cardboard and plastic bags. When it was our turn to rest, we instantly went to sleep in the filth.

The guerillas scored kills on March 23, and we delayed our movement. An Army company got lost and were nearly wiped out under mortars, small arms, and rocket-propelled grenades (RPGs) in Nasiriyah. After Marine tankers rounded up the survivors, First Battalion, Second Marines cruised into the city and captured two bridges. They lost eight jarheads. An amtrac carried the wounded north, while a Fedayeen RPG blew apart another amtrac and its ammunition, killing the squad inside. Other tracs took more fire. Then an Air National Guard–piloted A-10 struck a company of Marines believing they were enemy because our green MOPP suits made us look like Iraqis. No one ever took responsibility for that. As we drove through Nasiriyah, tracer blasts flickered over the burned out amtracs and Marine dead. The wagon train continued north.

Stressed out and beat down, we all began mastering the art of sleeping sitting upright. The white noise of the eight-cylinder engine helped me snooze. At that end of the cabin, the noise drowned out conversations.

"Ramp coming down!!!" We started taking fire.

Light filled the cabin and the ramp motor whirred as it dropped. My legs wanted to stay put but my hands pushed me off the seat. Up, out, into the morning light with my heart knocking into my vest, another Marine pressed behind me. I didn't see any muzzle flashes. The heavy weapons on the amtrac fired. Only one person started moving forward, waving and yelling. I grabbed Alcantar and charged forward, firing into the building where I heard gunfire at my front. Just short of the house one of my legs sunk into a mud hole. I screamed like a wild animal. It was an unrestrained, primal yell, and it surprised me, calmed me down.

I pulled myself out of the mud and then blew my top and yelled "FUCK" so many times that everyone busted out laughing. We cleared through the buildings and found no one and nothing. It passed so quickly I didn't understand how my body did it. Back in the amtrac, we did a head count, and I screamed my name over the revving engine. A fat, useless sergeant attached to us at the last minute in an anti-tank team thought I was talking back when I said my name. He crawled over the rest of the squad and popped me in the face. I blacked out and woke up five minutes later finding everyone asleep and my right eye swollen.

RCT-1 continued up Route 7 towards the river town of Kut. Iraqi grunts surrendered and we checked them for weapons or intel but found nothing. They looked malnourished and burned out like everyone else we met. We told them to go home and wait. On the road, we observed vans full of dead civilians and trucks with guerillas burnt black. Feet, otherwise ignored in regular life, had a special place in war. They could be severed and dozens of yards from their owner, but perfectly intact. Or fleshless and holding the same arch shape as when alive. There were plenty of feet along the road to look at.

The road trip worsened. Marines rear ended or side swiped one another. One Marine died in his fighting hole as a Humvee rolled over him in his sleep. Rank protected no one from accidents. Dirt kept piling up on top of and inside the trac. The leather in my boots dried out and cracked. My feet smelled worse than the dump in Nasiriyah. I wiped them down with baby wipes and changed into other dirty socks, each frozen stiff from foot sweat. Water and rations remained perilous. I constantly went for the bottled water. It stung, hot to the touch from cooking in clear bottles under the sun. I'd been taught to police up my shit—Marine speak for leave no trace—since boot camp, but everyone tossed trash onto the sides of the road or in someone's front yard. Graves of Charms candy—a US military staple since WWII—sat on the edges of Route 7, warding off bad luck.

Our asses felt less and less fleshy and more like flattened steel. The only semi-comfortable seat was the foam-covered ammo crate we turned into a shitter, but that was hardly luxurious. The flies didn't care.

On the line, we fought sleep deprivation by chewing on coffee grounds, Ripped Fuel (the weight-loss pill stacked with caffeine and soon-to-be-banned ephedra), slaps to the face, and push-ups. On top of the trac, the exhaust blasted your face. We kept munching on Doxy and taking our Lariam. At night, we dug the deepest ranger graves. Then we moved in an hour to new positions and dug fresh pits all over again. Knowing my soil types at this point, digging was easy. I expected Marine artillery to kill me long before a well-placed Iraqi mortar. In any case, I dug deep, and more dirt filled my lungs.

On the night of March 25, outside of Gharraf, we got bashed by the Mother of All Sandstorms. The brown-out killed visibility beyond thirty yards. Next, winter rains hit, turning the sand and dust first into bursts of damp powder then a cookie dough slurry. The rain turned to hail. Mud clung to every boot, finger, and weapon. The battalion was exhausted, and as the lack of sleep persisted, we started seeing and hearing enemies. Everyone imagined a troop of T-72 tanks prowling in the darkness and worried our limited anti-tank weapons wouldn't stop them.

The only thing keeping me awake were conversations with Alcantar. Every grubby decision, relationship failure, or bad piece of music you listened to comes back to life in an entrenched position. Alcantar took me through the rituals of Mexican adolescence and life in Louisiana. I riffed on camping, of all things, and how much I missed snow. Mud thickened during the night as the temperature dropped.

I was miserable, but somehow frustrated that I wasn't more miserable. This was bored misery, and the boredom made me want to get shot at. It wasn't hard enough. It wasn't bad enough. But I didn't tell Alcantar that.

THE OBJECTIVE OF RCT-1, MATTIS DIDN'T TELL US, WAS TO DRIVE UP ROUTE 7 AND destroy the Republican Guard Baghdad Division in Kut so they couldn't defend Baghdad. This would allow the main force of the US Army to advance swiftly on the capital from Karbala, from the southwest; the rest of our division would eventually bypass us and join the Army from the southeast. Kut was a head fake, and our regiment was the bait.

"Speed, speed, speed" kept Alpha Company dismounting in small towns to provide security as the rest of 1/4 charged through. In Shatrah, a town supposedly loaded with chemical weapons, the streets looked empty.

An empty town by this point indicated insurgents swarming for an attack. A single RPG shooter launched, missed, and then had dozens of 40mm grenades dropped on him. Then the town was silent. An hour later an old and unarmed man walked out of a building towards us. His baggy dishdasha dragged in the dirt. Maybe he was coming out to greet us or maybe he had dementia. He should have stayed inside. I prepared to yell from behind my berm and wave him back and didn't get the chance. Someone shot him in the guts, and he fell headlong into the street. Mosque loudspeakers called commands and I slumped behind the dirt. I felt sick.

We reached Kut on April 3. Chaos, General Mattis's callsign, sent the Iraqi commanding general a communique: "To the commander of the Iraqi forces in Kut. You are surrounded. There is no hope for your forces to be reinforced or re-supplied. We will continue to attack unless you choose to stop the unnecessary killing. If you choose not to surrender, all of the killing will be your responsibility and yours only." No one responded. No surprise. We edged into the city and blasted away at enemy positions for several hours as the Fedayeen poured mortar fire, small arms, and RPGs into us. Then we broke contact and turned around.

The Baghdad Division and accompanying chemical artillery we expected and diligently prepared against, I learned years later, were not even in the city.

After screaming two hundred kilometers back south from Kut, then to Numaniyah, we linked up with the rest of the division at the Diyala River crossroads. My squad leader told Alcantar and me to change out of our MOPP suits on the night of April 6. Twenty-two days in the suit and six potential gas alerts, combined with the word that had been coming down from on high in the previous weeks and months, didn't square with the orders. As we closed on Baghdad, our command warned that desperate Iraqi leaders would unleash chemical and biological shells at close range. If not the military, then it would be the legions of independent terrorists the Ba'ath Party had an apparent blood bond with. The Tuwaitha nuclear facility rested only eight kilometers southeast of the city, not too far from the holes we dug that night.

Now the command flipped the script. No need to worry. No MOPP suits.

I rolled my suit up tightly and pressed it into the bottom of my ruck. Still, the gas mask carrier stayed on my hip for another week, if nothing else to make my company gunny happy. The day after the no-MOPP order we cleared a compound loaded with unidentifiable artillery shells with zero chemical precautions and said nothing.

Our spring break continued inside the amtrac. Someone sacrificed one of their porn mags to decorate the lime-green walls. The face of the *charro* on the Tapatío bottle became dusty and begrimed. He still smiled through the dirt. *"Es una salsa . . . Muy salsa!"* He made MREs tolerable. We scrounged for bottled water and ate stale, half-eaten crackers and pound cake from roadside trash piles. Or we pilfered from the humanitarian rations that we and the Iraqis found equally disgusting. The day before we ripped off the MOPP suits, we dropped all our gear, made cardboard signs, and begged for food and water as other units passed us by.

We crossed the Diyala River at Numaniyah on April 7. Our trac, breaking down for the third or fourth time on the trail, needed a tow up to the shore. Our mechanical wizards and amtrac drivers, Corporal Edgecombe and Sergeant Eagle, repaired the engine before we crossed. Sergeant Mattmiller laughed at all of First Squad as we glided into the water.

"You fuckers better find every piece of MRE gum to patch up the leaks in this old can."

Unbeknownst to us, no one knew how seaworthy the amtracs were. No one inspected the seals or the bilge bumps before jumping on them in Kuwait. The desert didn't make you think hard about amphibious capabilities.

As soon as we hit the water, the cabin leaked. Drop. Drop. Drop. The leaks began spreading to different sections of the deck. I sat inside and felt the trac sink into the black water. Our packs floated, all still connected to the racks, and everyone cursed above me. Marines on the opposing shore cheered us forward and our squad cheered back. The treads hit the opposite bank and spun, grabbing the earth, and pulling us into outer Baghdad.

10

HUGGING THE DUST

I have always been attracted to creation stories. Take the Sumerian creation story, inscribed on tablets of Mesopotamian clay sometime in the third millennium before the Common Era. The story has many parts. My favorite deals with two goddesses, Lahar and Ashnan, who descend from heaven, drink too much wine, and then get into an argument about which is a better gift to the world, sheep or grain. Their disagreement is resolved when the higher gods of water and earth intervene on Ashnan's behalf, securing agriculture as the primary mode of subsistence for the Sumerians. But what stays with me is the description of the affluence the goddesses bring to the people of Sumer—near the present-day border of Iraq and Kuwait—before they begin to argue.

"In the house of the poor, hugging the dust," the tablets read, "entering they bring abundance."[1]

Hugging the dust. The way Alex tells it, it's an apt figure of speech for life in the lowlands between the Tigris and Euphrates rivers. Historically, dust storms have savaged the Arabian Peninsula with sufficient regularity and fury that the winds driving them have their own special words in Arabic. The *shamal*, a hot, dry wind from the northwest, typically sends sand and dust aloft and across the Gulf region in summer, while the *sharqī* wind from the southeast blows in the spring and fall, again kicking up dust storms and sandstorms that clog machinery and close down airports. As climate change has driven average daytime temperatures in Iraq upwards and average annual precipitation down, the frequency and intensity of those storms has increased. By 2009, the frequency of dust storms in Iraq had doubled the historical average, and that year the country experienced the worst dust storm event in living memory.[2]

On the wings of the *shamal*, dust and sand tend to travel together. But sand and dust are in fact very different things. Grains of sand are essentially small rocks, particles of minerals that fall into a size range somewhere between gravel and silt. Most sand is composed of silica in the form of quartz, and we typically measure it on the scale of millimeters, with grains somewhere between .05 mm and 2 mm. Dust, meanwhile, describes any fine particles of solid matter. Soil particles; airborne salts; products of combustion, explosions, and volcanic eruptions; human hair and skin; textile fibers; trace minerals; other forms of pollution; small flakes of fecal matter—all dust. Dust is ubiquitous and, from a health perspective, much more dangerous than sand.

When chemists and public health officials talk about dust, they often use the term "particulate matter," a slightly broader term that includes not just solids, but the whole mix of solid and liquid material suspended in air. Soot, smoke, chemicals, plant pollen, bacteria, viruses, mold spores, smog. Particulate matter, or PM, is like "dust plus."

The key to assessing the dangers of dust is size. It's all tiny; the smaller it is, the worse it is for you. Chemists measure PM in microns, a unit of measurement that describes distances six orders of magnitude smaller than a meter. A micron is one millionth of a meter, or a thousandth of a millimeter, .001 mm. The classic example of reference is a human hair, which is on the order of 50–70 microns—five to seven times larger than the classes of particulate matter that we're most worried about.

The two most important size categories of aerosol particulates—and two of the key EPA and WHO markers of air pollution levels across the world—are PM_{10} and $PM_{2.5}$, particulates of less than 10 microns and less than 2.5 microns, respectively. Whereas particles bigger than about 10 microns typically get lodged in the cilia (small, tube-like structures on the outside of a cell) and mucus of the nose and throat, particles under 10 microns tend to settle deeper in the bronchi and lungs. Particles smaller than 2.5 microns, meanwhile, tend to make their way even deeper, landing in the alveoli (tiny air sacs in the lungs), where the real business of gas exchange gets done. At sizes smaller than 1 micron, particulate matter can pass directly into the bloodstream. Scientists measure the concentrations of PM_{10} and $PM_{2.5}$ in micrograms per cubic meter, or μ/m^3.

When we talk about "air pollution," we are by and large talking about airborne particulate matter in the PM_{10} and $PM_{2.5}$ ranges. The composition of that particulate matter does make a difference, but for agencies like the EPA, air pollution is predominantly a sort-by-size phenomenon. High levels of PM_{10} and $PM_{2.5}$ are associated with a wide variety of health problems, from asthma and respiratory disease to heart disease, birth defects, and even diabetes.[3] In a survey of more than 300,000 Europeans, every increase of 10 μ/m^3 of PM_{10} coincided with a jump in lung cancer rates of more than 20 percent. For every 10 μ/m^3 of $PM_{2.5}$, the increase in lung cancer is upwards of 35 percent.[4]

The average American breathes air containing around 10 μ/m^3 of $PM_{2.5}$. In Iraq, that number is north of 60 μ/m^3. Iraqi air, in short, is really polluted. As is most of the air in the Persian Gulf. Rates of asthma in the more dust-prone localities of the region are off the charts. Even absent the *shamal* and *sharqī* winds, Mesopotamian air carries some of the highest loads of particulate matter in the world, and as of 2017, Iraqi exposure to $PM_{2.5}$ was the eleventh highest in the world.[5] Kuwait was thirteenth. Saudi Arabia, fifth. This is the air Marines and their Iraqi counterparts breathed when they stopped worrying about nerve gas and took their gas masks off.

In the wake of the First American War in Iraq, the government churned out reams and reams of research on soldiers' health. Among the myriad efforts to track exposures and outcomes associated with Gulf War illness was a prospective health survey launched by the Department of Defense in 2001 called the Millennium Cohort Study. The study was designed to track distinct groups of soldiers and veterans over time in an effort to assess the long-term health of service personnel. It was geared predominantly towards Gulf War veterans, but it quickly became a real-time assessment tool for soldiers fighting wars in Iraq and Afghanistan that the study's designers couldn't have predicted. To date, the study has attracted more than 200,000 participants, and researchers have made hay with the information participants have provided.[6]

One curious conclusion of the surveys has to do with respiratory health. It turns out that 14 percent of the Millennium Cohort participants deployed to Iraq came home with new respiratory problems. An independent study led by researchers at Stony Brook University in New York confirmed that number for veterans of both Iraq and Afghanistan: 14 percent. Veterans complained of asthma, trouble breathing, shortness of breath while exercising, coughing, wheezing, and tightness in their chests. For about 6 percent of the returning soldiers, the Stony Brook team was able to find empirical evidence of airway obstructions, about half of which they were able to relieve using medication that opens the bronchial tubes. Meanwhile, the researchers diagnosed 8 percent of the returning soldiers with other new lung diseases. Some soldiers' lungs looked like the lungs of transplant patients whose new organs didn't take. Others had high levels of iron and titanium in their lungs. The researchers called the phenomenon Iraq/Afghanistan War-Lung Injury, or IAW-LI. Most cases bore the marks of exposure to high concentrations of fine particulate matter: $PM_{2.5}$.[7]

IRAQ WOULD BE A DUSTY PLACE WITHOUT WAR, BUT IRAQ HAS BEEN A war zone more often than not for the last four decades, and its particulate matter reflects that. In war zones, there is at least *something* on fire most of the time. Where there's fire, there's smoke, and where there's smoke, there is particulate matter. Take, for example, the Rumaila oil fields. When the Iraqi Army pulled out of Kuwait in the winter of 1991, the first thing they did was set Kuwait's oil fields—including the Rumaila fields on the border with Iraq—on fire. The fires were both political and tactical. Saddam Hussein had long complained about Kuwait's flouting of

OPEC quotas, and the oil fires the retreating army left in their wake provided a potent political symbol in the two countries' long-standing conflict over oil policy. In this sense, the fires amounted to a big, black, sooty
"fuck you." But the fires also served an important tactical purpose. Bil-
lowing clouds of thick smoke rising into the lower atmosphere helped to
conceal troop movements and mitigate the vast air superiority of advanc-
ing American forces. Iraqi Army units not only lit wells on fire; they also
spilled thousands of gallons of oil into low-lying areas, creating oil lakes
and oil trenches that they subsequently lit to provide cover, stop troop
advancements, and generally wreak havoc on a key area of battle.

All told, more than six hundred oil fires blazed between January
and April of 1991, consuming more than a billion barrels of oil.[8] The
fires produced so much particulate matter that the United States' most
famous astrophysicist, Carl Sagan, publicly worried about an effect on
global temperatures.[9] Across the Gulf, temperatures fell by an average
of 4–6°C. Cities across the region suffered marked increases in respiratory ailments, and the acidic fallout from sulfur dioxide—alongside the
spilled oil and the fires themselves—devastated aquatic and terrestrial
ecosystems along the region's rivers and coastlines.

In 2003, as the United States prepared to invade Iraq again, the Iraqi
Army again threw a match on the Rumaila oil fields, this time on the Iraq
side of the border. The devastation was contained this time—fewer oil
fires were lit, and American firefighting teams had effective strategies of
putting them out—but oil and smoke continued to color the tableau of the
Iraqi battlefield throughout the American occupation.

And, of course, the local population and the occupying forces
breathed it all in, day after day.

MODERN IRAQ ISN'T JUST DUSTY; IT'S DUSTY WITH A PARTICULARLY
nasty brand of dust. A 2014 follow-up study on respiratory problems in
Iraq veterans in the *Journal of Occupational and Environmental Medicine*
by the same Stony Brook team that identified Iraq/Afghanistan War-
Lung Injury summed it up in its title: "Iraq dust is respirable, sharp, and

metal-laden."[10] Air samples taken from Camp Victory, the team found, ravaged the lungs of test mice, far more destructive than supposedly equally polluted air samples from the Central Valley of California and Montana mining country. As the paper's title suggests, the $PM_{2.5}$ dust in Iraqi is a particularly sharp brand of particulate matter. It also comes laced with trace metals, including not only titanium and iron, but also zinc, copper, cobalt, cadmium, nickel, and—you guessed it—lead. This sharp, metal-laden dust blends with the black carbon and other chemical particulate matter from the region's oil-heavy industrial centers—even when that oil is not burning out of control.

The dust in Alex Lemons's Iraq was war dust, yet another key component in a complex combat ecosystem shaped by the entwined forces of nature, history, culture, and war. War dust is sharp because it tends to be new. Whereas the soft-edged particulate matter of agriculture or of desert soil derives mostly from the slow erosive processes of wind and water, war dust comes off the treads of tanks and other heavy vehicles that fracture, crush, and pulverize rocks and soil both on and off roads. In Iraq, three decades of mechanized warfare has sent caravan upon caravan of dust-producing machinery across the desert, kicking up sharp particulates of silicon, calcium, and other minerals that circulate as particulate matter both locally and regionally.

That sharp particulate matter floats alongside the myriad particulates associated with the fossil fuels needed for transport. War dust is laced with metals because the chief medium of modern warfare is combustion.

Combustion in war is both exciting and mundane. First the mundane. The fossil fuels in tanks, trucks, amtracs, SUVs, and jeeps yield nitrates, sulfates, elemental carbon, organic carbon, lead, and sulfur dioxide. These "mobile-source" emissions from moving a military around have made the air around Iraq's military roads a lot like the air around the busier urban highways in California, with a couple of important differences. First, almost every heavy military vehicle in Iraq ran on JP-8, the diesel substitute aviation fuel that increases the amount of pesticides a Marine can absorb through her skin. For a diesel engine tuned to the stuff, JP-8 can outperform diesel in terms of certain emissions, but during the war in Iraq, there was no minimum sulfur content for JP-8, and only some military vehicles had been specifically tuned to the lighter aviation fuel.[11] Filters clogged, engine wear increased, and emissions remained high. And second, because Iraq never regulated the lead out of gasoline, most of the local fuel—especially the gas in civilian vehicles—still contained our favorite toxic heavy metal: lead.

In wartime, combustion is not always as mundane as a diesel engine. War dust also contains metals and sharp particulate matter because of dramatic instances of combustion—explosions. Consider the phrase we use when we destroy an object with an explosion: we blow it up. That is, a Marine uses the force of an explosive to turn something singular and solid into much smaller pieces that our colloquial phrase suggests can rise aloft like dust on the wind. Perhaps not surprisingly, some of what gets "blown up" does in fact become dust, a once-contained substance like, say, asbestos, suddenly liberated and made available for humans to inhale as a toxicant or carcinogen. On the roads after the invasion birthed the insurgency, armor-penetrating improvised explosive devices—IEDs, the weapon that will likely define the Second American War in Iraq more than any other—hit with enough heat and force to aerosolize metal, turning tempered steel, cadmium plating, and sophisticated electronics into respirable particulate matter for those nearby Marines lucky enough to avoid the blasts' immediate impacts. Meanwhile, every day, troops and civilians in battle-plagued cities like Fallujah and Ramadi and Basra inhaled the airborne remains of textile mills and fertilizer plants, pulverized cement, and the myriad household goods whose plastic bottles had suddenly become so many molten microplastics.

It is perhaps ironic that the leading researchers from the Stony Brook team that identified IAW-LI as a problem for American service personnel in Iraq cut their epidemiological teeth studying the respiratory effects of particulate matter on the New York firefighters who responded to the terrorist attacks on the Twin Towers on September 11, 2001. The respiratory illnesses of those firefighters struck them as remarkably similar to those of the returning veterans they studied a decade later.

Like most dust, Iraqi dust is not only chemical; it is also biological. Mixed in with and sometimes attached to bits of gypsum, calcium, and silica travel a veritable menagerie of microorganisms from as far afield as Turkey and Syria. Pollens from amaranth, prairie sage, cattails, date palms, and even pine trees blow with the dust alongside algae and the spores of fungi and mosses. Iraq is a tough place for a Marine with allergies.

It is also a tough place to keep from getting sick more generally.

Once again, there is a history to the dust that makes it so. As Iraqi exile doctor Omar Dewachi explains in his reflection on his country's medical history, Iraq once housed one of the most formidable health care systems in the world. Through the turmoil of the immediate postcolonial period, the Iraqi medical community maintained its ties to the British health care system, with doctors, medical students, information, and best practices moving fluidly back and forth between the two worlds. For all its paranoia and belligerence, Saddam's Ba'athist regime helped to maintain a high-quality medical system focused on public health up through the war with Iran, and for a time, control of disease overlapped significantly with a broader control over the Iraqi populace. Public health directives included literacy campaigns, and by 1980 literacy rates in Iraq hit nearly 100 percent.[12] Iraq was certainly dusty in the 1980s, but good roads, modern sanitation, widespread vaccination efforts, and clean hospitals helped keep the worst of the bugs out of the dust and out of Iraqi bodies.

Dewachi now teaches medical anthropology in Beirut. Iraqi doctors he knows, now sick, come to Lebanon for treatment because of lack of personnel, facilities, and security back home. Meanwhile, Iraq's hospitals, waterways, and air are factories of disease. Hospitals are rife with multidrug-resistant strains of bacteria—MDR, also known as superbugs—and rates of infection from wound care, simple surgeries, and emergency room stays have skyrocketed. Outbreaks of malaria, cholera, typhoid fever, and a variety of gastrointestinal diseases that had largely been controlled by the mid-1970s are now commonplace along the country's compromised waterways.[13]

And then, of course, there is the dust. A study published in the *Arabian Journal of Geosciences* reveals that microorganisms in the Iraqi dust include long-lived *Bacillus* species (including anthrax and a food poison called *B. cereus*); *Escherichia coli*; *Staphylococcus aureus*; the infamous MDR *Pseudomonas aeruginosa* (associated with pneumonia, septic shock, nasty urinary and GI tract infections, and burns and wound infections); *Proteus mirabilis* (associated with urinary tract infections); *Proteus vulgaris* (again, GI and urinary tract infections); *Aspergillus* (aka black mold); and a gut fungus called *Candida albicans* that may be familiar as a garden-variety infection but that can kill you in some pretty horrible ways when it gets out of hand. Alex tested positive for all of these microorganisms throughout the 2010s. The human flu virus can also travel with the Iraqi dust, and one study suggested that winter wind patterns could distribute the flu among both civilians and military personnel from hundreds if not thousands of miles away.[14] It's no wonder Alex had a runny nose for seven years.

IRAQIS SUFFERED AS MUCH AS OR MORE THAN MARINES FROM THE whirlwind of toxic exposures Alex reaped on his company's tear through Iraq and into Baghdad. For example, information from researchers on the ground in Iraq in the past few years has shown high levels of heavy metals in Iraqi baby teeth, suggesting widespread exposure to lead and titanium among Iraq's next generation.[15] Research has also suggested increased rates of cancer and child developmental abnormalities among Iraqis living around American military installations, as well as a host of other ailments plausibly related to the toxic legacies of the American wars in Iraq.[16]

Perhaps the best case in point for the differential in exposures between Iraqis and US service personnel lies in the Iraqi experience with depleted uranium. During the Gulf War, American forces began to use an ultra-dense byproduct of enriched uranium manufacturing as a key material in conventional munitions and armor plating. As the name would imply, depleted uranium is non-fissile (that is, not going to cause a nuclear explosion) and far less radioactive than enriched uranium. It is about 60 percent as radioactive as natural uranium. That said, depleted uranium is used in ways that allow that decreased radioactivity to easily enter the body. DU, as it's called, is almost 70 percent denser than lead, which made it appealing as an effective armor-piercing material for the 30mm and 25mm rounds used by fighter jets and heavy attack vehicles in US operations in Kuwait, Iraq, Kosovo, and Afghanistan. It also has a habit of lighting on fire on impact—and tends to aerosolize, adding a plume of suddenly accessible radioactive dust to the burning wreckage of whatever vehicle or building a pilot or gunner may have targeted.

US forces fired more than 700,000 rounds of DU during the Gulf War, and another 300,000 during Alex's war in Iraq, about 1,200 tons of it in all. Researchers have shown that veterans of the wars in the Gulf, Bosnia, and Kosovo, where DU was employed at a large scale, have up to fourteen times the chromosomal abnormalities you might expect from a control population.[17] A 2003 VA study revealed that female veterans deployed to the Gulf in the 1990s were three times as likely to have kids with birth defects than those not deployed. Male veterans were more than twice as likely.[18]

Iraqis fared much worse from DU, and their plight has been studied less. In 2004, Iraq saw a massive spike in leukemia cases, putting them among the highest rates of any country in the world.[19] The contested cities of Basra and Fallujah were hit particularly hard. By 2010, infant mortality in Fallujah had hit 13.6 percent, its increased cancer rates drawing comparisons to Swedes impacted by Chernobyl fallout in the 1980s and Japanese exposed to radiation at Hiroshima.[20] British researcher Chris Busby claimed that the people of Fallujah had "the highest rate of genetic damage in any population ever studied."[21] It's likely that the compendium of other toxic remnants of war have contributed to this disproportionate damage, but shooting nuclear waste into a war zone can't have helped matters. To the extent that records have been consistent and available, rates of cancer in Basra, Mosul, and Baghdad have all increased since 1991, doubling and even tripling for certain types of cancer associated with radiation. And those are simply measures of depleted uranium's potential radiation hazard. It is also more conventionally toxic, in line with heavy metals like lead, one of many affronts to body and brain floating on the wind after four decades of war and de-development.

During the war itself, Iraqis were likely as blind to the dangers of the combat ecosystem as the American invaders. For Marines, the existential threats of IEDs, mortars, snipers, and friendly fire superseded all but the worst dust storms and the most severe diarrhea. Alex recalls a vague awareness of the forever chemical fire retardants and an ill-defined uneasiness with the pills, but as in most wars, the fatalism bred by the constant threat of acute violence dulled soldiers' concerns over their long-term health. You didn't put the gas mask on because you were concerned about lung cancer twenty years from now. As Alex told me many times during our interviews, in his mind, he was already dead.

For everyday Iraqis, the acute violence of war accompanied the destruction of infrastructure, the erosion of law and order, the breakdown of a functioning modern society that had, with hard work, already largely survived two major wars. Four millennia after receiving the gifts of agriculture and animal husbandry—sheep and grain—a modern society in the land of Sumer rightly stood in disbelief as bombs, bullets, riots, looting, terror, and all manner of destruction left them once again hugging the toxic, radioactive Mesopotamian dust.

11

"YOU JUST DIDN'T THINK ABOUT ANYTHING YOU WERE DOING"

We entered the tightly populated eastern Baghdad neighborhood of Saddam City on April 8, 2003. It looked like a city within a city and a place we would never control. We cleared a block just outside the neighborhood before Bravo Company radioed for help. They had taken casualties, and we watched our wounded carried out on stretchers and stuffed into helos headed for the aid station. The Iraqis weren't giving up en masse. Dressed in track suits or in all black, they would fight, then break off and meld into crowds of civilians, and then pick up the weapons later when they had a tactical advantage. The engagements typically ended before they really started. Hit and run. Hit and hide.

We relieved Bravo and cleared several factories before reaching our limit of advance to our northwest along a berm with a single-lane road. I looked over the berm with the rest of my platoon into a rice field, ringed with palm groves. I watched one of our decrepit company Humvees out of my right, less swollen eye as it picked up speed on the road in front of us. Our homing pigeon was dead. The cage had been removed from the hood. Splashes of gunny sand and fluff along with white flashes hit behind the truck. I saw the flashes before I heard the crunches. The driver gunned the truck, and it sped past our faces as 155mm shells landed on us.

"Incoming! Incoming! Get the fuck down!" went out along our line. We slid down the berm and I buried my face into the earth and hid behind football-sized dirt clods. The ground shook for a couple seconds as two more shells punched us. Then it stopped.

I raised my head and listened. There was a silent break before I heard someone in Second Squad yell, "Corpsmen up! Corpsmen fucking up!"

McGuire raced up the line behind me and told us all, "Don't fucking look! Keep your fucking heads to the front and cover your sectors of fire!"

LCpl Anderson had taken shrapnel in the guts. I didn't hear any screams. Or maybe he did scream in his Appalachian dialect that I was still trying to learn and loved hearing. Our corpsmen worked their craft until they put him on a stretcher and dusted him off to the rear. Marine artillery had bashed us. We argued on the radio. They told us we looked like Iraqi Army grunts because of our green vests and ammo pouches over the top of our desert fatigues. Anderson survived but lost a kidney and then was retired on 100 percent disability.

The cattle drive into the heart of Baghdad ended at the British-built Sumer Cigarette Factory. My platoon led the company into the compound after well-placed shots fell into us from a multistory tower. We kicked into high gear and rammed the gates before dismounting and winding through a series of entries and fences. On the black marble of the main campus, I stepped over the body of a beefy Iraqi in a white shirt turning red. Flies surrounded the gut holes. He only had one sandal on. We climbed through floor after floor, sliding on marble and kicking in doors. We didn't find the shooter. We didn't find anyone. We rummaged through the offices and found nothing but cigarette packs, smoking advertisements, business cards, and paper clips. I had never seen so many ashtrays. The blue cigarette boxes contained a gold-painted Sumerian lyre and information about the brand. IRAQI & VIRGINIA BLENDED TOBACCO. THE STATE ENTERPRISE FOR TOBACCO AND CIGA-RETTES. My friends stuffed packs into dump bags, cargo pockets, and gas mask carriers and stole office equipment and Iraqi flags as souvenirs.

The command and the POGs ("Persons Other than Grunts") kicked our filthy bodies from our building to a grubby street near the warehouses a day later. We finally had a fenced compound to live behind, but as we wound down the war kept winding up. Outside, we let the looters loot. We let the arsonists burn. Mattis had told us in a letter he handed out forty-eight hours before the invasion kicked off, "Engage your brain before your weapon." In every other part of Iraq, we followed, or tried to follow, sets of rules to create order: rules of engagement, treatment of POWs, helping fleeing civilians. Now we encouraged bedlam. We were there to run patrols and look for bad guys and WMDs, not to manage the country now in full collapse. No brains were engaged. Our orders came from Coalition Forces Land Component Command under Army General David McKiernan, and then from CENT-COM Commander Army General Tommy Franks, who reported to the secretary of defense. I thought Mattis would fight back on this and put us back on the streets, but maybe, like us, he didn't have the rank.

On guard duty at the front gate, I watched children whipping donkeys mercilessly as they towed Jet Skis, television sets, and refrigerators on wooden carts.

"Missstah! Mistah! Good. Good." One boy smashed the animals' bloody back and gave me a thumbs-up.

I waved back, disgusted with the beating and confused about where you would float a Jet Ski around Saddam City in the middle of a war. McGuire couldn't stomach scenes like this. He swore at the cart drivers, and occasionally grabbed their jockey whips. Sometimes he said nothing.

The warehouses near the eastern part of our living area held hundreds of thousands of cigarettes. Some depots stood intact, and others were smashed from artillery. We didn't secure any of them. On April 11, one of the warehouses exploded. Everyone watched the flames twist upon themselves and turn red as the daily winds hit the factory from the north. Many smoked and gawked as the flames grew taller. Secondhand smoke blanketed nonsmokers like me and we watched. Ash and silver paper confetti sprinkled over the compound and our faces. It burned itself out by the end of the week.

Iraqis approached us at the compound gate confused and angry over the fires, looting, and general breakdown of order.

"Ali Baba," someone would say and point towards their neighborhood. Division brought only one translator per battalion. They were overpaid Americans who hadn't lived in Iraq for decades and knew nothing about local politics or even local dialects. We tried to make do without this key piece of equipment.

"Do I look like the fuckin' police?" one of my friends said, smoking a Sumer.

Actually, yes, I thought, we do.

Some Marines, most often the SNCOs and officers, fell in love with the fall of Baghdad. They overlaid 1945 on 2003. They listened to BBC accounts or watched statues of Big Smiley, McGuire's street name for Saddam, torn down throughout the city. We ignored conversations we didn't want to hear, as citizens swarmed us with hugs and kisses. They gave us flowers and tossed rice over us. We kept our gas masks on.

"Good Bush." Which in that moment was true for the Iraqi who said it. In Saddam City, nearly everyone was Shia and had battled Big Smiley for decades. Now he was gone. "You're welcome. It was our pleasure," went the typical Marine response. Mattis's "speed, speed, speed" felt surreal. We had just gone from cabin fever on the *Dubuque* to pissing in plastic bottles standing up inside our amtrac to having flower garlands draped over our necks and a plate of rice or a can of soda stuffed into our arms. People genuinely told us, "Thank you, Mistah. We love you America." But I smelled cordite and gunpowder from the night before throughout these scenes.

Our trac sometimes ripped up the pavement during one of our rare daytime patrols. People looked at the torn-up asphalt in disbelief. Water lines burst under the weight of the amtrac. Complaints were filed at the gate.

The second part of the conversations with Iraqis was more important than the hugs and kisses and falling statues. Baghdad natives had questions they asked in clear English.

"When will food and water arrive to my city?" What little food they did have wasn't enough. No one wanted the trashy humanitarian rations we had on board. Other Iraqis made historical references to occupation and the Crusades, and argued that we came for cheap oil. "Where is the power?

Food and milk will spoil for the children. Where is the security?" Resentment already brewed in the moment the regime was collapsing. We gave standard nonanswers. Our war had ended.

One of my interpreters from later in the war—during the surge—tried explaining this moment to me from the Iraqi perspective during the summer before Covid-19. Mortal (a nickname we used to cloak his real identity) is now my neighbor, and he runs a men's clothing store at a mall near my house. We were talking at a coffee house on one of his breaks. "Iraqis were in a cave their whole lives. Then the Americans knocked out Saddam and let them rush out of the cave with no transition," he took a sip of tea. Mortal cheered the end of the regime with everyone else. He immediately found the first Americans near his hometown and volunteered as a translator.

He explained what 2003 looked like from Iraqi eyes and I listened. "We went from dial-up phones to mobile communications. No transition. All Saddam, all the time. Then nothing. I mean, we weren't ready. How could we be prepared?" I hated knowing we opened the cells of one prison and led the Iraqis right into another one, mistaking that for liberation. "The crazies," Mortal called himself and other Iraqis, "were out."

He drank his tea, and I swigged my coffee under the 9,026-foot Mount Olympus in Salt Lake and we recognized it was too late. "You just didn't think about anything you were doing," he said, shaking his head.

Whatever else Iraq was at that moment, it was a mess, one that we made and didn't know how to clean up.

WE CONVERTED THE CIGARETTE FACTORY INTO CAMP PENDLETON. LONG HAIR posed a danger to everyone. Trimmers shaved heads. We cleaned out the trac and found piles of sand and grit. We broke out Q-tips and scraped every piece of rust and grime from our weapons. We washed our uniforms with some of McGuire's Tide powder. Our company gunny made us spray-paint blemished insignia. Someone made us present our nails for a bootcamp hygiene inspection. McGuire, doing an eyeroll, added one more instruction at the end of the hotwash: "You are no longer to call this Operation Iraqi Liberation (OIL). This is Operation Iraqi Freedom (OIF)."

My frustration and rage grew as we cleaned up and settled down. I wanted to fight. I felt untested. We found endless amounts of military equipment on the dust trail to Baghdad, yet few operators. Mail appeared in small batches along with three MREs per day. We plugged in speakers to CD and MP3 players and sang. Porn mags circled the company. My ex-Mormon shame kept my eyes elsewhere. We even heard rumors of getting back on ship and going home. It moved too quickly, and my skepticism wouldn't shut up. Most of my energy now went into talking back to my seniors and picking fights with my own tribe as the Marine Corps sucked us back into its micromanaging reach.

Still, our compound wasn't safe, and one of the threats was in the water. Backpacking at home had taught me the danger of untreated water. I'd watched how and where we got our water carefully since day one at Camp Inchon. The weather continued to get hotter as spring advanced. The heat and the presence patrols we ran demanded more water. All the extra gear and armor made the odds of becoming a heat casualty increase. We drank more water. As we sweated and no longer had the excuse of moving every night, our first sergeant noted our foul odor. We needed water, not baby wipes, and Division reconnected the showers inside the corporate tower to reverse-osmosis treated water from the Tigris. The same older-than-the-Old-Testament river we had floated across a week before, filled with trash, poop, and brown-purple blobs of oil.

I had not showered in over three weeks, but I thought the water might make me sick. I had picked up a case of giardia working on a buffalo ranch in Alberta as a teenager, and I wanted no part of waterborne diseases. I closed my lips, held my breath, and scrubbed fast under the showerhead with a bar of Irish Spring. Layers of dry skin broke off. The sand and grit behind my ears refused to budge without harder scrubs. I watched Second Squad push the brackish water into the drains where it backed up and then needed plunging. I dried off and put on a fresh pair of permethrin-laced utilities.

Next, we ran out of Kuwaiti water bottles and division trucked in fresh 400-gallon containers from the Tigris. The first day, I sniffed the water warily. It smelled like too much chlorine. I looked for plastic bottles and found none.

I thought about boiling it. I held off until I couldn't. The next day, canteens empty, I filled up and dumbly took a swig with everyone else.

From April 16 to 19 I endured a violent stomach illness. We nicknamed it "Saddam's Revenge." A burning sensation hit my colon first while I stood early morning guard duty with Alcantar. We wrapped up and changed guard with guys from Second Squad. "Fuuuck, Alejandro. You look dehydrated," Alcantar told me on the hike back to the lawn we slept on. He looked the same.

Something kicked me hard in the bottom of my stomach.

I rushed for the slit trench. I tried not to hit my boots as liquid poured out of my ass, then a different burn moved in the opposite direction. Flies swarmed around my anus. My stomach churned and belched another quarter gallon of fluid up my throat and out my mouth. I threw up between my legs as the diarrhea poured out. More flies danced around my body. This happened again and again. Nothing hit my boots. Then I pounded the chlorinated water to replenish fluids and began the process all over. We went back on post hours later. When our second watch ended after sunset, I stumbled back to where First Squad slept before I blacked out and collapsed on the asphalt.

"Alex? Hey Alex," a hand shook me, "you up?" Doc Newton asked me from above. I un-caked my eyelids and found myself inside our battalion aid station on a stretcher with an IV dripping into my right arm the next morning. Words came out slowly. "What happened, Aaron?" and then and more importantly, "Where is my fucking rifle?"

"Just kick back and relax, brother. We dragged you in here yesterday and your guys have your shit."

A dozen Marines lay beside me in the same state. The pathogen burned through 1/4. "Saddam's Revenge" fought us harder than anyone in the invasion. A year later the Navy studied Marine feces at the Cigarette Factory and discovered a gut pathogen gold mine. Norovirus and *Campylobacter* and *Shigella flexneri. Shigella sonnei, Salmonella, Cryptosporidium*.[1] They moved from water to vomit to flies and then hands munching on jalapeño cheese spread over plywood crackers where it all circled into our microbiomes and back out. The corpsmen treated us with a cocktail of Phenergan, loperamide, and the anthrax standby, ciprofloxacin.

I overheard hunches from the docs while I stared at the ceiling in the clinic and felt the second IV Newton started wash coolly into the same arm. Some said excess chlorine could make you sick like that. Others mentioned the company gunny's brilliant idea of distributing water less than ten yards from the fly-ridden slit trench. Dehydrated Marines around me called it a curse. Better theories might be had, but I racked back out as the city imploded and enjoyed my best sleep in months.

THE SEABEES CAME FOR A WEEK TO CONSTRUCT PERMANENT STRUCTURES AT OUR combat outpost in early June. Some fabrications improved our security and others our dignity and comfort. They built two wooden guard towers reaching thirty feet near the front gate and rear perimeter. They worked like ants, moving, sawing, carrying, positioning, and hammering beams into place as the platform grew upwards. Someone stupidly took this as a sign and gave the former Iraqi Army base in Hasyimiyah the name "Camp Twin Towers."

The Seabees ignored us. They kept working and towed in a modern outhouse. They had sawed and assembled a long bench with three partitions. Then they cut a triangle into the seat of each stall, hung curtain rods, and dragged clean-cut, half-sized oil drums underneath the other side. We added ponchos to the shower curtain rings. Sitting while you privately defecated into a barrel struck us as luxury after months of digging our own cat-holes and then crouching, sweaty-assed.

The shit barrels came with a catch: We would have to burn the waste inside with jet fuel and stir the contents down with a wooden or metal paddle.

The largest project came last. The Seabees climbed into their heavy equipment and bulldozed a fifty-yard trench out of the empty field inside our camp in the summer heat. They drove tan and drab green machines through the hardpan and dumped the earthen guts tidily at the other end. When the digging was done, they loaded the machines back onto trailers and left the next morning. We climbed inside or stood above the embankment of the pit. A geologist would have admired the clean-cut sides displaying history through the cake layers of sandy-orange dirt and gray-black clay down to fifteen feet.

For the Marines looking into the straightened trench, we saw a canal hungry for our trash.

The end of the invasion improved our living conditions, and improved living conditions increased our garbage. It had to be burned, we told ourselves, because it could either fall into enemy hands or we couldn't imagine another way to rid ourselves of it. Lithium radio batteries, blown-out tires, metal food trays, polyester socks, oil containers, AA batteries, unserviceable uniforms, and spent fuel cans. Many 3M products made of "forever chemicals" found new homes in the fire. Rifle magazines, gas mask cannisters, brass casings, and mercury-filled button cell batteries stacked up before we could push them into the new pit for incineration. We burned medical waste. We had plastics upon plastics from tiny gum packages to fifty-five-gallon trash bags.

We took breaks from the burn pits by continuing the search for nerve agents and nuclear material as spring rolled into summer. An Iraqi man, and it was always a middle-aged man, showed up at our outpost, with prime WMD intelligence. Not knowing who to look for, the Marine Corps handed us a package of "Iraq Most Wanted" playing cards containing blurry pictures or silhouettes of Ba'ath Party henchmen. I can see the misspelled names on the glossy cards in my hands right now. The only Iraqi woman in the deck is Huda "Mrs. Anthrax" Salih Mahdi Ammash, the five of hearts. It's also the only card displaying the initials "WMD."

"He says the Iraqi military buried weapons in February near the school. It was very suspicious," our translator informed the company commander. We looked like the fanatics who thought Elvis never died in Graceland when these chases ensued.

We drove to the school and dismounted. Mattmiller handed me a shovel. With two decades of war in the making and many of those weapons coming through my government's hands, we should have known throwing a rock in any direction would land on a trunk of ammunition.

"Shouldn't EOD [explosive ordinance disposal] be doing this? What about mines?"

We dug anyway. A few of my sergeants stood back out of potential blast range behind the truck. Iraqis gathered around us, happy their children might come back to the soccer field and the school once the weapons were gone and it was safe. One of us hit a wooden crate after we moved through a meter of dirt. We rummaged through seventeen surface-to-air missiles, six RPGs, and some flares, but no yellowcake or sarin shells. We either took the munitions back to base or called EOD to pick them up and destroy them.

We always came back empty-handed, and the burn pits asked for our attention. The care packages Americans tenderly and patriotically wrapped were often the first into the pit. Bibles, fifth-grade class drawings, *New York Times* and *Deseret News* editions, honey-smelling Swisher Sweets, and Brooks & Dunn paraphernalia had to go. *People* magazine, dreadful home-made cookies, empty boxes of Honey Nut Cheerios, *Reader's Digest*, Kid Rock compact discs, and the unconvincing letters written in support of the war all went into the well-oxygenated flames. We kept baby wipes and pens. I spared all Jack and Meg White material. Everything else burned.

The daily ritual of igniting junk relieved me of boredom and regret. I ran laps around the compound with LCpl Eddie Hernandez, our other company radio operator to Aguero. Eddie was from Texas and Texans behaved like the Marine Corps wouldn't be able to staff itself without the Lone Star State. We admired the shape-shifting towers of black smoke as we bitched about our laughable NCOs, our saltiness as combat vets—the real baptism was yet to come—and the decision-making process that brought us here. Eddie had been a high school cheerleader. He'd led cheers and flipped classmates in a better uniform than the ones we buttoned up. I couldn't believe he'd left that for our days of smoke and ash. He couldn't believe I had given up a college degree and the Rocky Mountains. After a run, we might launch a water bottle into the pit. It would expand, burst, and then fizzle into melting goo. I was wasting my life over here and all I could do was count down the days and watch plastic liquefy.

There were no rules. I can't remember instructions other than collect-ing that day's refuse and throwing it into the pit. We doused it in diesel fuel, the magical JP-8, and lit it with the matchbooks that came with our rations. It could all be burned and, we assured ourselves, burned safely. No one donned their gas mask or tried to seal the entryways to our rooms. Occasionally, one of us would turn a green T-shirt into a face wrap. Drenching the shirt in water slowed the smells. Mostly it just kept your mouth from drying out.

We tried to burn only in the day, but the trash embers roasted deep into the night. Iraq's night reminded me of desert escapades in southern Utah, where the lack of ambient light from buildings and cars made the galaxy look bigger and more welcoming. Iraq was not Utah. The constellations in both deserts were the same, but tracer fire and the Iridium satellite phone calls with my little brother and my folks always broke the spell and reminded me that we were strangers. So did the fires. In front of the darkened backdrop, plastic bags, paper strips, and sparks danced above the gas and light of the trench. Brown plastic spoons melted and folded into puddles of bubbly ooze. A *zZZzzzhhhh pooppPPP* went off randomly when one of the batteries exploded. It all appeared to shrink inside the pit.

I knew enough about chemistry to know that partial combustion usually turned big, bad things into smaller, worse things that were easier to inhale. We all knew the stuff we were burning was bad, but it probably wasn't just the stuff we burned that we should've worried about. None of us knew the history of the soil that burned along with our garbage.

But the trash had nowhere else to go. The biggest threats to my life were emerging roadside bombs, the hammer thud of RPGs, and rifle fire. Maybe my own side would kill me, mistaking my movements for the enemy. It didn't occur to me that there was friendly fire in the burn pits, too. None of it was my call anyway, so I burned and waited, burned and waited. My eyes watered, and the smell of burning plastic bags filled my lungs for the rest of the summer.

I STOPPED AT IRAQ'S UNOFFICIAL BURN PIT CENTRAL IN CAMP ANACONDA FOR FOUR days in 2008. It contained all the usual miseries and miserable people one could find on an American superbase in Iraq. Later renamed Joint Base

Balad and transferred from the Army to the Air Force, Anaconda housed more than 35,000 people, more than a quarter of them military contractors. It had a movie theater and an Olympic swimming pool. And it produced a lot of trash. The air there was different from that of other camps. It smelled like hairspray squirted into a burning Styrofoam cup. The air changed the color of day and night light. Brown and orange hues blotted out the daytime sky for minutes. Sometimes, it looked like black streaks painted over blue. Particulate matter refracted the camp lights in every direction and kept me awake at night. The smell and discolored light followed us into the gym, the Special Forces compound, the chow hall, and into our beds. Then we left and I forgot the place for years.

Infantry vets expect torn rotator cuffs, aching knees, and compressed vertebrae. Missing teeth, gigantic scars, and hearing loss. Other than battlefield wounds and the joys of PTSD, those aches and pains fill post-infantry life. You don't expect stories of coughs, headaches, and breathing problems. As grunts, I think some of us missed the worst of burn pits. A company-sized trash pile for a couple hundred Marines looks and smells different than a regimental one for a couple thousand, and even that looks different than the pits at a place like Camp Anaconda. The POGs always outnumbered us, especially at the bigger bases. They had more supplies, mail, and plastic. They had more time and space to burn trash. Then again, I hear stories from friends, and it seems like even snipers always end up with a detour that takes them through a world of trash and burn pits.

"Iraq was never a trashy place," Mortal says when I ask him about trash in his home country. I rely on Mortal, along with a dozen other Iraqi friends, to tell the story of Iraq before 2003, and to fill in things a Marine could never know. "You call us trashy? You don't even take your shoes off inside the house in America. Who is trashy? Gross."

"That's not what I meant, Mortal, and you fucking know it."

Mortal grew up depositing each week's refuse into a dumpster on his block and a garbage truck would dump the box in its belly, crush it, and drive west into the desert. The trash collectors buried it under rock and dirt. During the sanction-wrecked 1990s, trash collection still happened. The people on Mortal's block stuffed material into bags and threw them on a flatbed headed for the dump. The only things his family burned were clothes, paper, and food waste. Fear and punishment helped with sanitation. Mortal repeats that point as if he's quoting scripture. Saddam Hussein's very existence kept the streets clean.

We blew that system up. In our purge of the Ba'ath Party, even trash collectors made the hit list. The Coalition Provisional Authority (CPA), with blessings of the generals, fired them all, tossing the backbone of organized society on the street. The country became a litter freeway. Tied up with our own trash on the bases, we hardly noticed. Mattresses, blankets, boxes, diapers, chicken bones, and rice piled up on street corners or floated down canals and rivers. The flies feasted. Packs of wild dogs thrived on free food. Iraq began importing more goods with local business and state agencies wrecked by sanctions, war, and new CPA directives, and that brought more packaging and waste. The single-use plastic container replaced the recycled glass bottle throughout the country.

Meanwhile, for the few Iraqi sanitation workers left and for those who filled in the Ba'ath Party vacuum, trash collection probably became the single most dangerous job in the country. The best place to hide an IED was within roadside trash and the best way to keep trash in the streets was to murder Iraqi trash collectors. In areas where sectarianism took over state functions like Sadr City, the new name for the megacity where we lived in the Cigarette Factory, the Mahdi Army became the premiere waste management workers, and trash collection resumed haphazardly.

Yet for all the mountains of smelly, vector-loving garbage piles that accompanied the American invasion, Iraqis never adopted burn pits. I press Mortal on this point, but he says no, it never happened outside of American bases.

"The only organization that would burn trash that frequently now is the Iraqi military. That's because it's easier to keep records on paper. Easier to burn and forget." He thinks a bit longer. I check online newspapers and find only one report of someone randomly lighting trash piles ablaze outside Za'franiya neighborhood in Baghdad during 2019.[2] Enough of an aberration to make the news in a country full of newsworthy things. Not a pattern. There certainly hasn't been a nighttime special about the toxic effects of our burn pits on major Iraqi networks.

Burning trash still puzzles Mortal.

"We just wouldn't think to do that. I mean Iraqis will probably never believe the Americans would be that disorganized to, you know, make a burning pit." He paused, "I only know because I lived on FOBs with you."

12

BURN PITS

n 2018, Merriam-Webster added the informal term "dumpster fire" to its vaunted American English language dictionary. A dumpster fire, in common parlance, refers to an "utterly calamitous or mismanaged event or occurrence."[1] The metaphor is apt, the image vivid. A literal dumpster fire is in fact a pretty messy and unsavory thing, and I think we use the figurative term to describe exactly the sort of self-consuming but ultimately also self-contained, small-scale disaster that an actual fire in a dumpster represents.

Take a literal dumpster fire and replicate it over ten acres in the Iraqi desert, and you have the burn pit at Joint Base Balad (JBB), about forty miles north of Baghdad. The dumpster fire of all dumpster fires, minus the dumpster.

As the name implies, a burn pit is an area on a military base designated for the open-air burning of waste. They are probably the simplest of the four DoD-approved ways to deal with waste in the field. The other three—incineration (in an actual incinerator), burial, and "tactical burial"—require more infrastructure, more work, better planning, or some combination of those three things. Burn pits just require trash, a match, and some JP-8 fuel. Since 2001, the US military has established burn pits—usually run by contractors—in Iraq, Afghanistan, Kuwait, Saudi Arabia, Bahrain, Djibouti, Oman, and Qatar, as well as at several Middle East naval bases. The gigantic ten-acre burn pit at JBB was the largest and most notorious of these combustion fields, but Marines also created burn-pits-in-miniature just about everywhere they went, using the ubiquitous JP-8 fuel to help create a slurry of flaming shit and detritus in old gas barrels or metal boxes or holes in the ground in order to get rid of everything from batteries to medical waste in a way that would keep their quarters sanitary and keep their detritus out of the hands of the enemy.

In some ways, Alex is lucky that most of his exposure to open-air combustion came from stirring burning feces in old leaded gas barrels downrange. From a health perspective, it is the big pits like the one at JBB that have really caused the problems.

In the spirit of Webster's inclusion of "dumpster fire," the burn pit provides a perfect metaphor for everything that was wrong about the war in Iraq.

IF YOU STAND NEXT TO ONE, THERE'S NOT A LOT OF AMBIGUITY ABOUT the toxicity of a burn pit. Military personnel and DoD contractors describe the smell as the kind of unholy assault on the senses you might find in Dante, a mélange of chemical and organic plumes that, when the wind blew the wrong direction, sometimes brought them to their knees and made them vomit. When you consider what the military chucked into these open burn pits, you can see why. For starters, take everything that we have already identified as potentially toxic in the field, and light it on fire. Pesticide-soaked uniforms and pesticide containers. Fire retardants. Munitions and munitions casings. And, of course, JP-8 to make it go. Then look at Alex's list, and add a few items. Human waste, furniture and upholstery, dead animals, body parts, computers and electronics, chem lights, old tents, Gore-Tex jackets, asbestos, Styrofoam, rubber boots, old MREs, MOPP kits, flame-resistant FROG suits, tarps, nylon, rolls of wire, aerosol cans, paint, solvents, gas cans, whole vehicles, and a raft of loose plastic water bottles that would hiss like vanquished Harpies when they hit the heat of the piles.[2] And, perhaps for irony, gas masks.

In light of what was burned, it's not surprising that burn pits put off some seriously toxic smoke. When a 2012 National Academy of Sciences Institute of Medicine report sought to assess the long-term impacts of burn pit exposure at JBB, a committee assessed fifty-one different potentially harmful pollutants, from volatile organic chemicals (VOCs) to dioxins and furans to PM_{10} and $PM_{2.5}$ to heavy metals like lead, copper, mercury, manganese, and arsenic. If the invasion of Iraq presented a Marine like Alex with a whirlwind of environmental exposures, burn pits like the one at JBB were the eye of the toxic storm.[3]

Burn pits were nothing new when the United States invaded Iraq in 2003. Waste disposal has been a key problem for armies since the advent of war, and for almost as long as waste has been a problem, military commanders have found that burning it is one of the easiest ways to make the problem disappear. Burning trash can reduce its volume by more than 80 percent. It also tends to help prevent the proliferation of pests and the spread of disease. In Afghanistan, where the Taliban and other insurgents would scavenge for things like used batteries and other raw materials to use as triggers or other parts of improvised weapons, American troops found that burning trash also deprived the enemy of a possible source of matériel. Combat isn't camping, and even when Marines try to keep their footprint light, they're not exactly practicing the Seven Principles of Leave No Trace you know from your backpacking trips. In the early days of the wars in both Iraq and Afghanistan, everything from supply to communication to overall strategy was happening in a pinch. And in a pinch, burning trash is a pretty good way to solve an age-old problem.

In both Iraq and Afghanistan, however, the US military never ceased to operate in a pinch. The military described the operations in Iraq and Afghanistan as "overseas contingency operations," and that phrase accidentally tells a much bigger story than it means to. This is the first way in which the burn pits might stand as a perfect symbol for what went wrong in Iraq. In contingency operations, operational planning often happens on the fly, usually amidst a good deal of uncertainty. A contingency plan is plan B, the plan for when shit goes sideways. But in Iraq and Afghanistan, the DoD just assumed that shit would always be sideways. And you can see it in the trash.

The Iraq War was supposed to be short, and there's nothing like a burning pile of trash to suggest that you aren't planning to settle into camp. An off-the-cuff prediction by Donald Rumsfeld on a call-in talk show in November 2002 set the tone for the American military's expectations. "Five days or five weeks or five months," Rumsfeld said, "but it certainly isn't going to last any longer than that."[4]

The war in Iraq took eight years. Afghanistan took nearly twenty. Very few people in the military thought the US would be around long enough in Iraq for things like trash to be a major problem. But every day of the war, every soldier produced trash.

To be more specific, every individual service member in Iraq from 2003 to 2011 produced an average of about nine pounds of trash every day of their deployment. At the height of the US invasion in 2003, coalition forces had almost 178,000 people on the ground in Iraq and Kuwait, which amounts to about 800 *tons* of garbage every day. Some of that garbage was buried, and some of it was backhauled, but a lot of it found its way into burn pits at the superbases and forward operating bases that dotted the theater. By 2007, JBB alone was burning between 100 and 200 tons of waste per day.[5]

There were no DoD rules against burn pits as a form of waste management when hostilities in Afghanistan and Iraq opened in the early 2000s, but there should have been. After concerns about burn pits and other exposures related to combustion during the Gulf War (remember the oil fires?), the military had begun to find ways to transition away from open pits during combat operations in the 1990s. During NATO operations in the Balkans in the mid-1990s, the US military replaced open-air burning with incineration and other forms of waste management as quickly as they could in order to protect both local populations and troops stationed on the ground. The presence of other NATO troops may have had something to do with the quick move away from open-air burning. It's also worth pointing out the relative whiteness of the local populations in Bosnia and Kosovo in the American racial imagination. In Iraq, there were no such concerns—NATO wasn't around, and the Iraqis tended to fit more neatly into a racialized American worldview that posited Arabs as a racial "other." The DoD didn't install incinerators to replace the burn pits at JBB until 2009, six years into the war. And even though they are no longer supposed to, in Iraq and elsewhere, the DoD is still burning trash.[6]

IF THE BURN PIT AT JBB REFLECTS THE WAY CORNER-CUTTING CONtingencies became permanent fixtures for US forces in Iraq, it also highlights a couple of other major problems with the way the United States thought about and fought the war. First, like so much of the American warfighting apparatus in Iraq, most large burn pits were not actually run by the military. They were run by private American contractors. By 2006, there were more than 100,000 private contractors on the DoD payroll in Iraq, taking care of everything from food service to equipment maintenance to personal security to the training of soldiers. Many of these contractors were armed. Few of them were directly accountable to either military commanders on the ground or the Iraqi government. And that was even before Paul Bremer issued something called "Order 17" on his way out of Iraq in 2004, granting every contractor affiliated with the Coalition Provisional Authority immunity from Iraqi law.[7]

Perhaps the two most famous contractors working in Iraq during the war were Blackwater, a security company that made the news in 2004 for getting caught in an attack by Iraqi insurgents in Fallujah and again in 2007 when the Iraqi government tried to revoke their license to operate in the country after a car bomb incident in Baghdad, and a construction company tied to Vice President Dick Cheney called Halliburton. Halliburton is a private military contractor, but its services are different than those of Blackwater. Blackwater provides security services; Halliburton builds stuff. More specifically, Halliburton is a multinational corporation specializing in oil and energy services that in the run-up to the war won a noncompetitive $7 billion contract from the Department of Defense to deliver fuel to the military in Iraq.[8] A number of its subsidiaries also won contracts to build things like barracks and detention centers. One of those subsidiaries, Kellogg Brown and Root (KBR), was paid to feed the troops and take out the trash.

Since the 1990s, KBR has been accused of many things: corruption and waste in their handling of DoD contracts; bribing Nigerian officials; hiding money in shell companies in the Cayman Islands and using those accounts to avoid paying social security and benefits; price gouging; professional negligence and shoddy work; covering up sexual harassment and sexual assault within the company; and human trafficking.[9] KBR has also been accused of negligently exposing soldiers to smoke containing toxic chemicals from burn pits in Iraq and Afghanistan.[10] (KBR ultimately won the class action suit brought against it by veterans when the US Supreme Court decided not to hear the veterans' appeal in 2019.)[11] According to Alex, the near beer they offer service personnel in the Middle East should also be considered a crime.

Like so many other contractors operating in Iraq, KBR had no real incentive to do its job better. In fact, the longer it sustained the status quo—in this case, poorly regulated open-air combustion pits spitting toxic fumes across a landscape filled with soldiers and civilians to whom it had no accountability—the more money it stood to make. Military operations can revolve around priorities like troop and civilian safety and local and national political reform. For contractors, the bottom line is the bottom line.[12]

Military contractors operated in a constellation of bases strewn across Iraq to provide lodging and logistical support for American forces operating in the region. Superbases—technically called main operating bases or joint operating bases like JBB—constituted small military cities, with airfields, hospitals, post offices, training facilities, and in JBB's case, a Turkish café. Forward operating bases in Iraq were smaller and sometimes more specialized compounds that typically operated like heavily armed forts in enemy territory, but they, too typically housed contractors to provide security and amenities unavailable outside of the barbed wire.

Superbases and large FOBs both represent what was wrong with the American approach in Iraq. Both kinds of bases protected contractors and military personnel from insurgents, enabling American military personnel to interact minimally with Iraqi civilians. Other than being full of burning, toxic shit, they were relatively safe. But they also ensured that both commanders and grunts remained out of touch with the people they were supposedly trying to "liberate." Large FOBs, in particular, enabled the fiction that the US was not facing an insurgency in Iraq, and contractors running security, food service, and waste disposal enabled commanders and grunts to remain generally safe and comfortable on FOBs. As long as most American service people (alongside contractors) stayed on or around superbases or large FOBs, contractors like KBR had buildings to build and trash to burn. And in the meantime, as Thomas E. Ricks has noted in his book *Fiasco,* from 2003 to 2007 that FOB life also enabled groups like al-Qaeda in Iraq (which wasn't originally even *in* Iraq) and the Mahdi Army to recruit and mobilize among the Iraqi public that Marines on FOBs weren't engaging with.

The Mahdi Army sure as shit wasn't lighting their garbage on fire in FOB burn pits.

OF ALL OF ALEX'S POTENTIAL TOXIC EXPOSURES, BURN PITS HAVE probably drawn the greatest public attention. The class action suit against KBR that ended when the Supreme Court refused to hear the case in 2019 was only one of many flashpoints in veterans' ongoing efforts to get the government and/or the VA to recognize (and compensate) the impacts of burn pit exposure on the health of Iraq and Afghanistan war veterans. Among the nonprofit organizations like Burn Pits 360 and the Wounded Warrior Project, the investigative journalists covering the story, and the members of Congress actively pushing for better care for exposed veterans, the catchphrase is that burn pits are "this generation's Agent Orange."

Manufactured predominantly by Monsanto and Dow Chemical, Agent Orange was a mixture of two herbicides (2,4,5-trichlorophenoxyacetic acid and 2,4-dichlorophenoxyacetic acid) used extensively by the US military in Vietnam to help clear swaths of dense jungle in order to deny the enemy food and cover and force rural populations to move towards cities. It was the most famous of a class of chemicals called the "rainbow herbicides" with which the US military coated almost 40,000 square miles of South Vietnam at a concentration thirteen times greater than that recommended by the US Department of Agriculture. All told, the US dumped 20 million gallons of the stuff on Indochina. Think thirty Olympic swimming pools worth.[13] Growing up, my history books called these chemicals "defoliants," but as a biologist friend of mine reminded me, the distinction between a defoliant and an herbicide means very little to a plant. More importantly, perhaps, in Vietnam, they were sprayed on plants as a way to get at people. Once they cleared the leaves from the trees, they could more effectively bomb the people hiding beneath them.

Agent Orange became relevant to veterans after the Vietnam War when they learned that it got at people in some unexpected ways. Agent Orange contains dioxins, persistent environmental pollutants that can accumulate in bodies and act as neurotoxicants and carcinogens. You may have heard of pollutants like PCBs (polychlorinated biphenyls) and PBBs (polybrominated biphenyls). Those are both dioxins. Agent Orange contains a particular dioxin called TCDD (2,3,7,8-tetrachlorodibenzo-p-dioxin), a known carcinogen and according to the EPA the most toxic of the dioxins.[14] (Typically, when we refer to dioxin, we are referring to TCDD. Coincidentally, TCDD was among the fifty-one pollutants picked up in air samples at the burn pits at JBB between 2007 and 2009).[15] In the years following the war, the people of South Vietnam suffered cancers, skin diseases, deformities, miscarriages and stillbirths, and a raft of genetic diseases at rates well above background, in large part a result of the incursion of dioxin from Agent Orange into the country's food webs.[16]

When commentators say that burn pits are this generation's Agent Orange, however, they are not comparing the impacts of burn pits on Iraqis with the impacts of Agent Orange on the Vietnamese people. Maybe they should be. But they're not. As with burn pits, Agent Orange also stuck with American service personnel when they returned from overseas, eventually creating a public health crisis among American veterans of the Vietnam War. Most American commentators care about Agent Orange and burn pits because of their impacts on American veterans.

Beginning in 1991, Congress authorized the VA to declare a subset of the conditions associated with Agent Orange exposure as "presumptive." That is, rather than having to prove a causal connection, for any veteran who has been exposed to Agent Orange during their time of service and has developed one of these conditions, the VA presumes the exposure caused the illness, and gives them benefits. Symptoms of Gulf War illness now also trigger presumption for veterans who served in specific locations during the Gulf War, largely because of the precedent set by Agent Orange. Ultimately, veterans' groups concerned about care and compensation for personnel exposed to burn pits hope to establish presumption for burn pit exposure. When veterans' advocates call burn pits this generation's Agent Orange, they do so in the hopes that, unlike with Agent Orange, establishing presumption for burn pit victims won't entail decades of denial and delay.

As their impacts gain more traction with lawmakers and the public, the burn pits operated in Iraq and Afghanistan bring one final irony back from those overseas military operations. That irony was summed up in a 2008 report by an American defense think tank called the RAND Corporation. In a study called *Green Warriors,* RAND analysts assessed the US Army's considerations of the environment in overseas contingency operations from first boots off the boats to the business of winding down deployments after a conflict.

"Environmental considerations," RAND writes, "are not well incorporated into operations in any phase of an operation."[17]

The RAND study doesn't dwell on burn pits, but burn pits symbolize exactly the kind of things the military is missing when it fails to think carefully about its connections to the environments in which it operates. According to RAND, the Army was particularly blind to how things like soil types and agricultural practices, water sources and water distribution, and local natural resource management continually and dynamically worked alongside cultural relationships to the earth, air, and water to shape the Army's relationship to the landscapes it worked in and the people who inhabited those landscapes. When the Army thought about these things, it did so statically and independently. It did not, in short, think about overseas contingencies operations ecologically. It didn't think about forever chemicals like PFAS and PFOS. It certainly didn't think about the way an outsized concern over WMDs could enervate a toxic feedback loop between PB, permethrin, and DEET in a soldier's body. If it thought about dust, that dust had no history. And like their counterparts in the Marine Corps, the Army's planners definitely didn't think about the combined ecological and cultural impacts of burning hundreds of tons of trash every day.

The VA's approach to veterans back on the home front has largely recapitulated the DoD's broader environmental compartmentalization. Rather than looking at exposures comprehensively, doctors (and lawyers) fixate on simple, straightforward, cause-and-effect relationships between discrete substances and diseases. They treat Marine bodies as if Marines went to war in test tubes rather than in the complex, dynamic environments that characterize actual war zones. The VA has pioneered a number of developments in integrative health care over the last two decades, and they are a leader in treating what they call polytrauma from the Global War on Terror, but, from Agent Orange to Gulf War illness to burn pit exposures, the organization has largely continued to maintain the fiction of compartmentalized bodies and environments.[18]

The great irony is that more than almost anything else, burn pits have given the lie to the kinds of environmental simplifications the VA has borrowed from the DoD in their treatments of veterans' illnesses. The authors of the Institute of Medicine's burn pit study made clear that bodies don't operate predictably within the ever-changing toxic ecosystem of modern warfare.[19] But the study also confirmed something about the Iraqi environment itself: that even without the burn pits, the landscapes of the Iraq War presented troops with a whirlwind of toxic exposures, from particulate matter to depleted uranium to pesticides to tainted water. Those exposures, too, require a reckoning. When they refer to exposure issues, many veterans' groups now carefully refer to "burn pits and other toxicants," because they have come to realize that burn pits may be only the tip of the toxic iceberg.

CHASING THE GHOSTS OF TOXIC EXPOSURES DURING THE 2003 INVA
sion in Iraq can feel as convoluted and confusing as Alex's experience
with the invasion itself. First we're worried about WMDs, and then suddenly WMDs are a red herring. Around every corner in 2003 is a trace
of 1991, and behind that a hint of 1982 and maybe a brush with 1500
BCE. Lurking behind the Marine experience is an everyday Iraqi experience that, if obviously dire and at least partially the United States' fault,
remains opaque, especially from inside the walls of an FOB. The exercise
is doubly dizzying for Alex, who in helping me try to reconstruct his
exposures from his memories of the invasion has had to live the whirlwind twice. Worse still, there is no firm answer at the end of the second voyage, no certain statement that X, Y, or Z made Alex and other
Marines sick.

And yet, with all their uncertainties, the myriad exposures confronting Alex and his compatriots in 2003 remain central to confronting the
American wars in Iraq and their aftermath, both for Iraqis and for American veterans back home. You can only look at the war through the lens
of a gas mask for so long. When you finally take it off, you realize that
the same environmental myopia that failed to recognize the long-term
hazards of war in the Iraqi landscape also supported the obsession with
short-term tactical military achievements at the expense of the lasting
human relationships of an intact civil society. The war, in that sense,
was doubly toxic, and it would take Alex another fifteen years to begin to
unravel its tangled knots.

PART 3

HEAD GAMES

*Post-Traumatic Stress Disorder
and Traumatic Brain Injuries*

13

"ALEX. DEAD. ALEX IS DEAD."

Burny and I sat in darkness on the fifth floor of one of the hotels ringing the Imam Ali Mosque in the heart of Najaf. We punched out a loophole in the wall to shoot through before the sun rose. The raggedy square let in a column of dawn light. The adrenaline from the final assault the night before was gone, and days without sleep now sat on our eyelids. We were dead weight. Hours earlier, our platoon had pulled up to the ring of hotels to support the grunts. We had all endured nearly four weeks of the heaviest fighting in 1/4 since the battles around Con Thien, Vietnam, when the battalion fought off the "mini-Tet" in the spring of 1968. It was 0600, August 25, 2004.

From the beginning, we had done it wrong. Boxing three sniper teams and all our optics in one amtrac, Chief Scout Revert and I argued, would be the fastest way to kill us all. It would deprive the battalion of its eyes and ears. And yet we did just that the night before, boxed us all up.

Two IEDs popped into our amtrac, bouncing off steel wheels, too small to puncture the armor, but strong enough to rock the beast. Fateh 60mm mortars slammed into the walls above us. Small arms plunked away. Inside, I went through the plan of attack. I told myself to stay frosty. No conversations. I hugged my M40 and gave encouraging looks to everyone. The brakes squeaked and knocking treads stopped. My vest wouldn't let me take a deep breath. A pale green light illuminated our faces. I was the first Marine at the back of the ramp, and I waited for the obvious order: get out of the street and along the wall as fast as possible.

I sat. Nothing.

I looked at my platoon commander. His face had turned white under the green lamp. My platoon sergeant stuttered, "Sir, we, sir . . . We need to . . . We . . . We, we, we . . . " Sweat ran down his face and his head shook. He stopped talking. No help there. Together, they looked like green and white popsicles frozen in their seats. Junior Marines looked on, dazed.

I looked at Revert. He nodded.

"Let's go!" we yelled. "Everyone on your feet!" I grabbed the handle on the hatch, ignoring the frozen amtrac drivers who should have dropped the ramp by now.

As I twisted the handle, someone jerked me outside. Charlie Company first sergeant.

"What the fuck are you fucking doing? You need to get the fuck out of here and start shooting! We have wounded out here and need to evac them!"

We scrambled out running, following green and blue chem lights on the deck, lighting our way off the street and into the complex.

The building was better. The rooftop provided the ideal platform to overwatch the infantry and we moved upwards in a footrace. We split the bigger teams into two shooter pairs as we climbed to different parts of the roof. The darkness helped, but only some. As we settled into smaller positions, securing a perimeter, enemy mortars bashed the roof. We used night optics in one moment and day sights when explosions and the remaining streetlights provided enough light to look for targets. We stayed as long as we could, standing behind narrow roof lips.

I wanted to stay topside. I argued with one of the second lieutenants, telling him I'd move multiple times to keep my position unknown. I wanted the highest vantage point and needed to look down roads or into counter-sniper hides.

The lieutenant said no, paranoia in his boot eyes.

We moved into one of the rooms facing the mosque, built shooting positions, and started the tedious process of observation and range cards. In my team, I had laminated paper range cards, and now we marked them with colored dry-erase pens. We committed to 100 percent watch until daylight.

The darkness in the room contrasted with a growing external light. Burny and I planted our asses on sofa cushions after setting up the sniper rifle and spotting scope on a coffee table backed up from the loophole. The small, tan-and-brown camo-painted hammer of my rifle lay on the deck. My watch showed hours had passed since leaving the amtrac. It could've been seconds.

Outside, it sounded like a regular dawn in Najaf. A light breeze ruffled aluminum signs and blew plastic bags into the air. No humans. No rifle fire. We took a break to rest our eyes. Their muscles had stretched from strain, and blood vessels popped bright red in our corneas. The battery on my PRC-148 radio glowed warmly against my hip as the first situation report of the morning whispered ammo, supplies, enemy actions, and then casualties.

"Standby for KIA report." A pause, then lengthening to another one. "Alpha, Romeo, Romeo, Echo, Delta," the voice declared as if describing a batter strutting up to the plate, "Oscar, November, Delta, Oscar." ARRE-DONDO. Another pause. It called loudly as if everyone in Najaf was listening. The voice robotically dictated, "Alpha, Lima, Echo, X-Ray, Alpha, November, Delta, Echo, Romeo." ALEXANDER. Last four of his social security number came next.

Dondo. Dead. Dondo is dead. Alex. Dead. Alex is dead.

The voice submerged, other reports called, and I stared into the loophole, watching light blot out the last pieces of night.

Back to work. I checked on my ATL Simpson and the rest of the team. I picked up the scuttlebutt from other Marines. Then I went back to our hide with Burny and closed the door.

We went on. We were trapped in the same buildings. Our teams could be out there, I imagined, lurking, and wasting the enemy. But the risks terrified higher command, so we stayed in the buildings, moving floors and observing.

Later in the day enemy mortars dropped on our roof and on the ledges outside our window. They fired again in the night and on the second day. A forward observer, an eager but lost lieutenant, fired back with 81mm mortars, and I watched the rooftops in front of me break and shatter into dust and fragments. The mortars fell back towards our position, twenty-five meters away. The loophole filled the room with dust the way a blower would blast an old garage floor. Marines below and above me yelled as fragments hit them before someone yanked the radio from the lieutenant and the attack stopped.

For three days and two nights, we sat in the building with no kills. We observed. We watched. Then the cease-fire came with the Mahdi Army. We climbed out of the scarred and smoked buildings, loaded the amtracs, and rumbled back to FOB Hotel. The speed and violence of the previous four weeks turned into boredom and a daily grind.

Days later, Alpha Company's First Platoon made a surprise visit. Recognizing my friends, I left the noon chow line. I climbed the ladder on the tailgate. The number of rungs leading to the top of the seven-ton truck seemed higher than ordinary and I struggled to pull myself upwards. From my perch on the ladder, I saw everyone resting in the back of the truck. The senior Marines sat in back, velcroed and snapped in their gear and letting the sun hit their uncovered heads. Where I might find Arredondo, asleep or listening to the worst hip-hop, a gap stood out. I made eye contact with tired faces and registered the loss. There were hugs, but nobody spoke. The longer I stayed with them, the heavier my body felt and the more I sank into the depression settling in amongst the Marines in the truck.

I left the truck heading east. I had no appetite. I walked rapidly—fleeing the scene of a crime—until I reached one of the loading docks we had turned into a gym. I removed my blouse, smoothing the sleeves, and then folded it neatly. I unclipped my pistol holster and placed it on the deck with my faded cover sitting atop. I buried my watch in the pile.

I moved iron. I curled weights. I added more. I pressed until my body gasped and I started seeing stars. In the shade of the loading dock, I forgot about the war and the Marine Corps and heaved until time came back to remind me of my duties. I put my uniform back on and clipped the pistol holster into my belt. I still had no appetite. I didn't go back to the chow line. Instead, I went to the intel shop to find hunting missions.

ORDERS CAME DOWN THROUGH MATTIS THAT OUR PLATOON WOULD PARTAKE IN THE November assault on Fallujah. Though first, we would operate in Ramadi with Second Battalion, Fifth Marines, known to us as 2/5. The birds swallowed us in Najaf and chopped north until they delivered us to a camp on the outskirts of Ramadi. We dragged heavy rucksacks and sniper rifles off thumping CH-46s and then watched the birds dust off. We stared at each other in the darkness. Our holiday in Najaf had ended. We trucked over to the tiny outpost on the western edge of the city called Hurricane Point.

When 2/5 referred to themselves as beleaguered, you believed them. The Marines in Ramadi in 2004 raced from outpost to outpost along IED-packed roads and took mortars—often heavy mortars—almost constantly. They controlled nothing. "Fifty percent of the people hate us and fifty per-cent of the people try to kill us," a squad leader told me on day one. I marked an explosion every two and half hours for the rest of the day. The insurgents, whose existence our high command didn't officially acknowledge, refused to systematically engage. They wisely chose to shoot-and-scoot with small arms and RPGs before triggering IEDs and disappearing into the city.

During one of my first walks around the camp, the Headquarters and Supply first sergeant lit me up.

"Where the fuck are your neck and groin protectors, Devil?"

Neck and groin protectors were standard, but they made shooting the M40 more difficult, and they were cumbersome in the sprints we had to make to get to rooftops and secure positions. Heaviness, I said, kills. The first sergeant didn't care.

A skinny lance corporal walked me back to a rusty-white shipping container in the supply lot. He popped the door handles and pushed open the creaking door. Piles of supplies sat gathering dust in the dim light. "This is all KIA and WIA from 2/4," he said. 2/5 had taken over from Second Battalion, Fourth Marines, 2/4, in the summer. Some of the 2/5 grunts studied their 2/4 comrades in those first weeks, he told me, and called them murderers. "They had dead eyes." Now 2/5 had the same hollow look. I fished through the flak pieces. Many had blood mixed in with gunpowder and the CLP we used on our weapons. I picked the least bloody ones and left.

We made the boxcar run across the city on day three. The grunts from Weapons Company promised we would hit daisy-chained 155mm shells and small arms on the trip. We geared up in goggles, gloves, cock flap, neck, and throat protector. We stacked layers upon layers of police issue body armor along the bed and walls of our Humvee. Marines had creatively welded their own armor on top of the late-arriving armor kits.

"Don't look over the sides," they told us. Revert and I laid down in the bed.

When I looked at the map during the convoy brief, I assumed our travel time would take thirty minutes. The trip took under seven. We drove at what felt like fifty miles an hour with everyone buttoned up. When we turned into the eastern combat outpost, my nose glowed with the rancid smell of burning shit.

We checked in with the other snipers. Jeremiah Baro, a friend from sniper school, caught me up on operations and employment. Baro was even smaller than I was. His eyes smiled. He explained how to get off the FOB and get into hides, where his team had stacked up a few kills. He admitted separating foe and friend was damn near impossible.

We wondered what our sniper instructors were doing.

"Putting PIGs on the chain," Baro quipped. We kicked over our impending reenlistments. He wanted to get out. I didn't know, but in the short term I'd request my team get paired up with his. We nodded and hugged.

The grunts in Weapons Company knew what they were talking about. On the way back, I decided I needed a look. The add-on armor had small holes for picking it up by hand. I peered through the four-inch-long slots. It didn't give me enough of a picture and I raised my helmeted eyes just above the lip of the armor. Two shots whizzed overhead, accurate for a moving target. I dropped down. Thirty seconds later, a blast exploded a few feet in front of our truck.

Bang. Boom. Zreeeppp. The truck shook but didn't jump.

We drove through black clouds of smoke and dust. Brown and black powder covered Revert and me like snow. We sucked in kerosene and cordite. A second bomb went off seconds later, this time near the back end of the truck and it leapt. I floated upwards gracefully, momentarily weightless, and then slammed against the vests and metal where my helmeted head hit the truck wall first, then my back bounced off everything and I was flat on the truck deck. Another, darker cloud streamed upwards behind us as it crawled into the blue sky.

I laughed at Revert, hoping the grins would free my asshole from where it had lodged inside my throat. My head was starting to ache. He laughed back in his Jersey accent, our laughs going on for a half a minute, but the boom and crash from both blasts kept ringing in my ears as we sped towards Hurricane Point.

BEFORE RAMADI, THE FALL HAD RACED BY. I LOOKED BIGGER AND STRONGER according to friends. I drank two gallons of water a day and cut out one of our three daily meals. I didn't eat during the weekly platoon cheat day. In the chow hall, I would keep the portions small and eat quickly. With the terrible contracted food, no one noticed what was happening. Even the trained observers in my platoon failed to spot the trend.

By mid-October, I had lost ten and a half pounds. When we went to Ramadi, I weighed one-fifty. At some point during our Ramadi operations, I started measuring food as chunks of energy. I removed the easiest things first. I threw away the sugar-laden packets of Gatorade. If I kept any, I found the calorie-free varieties like Crystal Light. I started measuring food at the mess hall with my hands. I would only eat portions if smaller than my closed fist. With MREs becoming part of our daily rations again, I gave away the candy and cheese to other Marines. I carried more water and more ammo and less food.

On my fifth morning at Hurricane Point, I awoke early to cold air and rain clouds. The rain hit the aluminum roof in our shack for a minute and then stopped. Later that morning, I went over to another sniper hooch and gathered more information. The sounds of a Humvee downshifting and the brakes squeaking on the pavement outside broke up our conversation.

"Tamaran!" one of the sergeants commanded. "Get the fuck out here!" The heavyset corpsman rushed outside.

About five minutes later, Doc Tamaran returned and threw his rifle into a red folding chair, where it slumped until the armrest caught it.

"One wounded and one KIA from Weapons Company," he said matter-of-factly in the cold air. "The KIA is Whiskey 4. The other guy got hit in the throat." He stared into the wall speaking to himself out loud. He looked at no one. The day refused to warm up.

The dead lieutenant, Whiskey 4, was my platoon commander's friend. From what we heard, the IED blasting through the door of his armored truck removed his head and neatly placed it in his lap. The neck protector did nothing. I imagined the severed head's eyeballs open and staring through the front window, still surprised by the blast. My lieutenant wrote five letters home in a row that night. Mortars blasted us all through the next day.

At mid-morning, a 120mm mortar broke the quiet on Fallujah's peninsula. *Whomppp—clannnnggggg!* I located the sound 400 meters away to our southwest. No fire missions over the radio. I saw smoke leaving a doorway and the roof of a mudwalled home. A large crack from the foundation to the rooftop splayed the home open. Iraqis rushed towards the house as I called in to verify if we were firing or taking rounds. During the movement and communications, I saw a multicolored heap five or six feet from the door. A middle-aged man grabbed the fabric, and I watched a child's face and extremities slip out. The man carried the child with the purple shirt and pink pants south into the village where we couldn't see him. Another man ran out of the smoking house with a little boy. The boy's legs hung from his arms coated in red oil. We heard the call for the medevac bird: shrapnel peppered and then paralyzed his legs.

My corpsman, Doc Havig, begged to leave the hide and run towards them. "You're not fucking going anywhere," I said. The smoke from the explosion settled down and everyone disappeared.

Fallujah was car bomb central. We were there to destroy the factory. Sunni insurgents had cached munitions in houses across Fallujah and the surrounding countryside. The families gathered with neighbors in the wrong house that morning. The children found a stockpile and triggered a booby trap.

Fifteen minutes later we spotted the child with the purple shirt in the hands of the same man. He climbed out of a ditch full of tall grasses with healthy trunks of date palms behind him. He surprised us. We waved him towards our two-story observation house.

Almost immediately, I wished we hadn't waved him in. The Marines across the river in downtown Fallujah repeatedly found themselves tricked into an ambush or a suicide bomb by the pleas of a child or adult pretending to be injured. I pointed my smaller A4 rifle at his head and prepared to split it open.

Keeping my face on the rifle, I looked to Burny. He stared downwards, his eyes bulging out. He didn't have a hand on his rifle and I pounced, "Get your fucking weapon up, boot." I looked at my ATL Simpson. He was with me. The child looked dead. Why take the risk?

Burny wasn't having it. Neither was Doc Havig. The team had already started to come apart under the stress and fatigue of almost nonstop fighting since August 2. The week before, my battalion commander had added to the stress by deciding to tell us over the radio during a shootout that my tour was up and I was headed home in December, leaving the team to carry on in Iraq without me.

"I hate to let you down," Doc said, "but I'm going." He waited for me to agree so he didn't have to disobey orders. But he would've anyway.

I softened. I nodded and sent Simpson with them while I held the roof with my radio operator and I moved the rifle off the man's face and pointed it towards the deck.

The man moved closer. His thick black hair waved all over. He wore a tattered black shirt and stained black trousers. He stood in scuffed black, leather sandals, the straps cracked with whitish stems. Burny, Doc, and Simpson disconnected the Claymore mine behind the door and removed the barricade. My RTO and I checked our perimeter, all 360 degrees of it, still looking for a trap.

The man moved forward. Then he lifted the child overhead and slammed it into the dirt beneath me. He kicked dirt on it and began to curse. I understood enough, outside of words, as he pointed at me and at my rifle and screamed. He couldn't stop screaming.

I looked at the body as Doc worked knowing it was a waste of time. The right arm from the elbow down held nothing except shattered bone attached to red-taffy strands of flesh and cloth. The purple sweater had a Mickey Mouse face on the front. The father howled. I wondered if shooting him wouldn't resolve it all and stop the screaming. I kept looking at the body. It lay neatly and calmly on the ground. It had nothing to add.

THE RAIN WOKE ME UP AGAIN AT 0315 IN THE MORNING THREE DAYS LATER. AT FIRST, I imagined my feet getting wet in a dream and then I pulled myself up, half-awake, to touch my feet because the rain felt too cold, too real, for the dream. Water had soaked into my sleeping bag and onto my gear through the torn seams of the tent roof. The rain didn't bother me as much as the conversation earlier in the day with Burny.

"Did seeing that little kid affect you at all?"

"Why?" I growled and lied. Of course, it would.

"I keep seeing him," he whispered, "I keep seeing the Mickey Mouse face. I keep thinking maybe we should've done more."

Sure, I thought. I might have said the same thing my first time around. Now, I didn't know and didn't want to know. I convinced him to tear the sideview and rearview mirrors off and focus on the present.

The day the father threw his child at my feet was my last day in Fallujah. I handed my M40 to Simpson the next day as they sat packed inside Humvees pointing east across the Highway 11 bridge. I didn't want to let go of my rifle, but I gave it to Simpson and he nodded. They crossed the Euphrates. Dust kicked up behind the worn-out tires and the truck glided underneath the gray streetlamps as they charged into the city and the fight.

BACK IN THE STATES, ABSURDITY SAT NEXT TO TRAGEDY. THE BODIES CAME BACK in life and dreams. It all felt like a repeated stabbing, waking me nightly. To avoid the pull, I threw myself into work and exercise and starvation. I would train the Marines for sniper school and then transition through several schools myself.

My first job was to train the PIGs. I thrashed them and thrashed with them, taking them on four-to-five-mile runs across Camp Horno as Christmas approached. Between coaching on trigger control and helping them shoot through multiple bushes, burning the smallest windows, I caught myself wondering if I needed to be there at all. The war was still going on. Wounded HOGs at my sister battalion 3/1 said the same thing. "If I'm not killing people," one of them asked, "what good am I doing?"

During our training, I checked in with my instructors. I trotted towards the old shack and stopped, reminding myself that I was no longer a lowly PIG. I walked through the front hatch and then to the threshold of the instructors' office. The snipers sat inside joking and invited me in.

I tried to relax. "Can we verify their orders are good to go?" I asked. "I don't want any surprises." I needed trigger time, too.

Someone took me inside the SNCO hooch. It had two desks, a wall filled with publications and files, and the gigantic whiteboard containing all snipers in First Marine Division. I looked down, selfishly, at the carpet for the stained black-red pool of my blood from the three failed stabs of the corpsmen trying to insert an IV into my arm at the end of Hell Week the previous June. Still there.

While the instructor logged in and searched, I approached the board and checked on names. First Marines: 1/1, 2/1, 3/1, and 1/4. The names and ranks appeared on magnets that could be moved all over the board, tracking sniper assignments across our base spanning empire. The whole frame could've sat on an online database—and it probably did—but having the large visual gave you a more meaningful family snapshot.

I looked at the names of my friends in Fifth Marines and two jumped out.

2/5:

Cpl. Jeremiah Baro. KIA Ramadi 11/04/2004

Cpl. Jared Hubbard. KIA Ramadi 11/04/2004

I didn't believe it. I refused to believe it. I checked with the instructors. They walked into an IED and everyone else survived, they told me. "Negative.

I just saw Baro at the end of October." No one argued with me. I changed the subject.

———

MY ANTAGONISM TOWARDS FOOD ADVANCED AFTER THE HOLIDAYS. NONE OF IT felt out of control. I bought a scale and hid it in my room. Junk food, ground meat, salad dressing, and sugar disappeared. When I did eat, I derived no pleasure from it. I would look at my white plate inside the PFC Gary Martini Chow Hall and guestimate the calories, setting aside what I hadn't earned, removing all the unnecessary fats. If I overate, then I jammed two fingers deep into my throat and vomited out the contents in secret. The sense of control and command swelled as I stared at semi-digested junk.

The obsession mounted even as I struggled to prepare for my own training and future. My senior instructor from sniper school was slated to take over the platoon at 1/5. They were headed to Anbar, where things were still hot. I wanted to join them. I worked out now twice a day, six days a week.

At some point during a set of incline presses, I strained my right shoulder and had to stop lifting weights. The corpsmen placed me on light duty for weeks. My body temp measured at 93.7°F and resting pulse 40 bpm. Since I couldn't lift weights, I ran more often. My run time for the three-mile dipped to seventeen minutes and thirty-five seconds.

By early February, I had lost twenty pounds from my original one-sixty. I had to re-tailor my uniforms. A voice materialized in my head.

"You fat fuck," it said. "You don't deserve that. Put it down, you fucking undisciplined bitch."

I saw warped images of myself in the mirror and tried to control the curves of flesh. The controls intensified and the voice matured, engaging me in daily conversation. My energy began to fall. I responded by telling myself I needed to work harder.

My shoulder didn't improve with mandatory rest. The pain concentrated in a dime-sized space deep inside the joint. Regimental nurses and doctors bleakly told me to prepare for a discharge from the Marines. At the same time the doctors examined my shoulder, they ran labs to determine the cause of my fatigue.

I told my comrades I had a mystery illness. A virus or a toxic exposure, I said. I quoted the doctors and corpsmen. They had no idea what was happening.

I wanted a second opinion on my shoulder and, guessing my time in the Marines had ended, I set up an appointment with a sports MD in Salt Lake City. Regiment told me I would have to wait another month or two, too many wounded coming back, before the Navy hospital could see me, let alone operate.

The doctor called me the next week from Salt Lake. I sat in my truck and listened.

"It's as we suspected, Alex. Tear of the medial labrum from eight to twelve o'clock. You must have surgery and soon."

"How many months until I recover post-op, Doc?"

"You're looking at a minimum of five months until you could fully function again."

I hung up. I started crying. The salt streams disgusted me. I'd cried only once since joining up when my spotting scope was smashed during a patrol in the giant cemetery in Najaf.

Baro's face stared at mine through the windshield. Then Alex's. One of my School of Infantry instructors, Sergeant Reynoso, shot early in the cemetery, looked at me with the same accusing black eyes from years back. Failure and shame. I drove away from the crowds of Camp Horno, near blind. I drove down the road to an unused Claymore range and parked in the shade of a coastal oak. The crying only stopped when my tear ducts dried out.

BY LATE MARCH 2005, I WAS DOWN TO 130 POUNDS. ABS ON ABS AND EVERY RIB visible. I kept teaching and whipping the PIGs who would deploy with us the next year into shape. That part of me functioned. The regimental doctors admitted they had no clue what my body was doing, outside of the clear case with my shoulder, and sent me to Balboa Naval Hospital to see a viral specialist. They drew more labs, repeated the questions of other medical histories, and drew up a bone marrow biopsy.

My dad opted to come with me and stay in the room for the biopsy. I laid on the table, my skinny ass hanging out, and the staff prepped the area with a light numbing agent. They punched a large-bore needle through the skin and bone and then connected a device that looked like a door handle. *Crunch-Crunch-Crunch.* With each screw turn, the tap went deeper into my hip. I stared into the dull, off-white paint on the walls. I had trained for things like this, and I felt nothing. My sweet father turned ashen and nearly fainted. The corpsmen escorted him out of the room. The screw continued to turn deeper into bone.

MY DAILY ROUTINES WITH FOOD IN LATE MARCH AND EARLY APRIL BECAME MORE rigid, but I never made it below 127 pounds. I weighed pieces of food. I drank more water. Vomit became the last resort, but one I enjoyed. It worked until it didn't. I couldn't cut anything else out without causing blackouts or needing to crawl into my winter sleeping bag at night to avoid shivering.

Still, I went to the doctors, and didn't tell them about my war against my own body. I underwent another bone marrow biopsy a week later. The results yielded nothing. The lists and reports showed all the things I didn't have yet couldn't diagnose the problem. I waited another morning in the gastroenterology wing at Balboa Naval Hospital and a doctor explained how they would stick a camera into my esophagus and take out a sample of my pancreas. I pushed my body from appointment to appointment. I had starved myself, and little strips of evidence linking my anorexia to the mystery illness swirled around me. But the part of my mind that told me not to eat wouldn't let me see them, let alone tell the doctors about them. After the exam, we unearthed more information and still no clarity. "The tests and labs revealed no cancer. This is an eighty percent analysis. Some kind of virus whacked you and you're recovering now."

DURING THE FINAL ROUNDS OF HOSPITAL VISITS AND TESTS, MY MOM CAME DOWN to check on me. She stayed in San Clemente and I'd visit after work. Her eyes looked at me differently than any other point in our relationship. She made food for me in the small kitchen of her room at the San Clemente Inn. It took her time, as I sat in silence, to bring the plea to her lips.

I needed to eat, she said. And I needed to eat a lot more.

I had no answer. I sat, exposed, and couldn't invent a way out of it.

"It controls you and you don't control it," she blurted out. Neither of us named it. She didn't say anything else.

The lies weren't just lies to other people. They were lies to myself, too. And when my mom brushed the truth, I didn't want to believe it. But it tumbled through my mind in the days after. I looked at my latest medical history and took stock. I couldn't sleep past 0445. My body vibrated; my core temperature dropped. It took me ten minutes to move out of my rack and into my running shoes in the morning.

What had happened? I made a checklist of the most troubling, tangible problems. I could only do five pull-ups and my shoulder blazed in pain. I wasn't healing. I didn't have the stamina to get through the day. The checklist disgusted me. I was combat ineffective.

STARVATION CONTAINS A SELF-DESTRUCT BUTTON. A MALNOURISHED BODY, I learned from my VA counselors and other anorexics, going back through my mom, grandfather, and great-grandfather, will eventually countermand the brain, and force you to chow down. Maybe a specific weight is the threshold for this detonation. Maybe the body is trying to remind you of all the things it can't do on this regimen.

Standing in 0500 darkness, I looked at the loaf of bread I kept for breakfast. I uncinched the bag and closed my eyes. I moved the bread from the bag to my lips. No taste and no pleasure. I pushed it into my mouth and drowned out the voices telling me to spit it out. I forced myself to eat another. And then another.

Was I full? I didn't know. I left the room and went for a run. The chilly air ate on my lungs. I passed an isolated coyote on a side trail. A western screech owl stopped me and I stood nearby the white tree it perched in. I turned off my head lamp and listened to the owl in the darkness.

14

A WAR OF NERVES

Post-traumatic stress disorder is the one clear medical diagnosis that Alex walked away from the Marine Corps with. It is a diagnosis that I had no interest in challenging. It checked out. Even now, after deep dives into so many of Alex's other wartime exposures, PTSD stands out as one of the most important factors in his post-deployment physical and emotional struggles. It's not the only thing, but it's a thing.

I really only started looking into Alex's PTSD as a sort of due diligence. Alex had two personas in the early days of our relationship. In class, as a student, he was polite and reserved, and he left a lot of the Marine world behind him, despite the camo. In our one-on-one meetings, though, he wore his identity as a Marine Corps veteran on his chest, flirting with a set of military tropes that struck me as cliché. On the bad days, he would ramp up the Marine-speak and lean into a well-worn grudge against the civilian world that failed to respect and would never understand his experiences. On the good days, the caricature of the disaffected veteran would recede into the background of more thoughtful and nuanced reflections, but I was never sure what kind of day it was going to be, and I didn't have a grasp on where PTSD fit into the equation. I also worried that PTSD itself might make Alex an unreliable collaborator.

What would Alex's life look like once he finished his master's degree and left academia? Did he have triggers that I needed to worry about? I knew that he had been through treatments, but how messed up was this guy?

What I didn't understand at the time was how digging into Alex's PTSD diagnosis—and the history of PTSD as a psychological condition associated with combat—was a ticket into exactly the questions about other exposures that I was so eager to address. As it turned out, Alex's PTSD would help me start to understand how PTSD has blinded veterans and their medical professionals to other types of toxic exposures, even as it magnifies, mimics, and complicates those exposures in veterans like Alex.

When it was first given its current name, PTSD was described as a disorder of memory, a condition wherein traumatic stress compromises your relationship with your own mind through the vehicle of intrusive or unwanted recollections of that trauma.[1] An immersion blender of memory. It manifested, psychiatrists understood, in either a hypersensitivity to often repeated memories, or an avoidance of painful memories, or both. In practice, while PTSD is now also understood in terms of anxiety and stress, treatments like the immersion and behavioral therapies prescribed Alex by his VA psychologists continue to target the complex relationships between trauma and memory that characterize the actual experience of PTSD.

But the intensity of traumatic memories makes them no more reliable than any other type of memory. In fact, the opposite may be true. One way or another, along with probable exposures to a whole host of neurotoxins and pretty definite symptoms of traumatic brain injury (another memory killer), Alex's PTSD may compromise his reliability in recounting his own past. Which is one of the reasons I was worried about Alex's PTSD.

WHILE I WAS CONSIDERING ALEX'S PTSD DIAGNOSIS TOGETHER WITH his history of exposures, I moved a book on an otherwise perfectly alphabetical office bookshelf so that it was out of place. I put Ben Shephard's *A War of Nerves: Soldiers and Psychiatrists in the Twentieth Century* next to Jonathan B. Tucker's *War of Nerves: Chemical Warfare from World War I to Al-Qaeda.*[2] It's a convenient placement, because there is more room on the T shelves than there is on the S shelves. But I filed the book out of order as a hypothesis. The more I considered Alex's experiences in Iraq, and the more I dug into the environmental conditions of that war, the more I began to think that the two books belonged together. That is: the material conditions of the First World War and the psychological impacts of that conflict arose together in the early twentieth century. The coevolution of environmental exposure and psychological trauma has defined modern war ever since. PTSD and environmental exposures in Iraq and Afghanistan are the latest iterations of this history. From an exposures perspective, the Great War has a lot to say about the war in Iraq.

By any measure, the number of casualties suffered during the Great War is staggering. If you don't include the death and destruction wrought by the Spanish flu epidemic in the immediate postwar period, WWI saw about 20 million military and civilian deaths. That includes somewhere on the order of 10 million military deaths; it does not include another 23 million wounded soldiers, nor the untold number of civilians wounded or displaced in the conflict. The death toll of the Second World War—a mechanized conflict that ate between 70 and 85 million lives—quickly surpassed that of the First World War, but if death is your metric, WWI is the big break between past and present.[3]

The First World War wasn't just about a lot of people dying. Soldiers in the Great War died differently, subjected to differences in the scale and kind of munitions that separated the conflict from anything that had come before.[4] The most notorious new weapon on the western front was poison gas, mostly chlorine and phosgene.[5] But artillery and machine guns also introduced levels of destruction no general would have foreseen in 1900. Over the course of the war, combatants discharged more than 1.45 *billion* artillery shells.[6] That's more than 9.2 million artillery rounds for every day of the war from the guns of August 1914, to Armistice Day, 1918, accounting for more than 15 million tons of explosives, metals, gas, and other stuff hurled between sides during the course of the war. Meanwhile, the British and Americans alone produced more than

8.6 billion rounds of small arms ammunition from 1914 to 1918. And that's not to mention the barbed wire—U.S. Steel alone produced 2.8 million miles of it during the war, enough to circle the globe more than one hundred times.[7] This is what industrial warfare looked like.

The acute violence of WWI disturbed old-guard military men. The scale was troubling, but ultimately it was the indiscriminate and totalizing violence of artillery and machine guns that disturbed them most. A British solider faced a higher likelihood of death in the Crimean War than in the Great War, but the rain of shells and bullets and gas on the western front largely precluded valor and heroics.[8]

The slow violence of WWI got less immediate play. During and immediately after WWI, the only real focus on exposures revolved around exposure to chemical weapons. Military doctors near the front treated gas exposure as acute physical trauma, though at the rear and after the war they also worked to ameliorate the psychological toll of gas attacks along with the trauma of the war more generally. But all that military matériel comprised other forms of exposure as well. Immediately after the war, the French government mapped out a 460-square-mile area in the northeastern part of the country called *zone rouge* (the red zone), an area they deemed too physically and environmentally damaged to support human life. A hundred years later, French and Belgian farmers continue to pull hundreds of tons of WWI metal out of their fields after every plowing season, much of it in the form of unexploded ordnance. A 2011 assessment of soil samples around Ypres—site of some of the worst fighting in the conflict—revealed elevated levels of lead, copper, and zinc, a toxic legacy of the war that promises to last well into the future. A similar study along the Soča front in Slovenia revealed that shell and bullet fragments had also contributed to elevated levels of mercury and antimony there. At Verdun, geologists found further evidence of lead, copper, and zinc at the site of an ammunition burn pit. That site also contained significantly elevated levels of arsenic.[9]

And that's just the stuff that's still there. Each of the rounds responsible for the twenty-first-century soil burden in Ypres contained a lead-based primer that would have filled the air where the round was fired,

and every shell that burst across the trenches sent fragments of metal-
lic dust into the surrounding water. Historians have rightly dwelled on
the massive rates of disease and infection among troops living in close
quarters under unsanitary conditions, but few have considered the
extent to which the same circumstances of a largely stationary war must
have concentrated war's various toxic byproducts in the air and water of
the trenches.

The new weapons of the Great War didn't only foster widespread
toxic exposures and lots of traditional casualties. They also yielded new
types of casualties. In the early days of the war, British soldiers returning
from the front began reporting what many twenty-first-century doctors
would probably describe as symptoms of traumatic brain injury—ringing
in the ears, amnesia, headaches, dizziness, tremors, and a sensitivity to
loud noises. Initially, early twentieth-century doctors also assumed that
the symptoms had a physical cause, the result of the incredible concussive
power of the war's new artillery. The trouble was that very few of these
wounded soldiers reported or showed physical signs of a head injury, and
in some cases the nature and extent of the symptoms were profoundly
weird. In addition to severe amnesia, soldiers inexplicably lost their
vision, their hearing, and their power of speech. They couldn't sleep, or
developed strange, tremorous gaits, or entered full-on fugue states that
could last indefinitely.

"I wish you could be here," wrote an Oxford professor of medicine
to a colleague in the summer of 1915, "in this orgie [sic] of neuroses and
psychoses and gaits and paralysis . . . I wonder if it was ever thus in previous wars?"[10] Another British medical man, a Cambridge psychologist
named Charles Samuel Myers, described the condition as "shell-shock,"
and though British doctors continued to search for physical causes, the
condition was soon classified in a broader category of "neuropsychiatric
casualties" that plagued armies on both sides during the war. By 1916,
24,000 British troops had been evacuated back to the home country for
shell shock—and that was before the Battle of the Somme, in which as
many as half of the nearly 300,000 British wounded suffered (usually
along with clear physical trauma) some sort of nervous disorder.[11] Of the

approximately 320,000 Americans wounded in the conflict, meanwhile, 69,394 were classed as neuropsychiatric casualties. Perhaps even more disturbingly, almost a decade later there were still more than 68,000 Americans in veterans' hospitals with neuropsychiatric disorders.[12] This, too, was modern industrial warfare, on the back end.

Defined as a psychiatric disorder, the term "shell shock" quickly fell out of favor with the British military. In the absence of a physical cause, shell shock was simply a way to describe a soldier's inability to handle the stress of battle—largely and uncomfortably understood as a mark against the soldier's manhood, or quite simply a manifestation of cowardice. (That the rate of shell shock was higher in officers than enlisted men made this all the more uncomfortable.) You lost your nerve and that was that. Some military men also believed it a condition that could be faked, and thus a new front on the old war against malingering, the strategy of avoiding service by feigning sickness or injury.

As I stared at Alex's Post-Deployment Health Assessment forms in my office, however, I wondered if shell shock wasn't *exactly* the right term for thinking about the combined environmental, physical, and psychological violence of the First World War. The suite of shell shock's symptoms include many of the symptoms of lead and mercury poisoning. They also include symptoms of traumatic brain injury. Short of exhuming bodies and testing bones for lead—and really, even then—I have no way of knowing whether lead or mercury or any other environmental exposure caused an individual British soldier's shell shock. But the quantity of munitions expended and the circumstances under which they were fired provide good reason to suspect that the Great War exposed its trench-bound combatants to more lead, mercury, copper, and arsenic than any previous conflict in human history, and current concentrations of heavy metals in those landscapes help corroborate that speculation. A hundred years later, Alex's forms reveal the same tangled web of injury, trauma, and exposure that has characterized warfare since the Great War. And just as there is significant evidence that environmental exposures accompanied the many other horrors of WWI that may have led to that conflict's famous neurological conditions, Alex's exposure history provides at least as much evidence that we should be concerned about his environmental exposures as they do that we should be concerned about PTSD. I certainly think there is enough evidence for us to consider finally abandoning the either/or approach that dominates the search for physical and emotional causes for veterans' postwar neurological conditions.

The shell itself points the way, though it could just as easily be a WWI shell or a twenty-first-century depleted uranium shell, or an IED for that matter. A combination of potentially toxic things with the power to create the kind of indiscriminate, acute physical trauma that heightens the incredible psychological stress of a new type of warfare, the artillery shell and the modern IED both wrap symptoms and causes together into a perfect symbolic package of fast and slow violence. If toxicity is the capacity, in the right circumstances, to do harm, the shell is a toxic event in waiting.

15

"FIRST CIV DIV"

U nlike everyone I served with, I expected to come home with at least
one injury. War changes people, and rarely for the better. I didn't
expect I would be much different. Before I enlisted, I made it into
Westminster College in Salt Lake City on a biology scholarship as I chased
my dream of skiing in the 2002 Olympics. Once I was there, I struggled
with calculus, and ended up trading biology for studying American and English history and literature from 1900 to 1930. That literature inoculated me
against any romanticization of war. My two favorite poets were the English
grunts Siegfried Sassoon and Wilfred Owen. Sassoon grew up chasing
foxes on horseback and golfing. Owen grew up with a rail clerk father and an
Anglican zealot for a mother. They picked lice out of uniforms, censored mail
in their platoons, and led desperate missions during the First World War.

I paid more attention to them after enlistment. I probably heard "Suck it
the fuck up, Marine" a thousand times. Sassoon gave better advice:

. . . it's bad to think of war,
When thoughts you've gagged all day come back to scare you;
And it's been proved that soldiers don't go mad
Unless they lose control of ugly thoughts

That drive them out to jabber among the trees.

Now light your pipe; look, what a steady hand.
Draw a deep breath; stop thinking; count fifteen,
And you're as right as rain . . .[1]

My guide to Lost Generation literature was Robert Welsh, and he gave me the mental and spiritual preparation I needed when I joined the Marines. Bob had been a grunt and a sniper too, but in Vietnam. He taught classical studies and occasionally offered an early night class on the Great War or the Second World War. He told us sparingly about his survival on Hill 823 at Dak To with the 173rd Airborne Brigade in 1967 in order to get us into the minds of privates and generals in the Great War during class, though he didn't relish the details. Despite how much war surrounds American history and pop culture, we always get a sugared-up or moralistic version of it. Bob refused to give us easy views. He taught us that war is ultimately violent politics, but that the people experiencing the violence rarely had a spot at the political table. He knew how to connect struggles over resources above the battlefield to the generals setting policy, and then connect the generals to the grunt standing in a trench coat and trying not to get pneumonia.

He wasn't much taller than I am. He still had the same shaved head he had in Vietnam, the same one I would have in Iraq. Now the stubble was gray. Our class discussed *All Quiet on the Western Front* one night. "The worst scene for me was the screams of the horses in Chapter Four after the shelling," he said. He took a breath, "Detering, the farm kid, wants to save the horses before his friends, but the horses must be shot." He looked like he was ready to cry. Little things counted and hurt in ways you wouldn't expect on a battlefield.

Bob was the only person who knew what kind of help I needed after I came back from my last tour at the end of June in 2008. The transition had been fast, the fastest of my Marine life. One morning I was in a C-130 transport leaving Baghdad International Airport and flipping off the war through my tiny cabin window and the next I was shin deep in cool water on the Lost River of the Copper Basin in Idaho fly fishing. I should've been used to the trips and transitions, but this time felt different. Back in the Mountain West, the whole tour felt like it might have been a vacation. Everything at home felt the same. America still felt the same. The Snake River fine-spotted cut throat were identical. My dog Adriana was still the same. Nothing indicated the war was still going on.

Technically, Adriana wasn't my dog. I bought the dog, a blue nose pitbull, for my younger brother Mitch before I deployed in the summer of 2007. Mitch had struggled since I left. His success as a professional skier and X Games athlete was colored by run-ins with the law and episodes of depression. In the off-season, he painted houses. Some of those houses required abatement of lead paint in pre-1978 homes across Salt Lake and Park City. At one point he did what all little brothers do and tried to join the Marines. After my last deployment, we opened a skateboard company and moved in together, living and working out of a warehouse near the Salt Lake City International Airport. I hated it. I hated retail and the stress of trying to keep our heads above water amidst the financial crash. It was the only plan I could come up with as I transitioned back to what Marines call "First Civilian Division" or "First Civ Div." Still, I wanted to keep Mitch out of jail and out of the Marines, and the company kept my mind busy. I liked being my own boss and letting my hair grow.

Even living and working with him every day, I couldn't help but keep Mitch at a distance. I did it to everyone. The first woman I loved had been with me through two deployments, but when we tried to reconnect in Salt Lake my avoidance went into overdrive. Our conversations were stilted, and I embraced the silence as a form of sabotage. A few weeks after we broke up, she called me from the Denver airport to tell me she wasn't pregnant, and that was that.

Mitch tried harder to help me come back home. He set up a grill outside and cooked for us.

"Are you going to eat that?" he would ask now and then when I moved food around my plate. He was never pushy about it. He helped limit my drinking, which never amounted to anything because of our teetotaling Mormon upbringing. He noticed that I spent most nights staring at the ceiling tiles above my inflatable mattress on the floor at the warehouse. He gave me a little weed and sat me down to watch a crusty old samurai in *Sanjuro* and *Yojimbo*. Adriana laid between us on our couch and Mitch said, "You'll like this dude. He's a lot like you."

We built a team of amateur skaters, half in the states and half from Germany, and in November I sent Mitch off to Spain to manage the team through a film shoot. I can't remember what started the fight we had days before his departure. The real issue was right there at the surface.

"You know why I'm angry?" he shouted, fists clenched, ready to rain blows down on my know-it-all face. "I'm pissed off because you bailed on me. You fucking hung me out to dry and left all this unfinished shit for me." He stood there with his fists still balled together. I knew that Mitch hit hard, and I instinctively watched the hands more than I listened to the words. But I heard him. "You fucked me man." I didn't say anything. Now, I wish I had hugged him.

Adriana was the only stable relationship I had. She didn't need emotional support. She needed walks and chow. We left the office every day at closing time and drove to the south end of the dying Great Salt Lake. We cruised along deer trails and in between cattle while breathing in the smell of rotting algae turning into hydrogen sulfide gas. She sniffed, bit at brine flies, and then led me onward.

The Marine Corps sent me a warrant for my promotion to staff sergeant on the first of September. My ex-chief scout, Revert, called to ask when I could come back to the fleet and join his sniper platoon in Third Battalion, Ninth Marines pumping to Helmand Province in Afghanistan. Meanwhile, I visited an Army Special Forces recruiter and found out what it would take to leave the Marine Corps for good. My options were open. I kept everyone in the dark about my plans. The war was there, and it made sense. Every few days, I would catch myself dialing mobile phone prefixes of Iraqi friends. I missed eating with my hands, waiting for hot tea overloaded with sugar during meetings. I missed being with the boys.

Parts of my body started misbehaving as soon as I got back, and I went through the debate over what to do next. My allergies exploded in late summer. Plants and dander popped positive during skin tests. Box elder, Russian olive, and Fremont cottonwood; alfalfa, pigweed, and sagebrush; and cats, dust mites, and molds. My allergist diagnosed me with seasonal allergic rhinitis and conjunctivitis. I went in for routine allergy shots and the immunotherapy proved ineffective, so I gobbled up antihistamines, squirted nasal sprays, and mostly stayed indoors. Migraine headaches flashed in and out when the pollen count was high.

My body cooled down. At a Wynton Marsalis concert at Red Butte, my father and I watched the band move through difficult and physically demanding sounds with ease and grace. It was good music. The yellow guts of the copper mine splayed out in the west under a sunbath. The botanical gardens smelled sweet and dry, fed by a fast, deep creek. I watched in shock as concertgoers swayed and danced. It was the first event I had attended in more than a year where no one was searched or detained. It was bizarre to see a large group of people in control of themselves without barbed wire and armed checkpoints. The size of the crowd, the amount of sound and movement, wore me out, and I started to get cold. It was eighty-five degrees out once the sun set, but I was freezing. We left three-quarters of the way through the performance, and I was shivering.

What kept me stateside as 2008 slinked into 2009 were my feet. I rolled out of bed in the mornings and the first steps felt like standing on broken rum bottles. It had started years earlier after a fall and slowly became worse. I had developed plantar fasciitis, and it didn't respond to manual massage or stretching. I refused to take painkillers. The podiatrist made the decisive call. The scar tissue was too thick. I needed to undergo surgery followed by injections of my own blood and fat to restimulate tissue growth. I knew what it meant. I knew I couldn't be a Marine forever. The pain made the decision for me.

My feet healed more slowly than the doctor had ever observed. New problems started to show up. My left eyebrow shrank and square patches of scalp hair fell out. I picked up a respiratory infection that laid me out for a week in October. Insomnia disrupted my recovery, and when I did sleep, nightmares kicked me awake. I never remembered the dreams, just the faces of missing friends. Staring at the ceiling again as the first snows hit the mountains, I admitted I had never felt this weak before. What was happening to me?

Bob invited me out to the bar at nearly the same time. We sat in a booth near the college where he'd taught me history and Latin a few years before. I ate some of the chicken wings and we shared a pitcher. Bob had spent most of the 1970s trying to escape his war through alcohol, drugs, and motorcycles, but he had eventually found a postwar life worth living. He asked me to come out for a beer to check in on me and try to talk me into grad school. Instead, he talked me into getting treated for PTSD.

I stared at the tiny bubbles in my glass. I wanted to growl back and pull rank, but Bob's eyes made the decision for me.

"If you don't deal with these things Alex," he said, "they'll deal with you."

I STEPPED INTO WHAT THE VIETNAM VETERANS CALLED "THE TANK," A GRAY-BROWN temp building like you'd find behind a crowded elementary school, on a late February morning in 2009 at the George E. Wahlen VA Hospital. The Tank housed the PTSD clinic. I arrived fifteen minutes early and couldn't find a parking space. Stopping near the baseball diamond, I walked uphill, a half mile, towards the dull building. In the parking lot, I looked up at the flattop, breathing heavily from the fast walk, and exhaled in the cold.

I sat on a thinly cushioned and faded blue chair inside. The Vietnam vets eyed me curiously, someone decades too young for a visit. I still wonder if they thought I was there to pick up my father. They said nothing and we all sat in the windowless room. Eventually the attendant bought me a clipboard with a PTSD scorecard on it.

I moved the pencil down the list of questions. It quizzed me about hyper-vigilance, sleeplessness, rage, guilt, and depression. Pretty much what you would expect on a PTSD scorecard. Farther down the list there was a series of questions I didn't expect that stopped me. They were questions about starvation and body image. I moved down the list and stopped again, then moved back up to the eating questions. I was here to get better, wasn't I?

I checked the box next to "Anorexia Nervosa." I looked hard at the shiny graphite calling attention to what had until only recently been a secret even to myself and played with the eraser. I left the mark and finished the form. I scored an 85 percent.

Eventually the attendant called my name, and I went back, following the psychologist, who was nearly my age.

"It's hard to get any vets from our generation in here," she said "I think your suspicions of psychologists are higher than any other group we treat."

Then she explained how I could either take a soft approach over a long period of time or jump right into intensive therapy. Behavioral therapy and meds. Get back up to weight and fight the nightmares on the fast track. Predictably, I chose the intensive approach.

"We're going to double you up with an eating disorder specialist."

I hated hearing it. I agreed anyway.

PTSD treatment was all about memory, and immersion therapy made up one of many techniques to recall buried memories and bring them safely to life. She wanted me to locate recollections that I avoided or the ones causing the recurring nightmares since my redeployment the previous fall. Medications, and occasional weed from my brother, would only take me so far. With time and a sympathetic witness, the veteran might recall more information and respond to it in a way they couldn't during the war, eventually realizing the past was no ongoing experience and that I could finally grieve all these losses. Or at least that's how she explained it to me.

I came back to the hospital and entered another wing a week later to get weighed by a different doctor. I barely made "adequate" when I stood on the scale. I don't remember the number of pounds in the display box. Every room felt cold to me then unless it was seventy-five degrees and my heart rate always beat slower than 50 bpm. We sat and discussed the next four to five months.

"My sense of hunger is totally fucked up. I can't 'eat when I'm hungry' because I have no idea what that means." I struggled to explain this, but she understood.

I had to eat, though, and try and be less restrictive. I had to get off the roller coaster.

"You're still constantly exercising even though you're going through these surgeries on your feet?"

I nodded. I swam when I couldn't run. All that winter I had been seeing an acupuncturist to manage the pain in my feet. What kept me going to those appointments was less a belief in what all the pins dotted in my legs and back did and more that it was the only place where I slept deeply.

She didn't tell me to quit, just to try and relax the routine.

"As you retrieve old memories, you're going to have flare-ups. The medication should help."

I left with a container of 100 mg tablets of sertraline, aka Zoloft, and resentfully started taking them that night.

I went back into The Tank in May once I had a more stable relationship with food and my weight. Something clicked in the weeks of weight check-ins and food reports and journaling, where my thoughts were protected and camouflaged from everyone. I wasn't going back to whatever I had been doing for the past five years with my body, but it wasn't clear what was next.

16

BOTH/AND

Alex was diagnosed with PTSD, which psychologists today understand very differently than Great War psychiatrists understood shell shock. And with Alex in mind, I think it is worth considering more carefully just how modern psychiatrists define PTSD. On the surface, the diagnostic criteria are relatively straightforward. There are eight main criteria, A–H, but the really important one is Criterion A. To meet Criterion A, a subject must have been exposed to trauma. Couldn't be more obvious; it's right there in the name.

Once they meet Criterion A, the subject must also report or display some combination of symptoms from four main symptom clusters to be diagnosed with PTSD: Criterion (B) symptoms related to re-experiencing the trauma, usually called "intrusion"; Criterion (C) symptoms related to avoidance or emotional numbness; Criterion (D) symptoms related to negativity and negative self-perception; and Criterion (E) symptoms related to hyperarousal. Symptoms have to last more than a month (Criterion F); they have to mess with your life in some way (Criterion G); and they can't be the result of drugs or another medical condition (Criterion H). Not quite as self-evident as Criterion A, but also not rocket science.

Look under the hood, however, and PTSD is a mess.

Psychiatrists have recognized mental disorders resulting from acute, often life-threatening stress as a special category since as early as the late nineteenth century, but PTSD as we know it didn't enter the diagnostic lexicon of the American Psychiatric Association until 1980. Its inclusion in the third edition of the APA's *Diagnostic and Statistical Manual of Mental Disorders*—the DSM-III—was not simply a matter of plodding scientific advancement. Rather, it came about through the intense lobbying efforts of a coalition of Vietnam veterans' groups and women's rights advocates, all focused on describing a category of mental illness with a clear set of causes that might impact anybody exposed to trauma in just the same way.[1]

For veterans, medicalizing postwar mental health disorders under the name PTSD created opportunities for former combatants to claim compensation and receive treatment for psychiatric injuries. For groups like Vietnam Veterans Against the War, lobbying for a PTSD diagnosis in the early 1970s also served as one of many ways to oppose the war itself. For women, meanwhile, PTSD provided a way to recognize the psychiatric impacts of sexual assault, not just medically but also socially and legally. PTSD patients weren't inherently crazy. They were, in a word, traumatized.

The needs of the unlikely coalition of women and veterans meant that the first iteration of Criterion A had to encompass the psychiatric stress of combat historically described as shell shock or combat fatigue and the mental health toll of sexual assault in the same, actionable diagnostic category. In 1980, the DSM-III said that PTSD required a "recognizable stressor that would evoke symptoms of distress in almost everyone."[2]

Criterion A is what makes PTSD PTSD. Unlike just about any other disorder listed in the current DSM—the DSM-5—PTSD requires a specific etiology, or causal origin: trauma. You can have all the symptoms in the world from Criteria B–H, but without Criterion A, it isn't considered PTSD. But by the standards of the DSM-III and later DSM-IV, "trauma" proved almost infinitely expandable. Under the updated DSM-IV guidelines, for example, anyone in the United States with a television could have been diagnosed with PTSD following the terrorist attacks of

September 11, 2001. How useful was that really? Meanwhile, the same condition used to diagnose the trauma of car accident victims and Holocaust survivors could, its critics complained, apply to teenagers who have played too many violent video games or white-collar employees who have heard too many dirty jokes at work.[3]

In the main, the diagnosis did its job by providing a framework for legal protection, compensation, and legitimacy for veterans, sexual assault victims, and survivors of other violent experiences like car accidents and mass shootings. But even after they cleaned things up to exclude violence on TV in 2013, the DSM-5's definition of "trauma" has remained central to critiques of the diagnosis from within the psychiatric community.[4]

The focus on "trauma" and "traumatic stressors" has also created a logical problem in PTSD diagnosis. As Marilyn Bowman and Rachel Yehuda pointed out in the early 2000s, the phrase "traumatic event" presupposes an outcome, assuming that an event that might be traumatic for some is experienced as traumatic for everybody. (This assumption was in fact baked into the DSM-III's definition of trauma on purpose, serving to validate survivors' responses by suggesting that anyone else might have responded the same way.) But people only *sometimes* experience the car accidents, combat experiences, and sexual assaults lurking in PTSD diagnoses as trauma, and these events only *sometimes* result in symptoms of PTSD. The rates are actually lower than you might imagine. A famous study of residents in poor, largely black neighborhoods in Detroit in the late 1990s revealed that while almost 90 percent of the subjects studied were exposed to the kind of trauma that fit the DSM-IV's Criterion A, only just over 9 percent developed symptoms of PTSD.[5] Surviving or witnessing an experience threatening death, serious injury, or sexual violence is thus necessary but not sufficient in diagnosing PTSD.

The research world is full of awkward terminology, and an inelegant phrase like "potentially traumatic stressors" might have done the trick here, but Bowman and Yehuda chose something I find much more appropriate to talk about the incidents that can lead to PTSD. They began to refer to the incidents in question as "toxic events."[6]

The quagmire of PTSD diagnosis doesn't stop at defining trauma in

Criterion A. There is also a strange binary cooked into the PTSD diagnosis in Criterion H that it has inherited from the days of shell shock in
WWI. During the Great War, the binary was a big part of the debate over
the disorder. Was there a physical cause of shell shock, or was it purely
a psychiatric disorder? One or the other; surely not both. For a condition to count as PTSD, the DSM-5 requires that symptoms cause such
a disturbance that they impair a patient's functioning in daily life. Criterion H says that the "disturbance is not attributable to the physiological effects of a substance (e.g., medication, alcohol) or another medical
condition."[7] It's either PTSD or it's something else, and never the twain
shall meet.

But the fact is, PTSD often shows up with a variety of fellow trav-
elers, and a PTSD patient's other ailments are often wrapped up in the
same trauma responsible for post-traumatic stress. This is especially true
of PTSD from combat, where physical and psychological trauma often
occur in the same harrowing moments. Bullets and explosions, it turns
out, cause all kinds of damage, all at the same time.

Fortunately, researchers interested in the relationships between
PTSD and fellow-traveling conditions of exposure aren't bound by strict
rules of psychiatric diagnosis. Criterion H has only so long of a reach.
This is especially true of military health researchers like Cynthia Leard-
Mann who are more interested in assessing the outcomes of PTSD than
they are in wading into the minefields of debate about its causes. Leard-
Mann works on the Millennium Cohort Study, the massive long-term
prospective health study I mentioned earlier that arose out of concerns
over Gulf War illness and launched at the Naval Health Research Center
in San Diego beginning under the Department of Defense in 2000.

The MCS almost accidentally created the perfect framework for
tracking the health impacts of the American wars in Iraq and Afghanistan. They are one reason we have reasonably good data on PTSD in
the military—data that is far more detailed and useful than Alex's Post-
Deployment Health Assessment forms. Using MCS data to look at PTSD
outcomes—that is, the type of down-the-road physical health risks that
tend to crop up more frequently if you have a PTSD diagnosis on your

medical rap sheet than if you don't—makes it clear that it's impossible to draw hard-and-fast distinctions between psychiatric disorders like PTSD and the myriad related ailments that, as in Alex's case, often accompany them.

LeardMann and her coauthors have drawn some astonishing links between PTSD and four relatively common autoimmune diseases: rheumatoid arthritis, systemic lupus erythematosus, inflammatory bowel disease, and multiple sclerosis. Autoimmune diseases occur when your body, often for no apparent reason, deploys the mechanisms it has to fight disease against its own healthy cells and tissues. Autoimmune diseases tend to be rather mysterious illnesses, though their increased prevalence—especially among women—in the last few decades has led to a much greater understanding how they work.

I was surprised to find there was a link between PTSD and autoimmune diseases. It turns out that if you have PTSD, the likelihood that your body turns on itself goes up dramatically. Drawing on a sample of more than 120,000 military personnel, LeardMann and her group found that the risk of developing an autoimmune disease went up 58 percent for those with a history of PTSD over those with no PTSD diagnosis. The study corrected for a variety of other risky behaviors also associated with PTSD—smoking, obesity, problem drinking—and acknowledged the possibility of some self-reporting bias issues. But 58 percent is still a pretty robust signal in such a large sample group. The association, the group suggested, is "more likely due to biological changes that occur in the body among those with PTSD" than it is due to any behavioral disorders.[8]

LeardMann's conclusions brought me back to Alex's Post-Deployment Health Assessment forms. Both autoimmune disease and PTSD tend to manifest in many of the same ways as the other types of toxic exposures Alex confronted during his time as a Marine. Symptoms of PTSD and toxic exposure not only coincide with autoimmune disorders; they both may actually contribute to autoimmune disease. LeardMann's group confirmed a growing body of research that suggests that PTSD is a major risk factor for developing lupus, multiple sclerosis, and irritable bowel syndrome. So too is exposure to heavy metals implicated in immune system malfunctions.[9]

In fact, PTSD and heavy metals even share a common mechanism for messing with a person's immune responses. PTSD tends to affect the relationship between an organ of the brain called the hypothalamus and two sets of glands, the pituitary and adrenal. Tied to the thyroid, this structure is called the hypothalamic-pituitary-adrenal (HPA) axis, and it helps to regulate both the immune system and the body's physiological responses to stress. PTSD tends to cause the HPA axis to malfunction, contributing to the type of immune system problems at the heart of autoimmune disease. So too have heavy metals been shown to cause dysregulation of the immune system through the HPA axis. Lead, mercury, pesticides. PTSD and TBI. Autoimmunity. The HPA axis of evil.[10]

By the time I talked to LeardMann, I was no longer surprised that while groups like hers have established links between PTSD and autoimmune disease, and environmental health specialists have found clear connections between toxic exposures and autoimmune disease, almost nobody has tried to establish a relationship between exposure to heavy metals or toxicants and PTSD.

I asked LeardMann if I was missing something—whether perhaps this was something that someone had looked into and found to be pretty definitively not a thing.

She laughed genially. "Listen," she said, "we're used to working with imperfect data. If you're looking for it to be perfect you're never going to do the work. But sometimes there is such a thing as data that's just too uncertain." The near impossibility of pinning down good data on exposure, she explained, is probably why you don't have a lot of people looking for an association between toxic exposures and PTSD. Marines aren't exactly clocking in and out of pollution plumes while they're deployed. The DoD certainly wasn't monitoring active-duty personnel's average daily exposure to burn pit exhaust and pesticides and jet fuel, adjusted for proximity, wind direction, intensity, and duration in the way we might want during more than 200,000 individual deployments. Reconstructing exposure scenarios ex post facto hardly makes for the kinds of rigorous public health studies researchers like LeardMann are in the business of conducting.

"I'll leave that problem for you and Alex."

LIKE ENVIRONMENTAL HEALTH CONDITIONS RESULTING FROM things like lead, mercury, and pesticides, PTSD is fundamentally a condition of exposure. We think of the impacts of PTSD as primarily psychiatric and those of something like lead as primarily neurobiological, but the borders between those two ways of understanding a disorder are always fuzzy and contested. Ultimately, both PTSD and environmental poisoning result from components of our external environment that, over time, put us at risk for certain types of harm. And that is in fact the very definition of a toxic substance: something that, in the right doses or the right situations, can take a healthy body and brain and make them less healthy. One look at Alex's post-deployment health forms and you can see that even if the DoD doesn't see them as directly associated, we understand and screen for these two types of exposure—environmental and traumatic—in very similar ways.[11]

And yet, among conditions related to exposure, PTSD is also different. The symptoms of PTSD are bound to culture and context in ways that the symptoms of other environmental exposures simply are not. Doctors continue to try to figure out why people who have received the same doses of toxic substances like lead or radiation often develop widely varying degrees of symptoms, or sometimes none at all. But for conditions associated with psychiatric trauma and stress, that puzzle is not just about severity. For combat-related stress disorders in particular, the nature of the symptoms has changed significantly over time, and tends to vary widely with culture. The fugue state is out; flashbacks and self-harm are in. Presumably, the underlying conditions of shell shock, the "combat fatigue" suffered by soldiers in WWII and Korea, and PTSD from Iraq and Afghanistan are at least mostly the same. But the symptoms of these wartime conditions have been different enough over time that reading a PTSD diagnosis back onto a WWI soldier feels anachronistic.

For some researchers studying combat-related mental disorders, differences in the way combat stress has manifested over time and in different cultures is the result of a process called "looping." Take a member of
the British Expeditionary Force at the front in WWI in 1917 as an example. By 1917, that soldier has either seen or heard about traumatized comrades with "bad nerves" or shell shock. The symptoms of shell shock are
culturally available. And when that British soldier begins to suffer from
a stress-related disorder, it manifests in exactly this, culturally available
form: as shell shock. Numbness, inability to speak, the shivers, sensitivity
to noise, and a haunting steady stare. That soldier's shell shock, in turn,
influences future manifestations of combat stress among other British
soldiers. And so on. Half a century later, Vietnam veterans increasingly
expressed their postwar anxieties and disorders in ways that reflected the
media's portrayal of disturbed veterans in the post-Vietnam era. Depression, irritability, hyperarousal, disaffection. Those very symptoms would
come to help define the condition of PTSD, which in turn has entered
popular culture in ways that, if you believe in looping, have influenced
the manifestation of PTSD since then.[12]

PTSD is not the only culture-bound mental disorder in the DSM-5,
nor is it the only culture-bound disorder of concern to veterans. In fact,
PTSD frequently serves as a risk factor for developing other psychological or behavioral disorders with a major cultural component. The most
obvious set of these is addiction and substance abuse, mediated in part
by cultural images of addicted veterans and in part by the availability of
certain substances. (Alcohol has almost always been the drug of choice;
after all, the Marine Corps was born in a tavern.)

One that is less obvious—and that surprised me in its relevance to
veterans—didn't just travel alongside Alex's PTSD, but helped to define
it. That disorder was anorexia.

Alex's anorexia didn't show up on any PDHA form he filled out as a
Marine, and it didn't come up in our initial marathon interviews. I was
just as fooled by Alex's "mysterious illness" file as his doctors had been.
Alex's weight loss and his lowered body temperature looked like autoimmune activity, or like exposure, or maybe like one of the many physical

manifestations of PTSD. And it may have been all three of those things, but I didn't think to ask about his eating.

Eating disorders are more common among Marines than I expected, especially among Alex's female peers. Between 5 percent and 8 percent of female service personnel are diagnosed with an eating disorder during their service. If those numbers seem unremarkable, consider that a history of eating disorders can be a disqualification for recruits, creating an extra incentive to avoid detection. Regular body-fat checks and weigh-ins, a codified attention to physical stature and ability, and severely regimented eating patterns likely combine with a larger cultural fetish for thin, fit bodies to create significant body image anxieties—manifesting in diagnosed eating disorders or not—in both active-duty personnel and veterans, male and female.[13]

More than the overall numbers, what struck me most was the measurable increase in eating disorders among veterans exposed to military trauma. Women who saw combat were almost twice as likely to develop an eating disorder after deployment, and more than twice as likely to sustain significant post-deployment weight loss of 10 percent or more.[14] Buried within these numbers is an even more troubling set of statistics that associate eating disorders with sexual trauma, which women experienced at shockingly high rates during the Iraq War, especially in combat units.[15]

The numbers are troubling for men, too. While only a fraction of a percent of male service members receive eating disorder diagnoses, a full 4 percent of trauma-exposed male veterans meet the criteria for an eating disorder.[16] Outside the military, enough research has associated trauma with eating disorders that some doctors now include PTSD therapies in treatments for anorexia. In Alex's case, the opposite was true; treatment for anorexia was a prerequisite for his PTSD treatment. Alex may have a family history of disordered eating, but his condition also makes plenty of good sense in light of his traumatic history of combat.

———

IT'S IMPORTANT TO UNDERSTAND THAT BEING A CULTURE-BOUND disorder doesn't make PTSD any less real. Today, neuroscientists can measure damage to gray matter in the brains of patients suffering from PTSD, and again, the HPA axis gives us at least one mechanism for how PTSD might, at least in part, work. But even short of these biological markers, I think it would be a mistake to discount the suffering of veterans with PTSD simply because it manifests in ways that respond to its cultural moment. Pain is pain. Too fine an analysis of its categories of manifestation threatens to blind us to the human suffering we are trying to categorize in the first place. For all its cultural baggage, definitional squishiness, and alleged invitations to malingering, the modern PTSD diagnosis provides suffering veterans and survivors a framework for understanding—and hopefully healing—that pain. And it does so with less stigma and far more dignity than designations like shell shock, bad nerves, and combat fatigue that came before it.

For these same reasons, it is important to understand that the overlaps between the mechanisms and symptoms of PTSD and other types of exposure are not meant to suggest that Alex's or any other veteran's PTSD is somehow not real. The Criterion H binary is infectious; when you hear that PTSD symptoms like memory loss or irritability may also be caused by lead, it is easy to jump to the conclusion that somehow it's *not* PTSD that has caused Alex's symptoms. As if toxic exposure were the answer, and PTSD a false diagnosis.

But that line of thinking is dangerous, maybe more dangerous than the failure to see toxic exposures in the first place. Taking environmental exposure seriously means looking for another contributor to PTSD, not an alternative diagnosis to it. Forget Criterion H. Think "both/and." For veterans, heavy metals and other environmental exposures travel together with the kinds of traumas that we recognize as causes of PTSD and TBIs: explosions, car crashes, firefights, and even training exercises. The shell that contains the necessary precondition for a Marine's shell shock also contains lead primers and copper residues that might contribute to that shell-shocked Marine's symptoms and, untreated themselves, might also interfere with that Marine's psychological recovery. Recognizing lead, mercury, pesticides, and particulate matter as potential contributors to veterans' mental health issues isn't a way to cheapen or supersede their PTSD diagnoses. Rather, taking exposure histories seriously, testing for those exposures whenever possible, and studying the connections between those exposures and PTSD should facilitate a more holistic approach to veterans' health.

Or, to put it in terms of recovery: no amount of PTSD therapy in the world is going to cure lead poisoning, and no amount of chelation is going to cure PTSD. But if Alex's experience is any guide, getting the lead out may be just what you need before you can really deal with the memories.

17

"HELMETS ARE EVERYTHING"

y first visit to the George E. Wahlen VA hospital overlooking the city and the Great Salt Lake in 2009 was not the visit to the head-shrinkers in The Tank. Before anything else, I underwent a screening for a traumatic brain injury.

A company of drivers and supply gurus from the Utah National Guard filled up a waiting area and we went through the examination together a week after New Year's Day. I respected the reservists. They received some of the roughest assignments, moving luggage, supplies, and sometimes my team from Kuwait to Baghdad during the surge, all the while dealing with foot-dragging and abusive contractors. The car crashes and monster IEDs they ran into over fifteen months guaranteed knocks to the brain. Compared to them, my concussion past didn't look horrific. The screening felt like checking off an item from a grocery list so I could get into the VA system.

The Department of Defense only started taking head injuries seriously in late 2007 when they launched the Blast Injury Research Program. A RAND study released during the same month of our screening found that 320,000 vets from Afghanistan and Iraq between April 2007 and January 2008 came back with TBI-like symptoms.[1] (No one checked our Afghan and Iraqi counterparts.) Head injuries from roadside bombs increased as the insurgencies we created blossomed. The DoD tracked head injuries in the hope of finding tools, apart from better strategies or ending the wars, to decrease them. So post-deployment health assessments began including TBI testing, and the VA booted up a first-generation exam the reservists and I endured.

The medical team asked questions like the ones I answered in every post-tour form, along with new ones about my brain. They took blood and urine samples. Then we played memorization games to evaluate my short-term recall. I talked and they documented. Remembering my conversation with Bob Welsh, I held nothing back. Not surprisingly, they asked if I'd suffered a concussion.

The VA team ended the screening by measuring our hand-eye coordination and inner-ear balance. In one of the tests, four orange cones stood in the hallway and the physicians had us trace turns around them, like you might in driver's ed, but on foot. One reservist couldn't make the turns and hit the cones as he stared down at them. The cones slapped the floor and flipped when he bumped into them. Disgusted, he tried again. In a stairwell, I watched other vets miss steps or concentrate extra hard to get the timing right as they went up and down. Some of them stopped midway and seized the rail, resetting their legs and hips before they tried again.

I cleared the battery of tests and walked out two hours later with nothing more than a prescription for three months of 2 mg tablets of the drug prazosin (a heart medication that might alleviate some of the nightmares).

THE ONLY TIME I FELT AND KNEW I HAD A CONCUSSION HAPPENED IN NAJAF ON August 12, 2004, during my second tour. I fell through a roof, hit my head, and wrecked my feet during an operation to capture or kill the spiritual and political leader of the Mahdi Army, Muqtada al-Sadr. The story would get retold by other Marines over the years. Tellers would stretch the truth or miss details. The corporal in their stories sounds bigger and tougher than I am.

Our mission was born from a set of ideas developed the day after September 11, 2001. The logic went like this: capture or kill the leaders—Osama bin Laden or Saddam Hussein or their high-ranking staff—and the resistance will fall apart. The first set of targets in Iraq came from the deck of cards with pictures of Ba'ath Party leaders on them that the high command passed out in 2003. But even as those leaders were arrested or killed, the war kept growing.

There was in fact no monolithic block of resistance in Iraq. There were nationalists. There were more than a hundred tribes with histories older than the Hanging Gardens of Babylon. Iraqi elites split into camps, some wanting democracy and others wanting slices of the Ba'ath pie. Mosques stood as the only institutions intact and upright after the invasion. They housed religious sects that gave meaning to everyone's lives. They also possessed the money and weapons that could create security and divide the country even further. And there were disenfranchised and unemployed Iraqis. Arguments about the past and future after decades of dictatorship, wars, and sanctions tended to ignore that Iraq didn't have a functioning civil society. It didn't exist; our generals and their civilian counterparts dismantled the state down to the footings. Iraqis called this broken moment, flooded with new voices and movements, *faudha*, or chaos.

When we reached Najaf, Muqtada al-Sadr was the ultimate target in our flawed thinking. Sadr was a religious scholar from a family of Shiite martyrs. The Ba'athists executed his father-in-law and uncle for organizing one brand of political resistance. He became a political survivor, a Jerry Falwell with a Kennedy pedigree, until 2003 deposited him into the leadership vacuum. Without him, many in the high command told themselves, the Mahdi Army would dry up and we could guide the Shiite faction of *faudha* before the emerging civil war got any worse.

We didn't think much harder about this than the command. The grunts had fought hard in the cemetery for three days, and then pulled back. Now the kill or capture raid against Moqtada was a go. We did, however, have a tactical problem. As sniper teams, we typically inserted hours, sometimes days, in advance to set up hides. How could we jump into an operation that was essentially already under way?

Clearing a building through the front door is a guaranteed way to get shot in the face. No matter the depth of your training or the strength of your weaponry, advantage always rests with the defenders. They can construct booby traps and barriers or hide in blind corners. We learned repeatedly that clearing a room from the top down could create enough surprise to level the playing field. We wouldn't have time to fly in helos and fast-rope out or drop the ramp onto the roofs, though. With Charlie Company clearing buildings, we scratched our heads thinking of ways to get to the highest vantage points to support them.

The Reconnaissance Platoon had an answer. A recon Marine found a stack of thirty-foot-long sprinkler pipes near one of barracks at FOB Hotel and started playing with them. I knew the galvanized tubes from carrying them across alfalfa and spud fields in the summer.

"Why not pole-vault some fucker up there?" he asked.

"That wouldn't work," another huffed. The pole was too long and too heavy for one person to carry.

"Flip it and stack a shitload of guys on one end to push the other one up like some Spiderman shit," someone else commented.

We ran tests. Five or six Marines held the end of the pipe while I stood alone at the other end facing the wall. We started twenty-five yards back, signaled, and then charged towards the two-story wall. At the last minute I jumped and placed my feet on the bricks as the rest of the team pushed me up. It worked. I was on top of the roof and peering into the cemetery and the desert. We were in the fight.

We moved into the staging area the night of August 11. An 800-yard empty boulevard led to four buildings: a school, a hospital, a guard building, and Moqtada's house. According to intelligence reports, the school and hospital contained roaming militiamen armed to the teeth. No students or patients. With three platoons of Iraqi National Guard, we could only conduct the operation in daylight. They had no night vision capabilities or night training. Some of them had already abandoned their uniforms and joined the Mahdi in the cemetery. A few would probably call their friends and tip them off. Charlie Company would take the buildings by platoon with the Iraqi National Guard led by their Green Beret advisors in the morning.

A Huey-Cobra team thumped over the column as we kicked off the assault at 0800 on August 12. Our teams crept along in the back of the convoy through the empty streets of Najaf. Ahead of us, I saw helicopters dive as single blocks of orange—RPGs—zapped towards them, followed by the *pop-pop-pop* of small arms fire. We had nearly reached the objective. A few minutes later, a pleasant *thunk-thunk-thunk* broke the sound of our engines and radio traffic. Those were our sounds. Forty-millimeter grenades from an MK19 bashed into something and then exploded. A fuel truck now roasted on the street ahead of us and a black column circled upwards before the wind broke it apart. The brakes in our truck squeaked and stopped near the first building at the west end of the boulevard. Our two five-man teams piled out. Half of us provided security as AK and 5.56mm fire erupted, while the other half dragged the sprinkler pipe from one of the seven-ton trucks.

This was only the second run with gear on. Each Marine added a hundred pounds to their uniformed bodies in the form of vests, helmets, and mountains of ammo. Add that to sweat or fear or excitement and you had one heavy-ass Marine. We set up and aimed the pipe at a building with what appeared to be 600-yard fields of fire.

"Ready?" I yelled back. Tired eyes and huge hands wrapped around the aluminum. The pipe had already warmed up in the morning sun.

"Set!" the screams came back to me.

"Go!"

The whole thing happened faster than in any of the trial runs. When all I could see was the white and brown of the building, I lifted myself up and planted my boots against the brick. My rifles and gear pulled me down as I took quick steps up the face. Smoke filled my sky view. A few more steps and I reached the top. I pulled myself up and over. Nearly two stories and the viewpoint was deadly. I saw a twelve-inch wall twenty yards away across a sheet of corrugated metal, perfect to fire from the prone. I oriented towards it and cradled my M40 sniper rifle. Charlie Company cleared buildings and blew something up across the street.

Move. I started, crouched low, and took light steps. My heart slapped against my vest and made the frags bounce. Sweat dripped down my helmeted forehead and stuck on my nose and mustache. Halfway across, I saw softball-sized rocks dotting the metal. I'm on the crossbeam, aren't I? Yes, keep moving.

Five yards from the position, I went through my prep checklist. Wind isn't heavy. I could see the hospital ahead. Almost there. Pop the bipods, set the turret at 500 yards, and then cover for Burny. Look for targets to your east and north when you get into position.

The next footstep felt mushy. The metal peeled and the ledge in front of me vanished. Nothing but gravity.

I know how to fall, and it's not something I picked up in the Marines. As kids, Mitch and I jumped from roofs, trees, and cliffs with frightening regularity. It's a hard skill to teach, and sometimes tough to learn, but if you have it, you never have to think about it again. Dropping, I held my M40 tightly and relaxed the rest of my body.

The cement floor pushed up into my ragged legs and dust and rocks fell around me in the dark room I crashed into. I hit my right shoulder hard against the wall. Then I slumped forward and slapped my helmeted head against a set of pipes leaning in the corner. I saw red, then black, then red again. Then black. My legs disappeared underneath me. I tried to concentrate on the bricks in front of my face.

My head felt like it was under water where I heard the buzzing sound of pool lights. Dust and light swirled around the room. As I took deep breaths to get my heart rate under control, I heard footsteps and the voices of young Iraqi men on the other side of the lone door of the closet I crashed into. Armed and dangerous? Were those AK bolts I heard racking? The voices raised.

I yelled at my legs, "Tighten up!" and set my M40 down to prepare for the assault. Get the fuck up, Alex. Black and red screens turned on and off. I knew the feeling of a rung bell from knuckles and pugil sticks to the face and botched landings. Not the time to lie down. I left my pistol holstered and pointed my 5.56mm A4 rifle at the hatch. Get the fuck up. Fight. Fight. Fight.

Then, nothing. Nobody. On the cement floor, my legs began to respond. They moved. I stood up. My skull hurt and my eardrums rang. I kept my rifle pointed at the door when all I wanted to do was stop fighting and sit down.

With my rifle still aimed at the door, I heard the beautiful sounds of four-letter words and incomplete sentences in Marine-speak. More skull pain and the ringing came on in waves. The door opened and I saw the dip-stained smiles of my crew.

Our movements sped in a blur. I remember the sounds more than the story. My feet scraped against the dirt as I re-slung my A4 and exited the building. Outside small arms fire and screams lashed out. Broken bricks and sand on asphalt slid under my boots as Burny and I moved to a dirt berm and searched for shooters on the roofs. The sprinkler pipe lay behind us on the street. Hellfire and 2.75mm rockets smashed into something from the Cobra. RPGs whooshed back. We bounded between streets and torn-up buses and shot off the hoods of cars as the company worked its way into the objectives.

Hours later, four of us huddled on a roof overlooking the long boulevard and the hospital. No kills. Over twenty wounded on our side. In the hospital, Charlie Company found a room of unharmed newborns. At the school, the Iraqi National Guard encountered a platoon-sized force of Mahdi troopers. The defenders wounded twelve Iraqis and killed one of the Green Berets and an ING trooper when he entered through the front door. Marines swarmed the building and tried to clear it. More casualties ensued. They dropped a 500-pound bomb on the building. It refused to detonate. They called the fast mover in again with a second bomb and leveled most of the school and silenced the defenders.

Moqtada wasn't home. The raiding party found movie posters of *Indiana Jones*, *Die Hard*, and *Dirty Harry* plastered throughout his bedroom. Sadr continues to have a long and impactful life in Iraq, but even if we bagged him, other versions would've taken his place and roadside bombs would've kept blowing up.

We all caught our breath and calmed down.

"Lemons, what the fuck?" Revert asked. "Why the fuck are you bleeding? You've got blood all over your rifle."

I had my helmet off and a green cravat tied around my neck mopped up sweat. The right side of my temple throbbed and taking the kevlar off relieved some of the pain. My feet ached. I looked at Revert and then looked down on my rifle. Dry and fresh blood streaks covered my tan sleeves and light green camouflage on my vest. More blood stained my M40. I had no clue where it came from.

"Are you hit, Goose?" he looked at my face and then my arm. "Check your wrist, dawg."

Thomas and Burny stared at me and smiled. They saw the blood on my left cuff. I pulled it back and looked at a red-black one-inch gash. I put my rifle down and snapped my bucket back on. Then I pulled off my cravat and secured it around my wrist.

I slashed my left wrist on the corrugated metal when it broke underneath me. I hadn't looked for the beam. I laugh now. I fucked up. Poor roof-reading skills. Later, we discovered the building I fell through was an ice cream factory. Over time, the foot pain worsened until I felt like I was walking on glass. Years later I was diagnosed with severe plantar fasciitis. It was all for Booza, a stretchy frozen treat made at the factory, and Clint Eastwood memorabilia.

I'D TEACH A PLATOON OF JUNIOR MARINES AT LEAST ONE LESSON ABOUT MY ROOF fall in the classroom today. Helmets are everything. If you pay attention and fight long enough, you learn the rifle is secondary. The ultimate weapon on a battlefield is your mind. A helmet protects it from the strike of a round traveling twenty-six hundred feet per second and causing immediate incapacitation. It shades your head. You can pound tent pegs or faces with it. A good helmet lets you hide smut or the photos of loved ones. You might even shave or bathe in it. And if you need to warm a dreaded MRE, then you've got something to rest it on as the heater charges.

From the Second World War through the American War in Vietnam, the Army and Marine Corps used the steel one-size-fits-all M1 body with plastic helmet liner to protect skulls. After defeat in Vietnam, the Army started looking for a lighter bucket that could stop faster rounds and shrapnel. Designers soon turned to Kevlar, five times stronger than steel and capable of being shaped to head contours. Olive drab green with a half-inch gap between the skull and the helmet, the Personnel Armor System for Ground

Troops (PASGT) helmet had a futuristic G.I. Joe flavor when the prototype emerged in 1972.

I wore the PASGT from boot camp through 2004 and it wasn't any lighter or comfier than the M1. The M1 weighed 2.85 pounds in 1941; the PASGT arrived in 1985 at four pounds. Instead of steel, the PASGT contained nineteen Kevlar layers and a resin laminate to finish it off. A web of straps held the skull tightly with a leather band circling the forehead. You added an aftermarket, quarter-inch foam pad into the crown to improve comfort. The foam smelled like dog piss after breaking it in with sweat and anger and didn't stop the helmet from making your head hurt.

The PASGT dominated the Army and Marine Corps throughout the 1980s and 1990s. I wasn't the first to complain about its heaviness. Special Operations Command looked for alternatives after gunfighters in the Battle of Mogadishu grumbled. Shooters tossed the PASGT for lightweight kayaking helmets loaded with adjustable foam pads and chin straps that didn't chafe. USSOC noticed. They wanted the lightness of a kayak helmet with the protection of Kevlar wraps.[2] The command had French helmet maker CGF Gallet build the Modular Integrated Communications Helmet (MICH) soon thereafter. The MICH came with two-inch padding from Oregon Aero and covered less of the ears so you could hear. General Mattis wore one throughout the war—the unique black chin strap gave him away when we bumped into him on camp or in convoys.

MICH helmets had an unknown side benefit to any grunt: they dissipated blast energy to the skull more effectively than the PASGT.

Helmet researchers use g-forces as the key to figuring out when our brains get concussed and how to prevent that from happening. We experience the day-to-day force of gravity as 1 g. The 4 g on the Knott's Berry Farm Xcelerator roller coaster presses you into your seat or throws your stomach up into your throat. It's fun, and safe, and it's why ski racers trying to carve turns at 60 mph spend so much time on the squat rack. Impact from collisions, explosions, and projectiles produce much higher g-forces, and brain experts have determined that serious brain dysfunction starts to occur at 90 to 100 g.

G-forces are all about acceleration. Starts, stops, changes in direction. In a fall like the one in Najaf, the old coach's joke rings true: it's not the fall that causes the concussion, it's the sudden stop at the bottom. My body stopped when I hit the floor. When it did, my helmeted head bounced off a pipe, leaving my brain to bounce off the inside of my skull, a case in point in the g-force/concussion equation.

The helmet is an important part of that equation. Acceleration is a change in velocity over time. When I hit my head against the pipe, the PASGT increased the amount of time it took for my skull to come to a stop, decreasing the g-forces I experienced.[3] The MICH would've done it better, in part because of the way the Kevlar deforms on impact, but also because of the way the superior Oregon Aero pads push energy back instead of passing into the skull. The stock MICH had a rating of 150 g. Still enough to cause a concussion, but not bad if you consider we're talking about explosions and projectiles. USSOC confirmed the benefits of the MICH two years into our Afghanistan adventure: their shooters reported few concussions in the MICH versus ten per day among Marines in the PASGT.[4]

WE PLAYED A CAT-AND-MOUSE GAME WITH HIDDEN BOMBS IN AFGHANISTAN AND Iraq. The IED distributed pain equally on every military occupational specialty. When it exploded in the same vehicle carrying the grunt, the cook, and the IT specialist, decked out in the same helmets, the physics operated on every brain identically. Concussions ensued. We responded by welding scrap metal and ballistic glass into Humvee doors and panels. We had siblings mail us remote-controlled cars and took the controllers on patrol. We turned them on and duct-taped the throttles down to trigger explosions, hopefully, a hundred yards away. Insurgents countered with deadlier bombs hidden in trash piles or pavement. Congressional dollars bought bomb detectors and $475,000 mine-resistant ambush-protected (MRAP) trucks. The insurgents had a budget and rolled out explosive force penetrators that punched holes in said MRAPs for the price of a new iPhone. We responded with PowerPoint classes, man-tracking, snipers, and robots. We treated symptoms, not the disease. The arms race continued as bombs became bigger and our defense more elaborate. We put garage door infrared sensors on poles welded to the front bumper to set off bombs ahead of us or electronically jammed them, and the insane game went on. More concussions ensued.

IED blasts had two flavors every time: visible and invisible. Genital-ripping shrapnel and flames came right at us. But a blast also compressed air from the explosion at supersonic speed. That wave might bend or twist the plates in your skull, changing the flow of blood and waste into and out of your face, or shift the tubes in the middle ears needed in hearing and balance. Most of our helmets had circumferences greater than the size of our heads. When the shock wave hit, the bigger helmets acted like an oversized outfielder's mitt and caught more of the explosion, yanking the helmet and your neck in unforgettable whiplash. Oregon Aero padding in the right formation, even in the oversized helmet, stopped the air gap between the skull and the Kevlar. If you stopped the extra flow of air from pulling the helmet and dissipated it, then you improved your chances.

Hillbilly armor and retrofit helmets were by-products of the system everyone at home wanted. It was all about outsourcing and privatization. The M1 helmet, the same bucket my homesteader grandfather wore in Korea, cost $3.00 per. The Army Infantry Board and Ordnance Department designed the M1 in early 1941 because 60 percent to 80 percent of the new war's wounds came from deadlier bullets and shrapnel. They delivered their design to McCord Radiator in Detroit, along with Schlueter Manufacturing in Wisconsin, who moved from cars and dairy equipment to war matériel and built over twenty-two million steel buckets by 1946. The companies made money, but with senators like Harry Truman arguing that wartime contractors' "greed knows no limit" and taking back lavish payments in the Renegotiation Act or threatening to nationalize them for shoddy goods, defense industries played fair. When the Army wanted improvements in the shell strength, better balance, or lightness in the M1, they got them quickly.[5]

Since the end of the Vietnam War and full tilt after 1991, the US military outsourced control over safety and supplies to contractors. When it came to selecting helmets in the 1990s and beyond, a few military personnel worked alongside civilians under helmet czars at the DoD with little or no Congressional oversight or public transparency. The line between insider trading with helmet makers, the military, and government officials disappeared, but at least taxes stayed low, and the headaches of governance largely stayed out of the headlines. This arrangement worked fine for the relatively small runs of MICH. Elsewhere, companies promised better designs against blast injuries, ran up costs, and failed to deliver. The Corps, for instance, punched out their own Lightweight Helmet (LWH) in mid-2003. It weighed less and had greater ballistic impact than the PASGT but gave everyone headaches and only reduced blasts to 158 g. But the companies created high-paying jobs in an era of manufacturing flight. The PASGT plant in North Dakota and the LWH line in Pennsylvania kept churning out buckets and the military kept buying them, so few Americans complained.

Head injuries are a permanent feature of combat. You can't make war safe, but you can think about the nature of the risk. Booby traps and anti-personnel mines tore up Vietnam veterans I know. Northern Ireland belched out roadside bombs for decades. Soviet Army reports, barely collecting dust from their war in Afghanistan, detailed first-generation electric pressure plate IEDs. In after-action reports from the 1992–94 Somalia intervention, GIs detailed explosive devices and car bombs. It didn't take a rocket scientist to expect IEDs in the Global War on Terror.

On the ground we adapted. We built armor and bought our own helmets or padding. Eventually, I dumped the PASGT and the LWH in 2005 for a MICH with ballistic liner and suspension system pads from Oregon Aero. This setup lowered the impact of an IED on my brain, simulated in the lab, to 62.8 g.[6] I knew nothing about head injuries. I only knew comfort and perfecting my shots. My team bought us and our translators the MICH during the surge. I lent that MICH to my spotter Burny when he was sent into Helmand Province Afghanistan for another failed surge in 2010. He survived and returned the helmet. Now it sits on my bookshelf next to an Iraqi Kevlar from the Iran-Iraq War. It's also the helmet on the cover of this book. I used to think they were cool trinkets. Now they collect dust as a reminder of saved brains and alternate futures. Weirdly, they make me think of my brother.

THE MARINE CORPS OFFICIALLY DISCHARGED ME IN OCTOBER OF 2009. I DID ALL THE things that I was supposed to do through the winter and into the spring of the new decade. My counselors eventually stopped my medications and let me steer the bike on my own. I kept getting injections of my own fat and blood into my feet and stayed off them, not even pushing a skate deck around. I watched friends leave for Afghanistan and email me how much I was missed. I stayed in my office with my brother. I bought a new fly rod. I tried making new friends and dated again. I fell in love with an ex-Mormon, the first woman I'd ever dated from the religion I didn't practice but knew I couldn't escape. She didn't need me to play caretaker. She told me over the phone, "We were made in the same factory," and this time I could share every part of myself without running away. When she broke things off, I felt a level of pain that seemed like the first heartbreak of my life. I was glad I could feel the sting and happy I wasn't so dead.

I knew enough from my own journey, the war poets, and Bob Welsh that I would never be the same person again and there was nothing wrong with that, but still, something was missing. I battled with myself over food less and didn't run from any nightmares, knowing they were messages I needed to decode from my subconscious to get better. And yet, my body kept misbehaving. Progress on my feet was slow. My allergies didn't subside, and I needed to use a neti pot twice a day to keep my nose open. New migraines arrived without a schedule or explanation. My right wrist felt sore during the spring. One day I woke up with a large cyst bulging over the joint. X-rays revealed nothing and when the doctor opened it up, they found a wood splinter. I still don't know where it came from. Getting it out didn't change much. My body still felt colder than usual, and half of my left eyebrow was missing. My sleep was different, too. I started dreaming less as spring turned to summer and woke up after eight hours unrefreshed.

I was supposed to be better, wasn't I?

IT SEEMED LIKE THE RIGHT TIME TO GO BACK TO SCHOOL AND USE THE GI BILL BEN-
efits that came with honorable service. My brother and I both needed a
change of pace and a clean slate, and we moved to Portland. The one connection I had in Oregon was the woman who had dumped me, and I still
hoped it might all restart. We found a house with a big back yard for Adriana
and a new dentist who gave us each another set of mercury fillings. Mitch
started studying German at Portland State University and made plans to
leave the states to run the skate team after he finished his degree. I climbed
into grad school with a lukewarm commitment.

In June 2010, I went on a hike in Portland's Macleay Park with one of
my closest friends from the battalion, Doc Newton. Doc had come down
from Seattle to catch up before he marched himself into rehab. He'd dealt
with the drinking for a long time, and I watched his transformation from god-
like medic and stable friend to a man who stashed bottles of alcohol inside
boxes of laundry detergent and tool kits. My own struggles mirrored his.
Over successive tours in Iraq, he had become secretive, and even cruel.
Now he was ready to face the music. We walked through the park one early
afternoon trying to catch our breath and figure out what would happen next.

I'm sure in retrospect Doc needed something from me on that trip, but
whatever it was, I didn't have it. He talked and my mind drifted. I talked and
my voice felt like it belonged to someone else. The shade of Douglas fir and
vine maple in the forest felt cold when I dipped my hand through it as we
moved along the trail, but that was all the external feeling I could muster.
Internally, I could feel scratching against my organs. The blood in my veins
heated up. Electricity pulsed through my bones and flesh, and no amount
of shade could slow the warming.

I stopped walking. My boots sank into the drying mud and my cold
fingers stiffened. My arms wanted to fall from their sockets and a haze
powdered the inside of my skull. I wondered, almost aloud, how far we had
marched, how heavy my pack was. Twenty miles with 125 pounds, maybe?
I looked at the ground. No pack. We had only traveled three miles. Spaces
of light blasted through the shifting tree limbs and leaves. I looked at the

blotches of light on the canopy floor and Doc's voice disappeared. Was I moving down the hill or up it? Where were we?

"Goose, are you lost?"

Of course I wasn't lost. I don't get lost. I'm a human GPS. On patrols on Camp Pendleton or in Iraq, I only had to see and walk a place once to remember it. I used to hike alone in the Utah wilderness for days at a time, confident in my location at every step. Years later, before my third deployment and long after we had moved to Salt Lake, I was able to lay out the curves and lengths of roads and colors of homes for five miles around my childhood home in Denver.

I spun the printed map and my phone map around and around. I couldn't even find north.

"You don't get lost. You all right?"

I waved him off. Just messing around. I recognized some folks from the parking lot and secretly followed them back towards the car. I changed the subject. We walked back and drove home.

Doc Newton bounced at 0400 the next morning, and when he pulled away from my house for three months of rehab, I could barely figure out how to wave. I didn't know what to say, what to feel. My body gave me no clues.

The moments of drop-down fatigue and brain misfirings happened more frequently as the summer progressed. My fishing trips on the Clackamas River grew shorter as the featherweight fly rod became heavier and casting harder. I felt like one of my grandparents, creaking and sore, as I shuffled around the house. My allergies intensified as summer dragged on. I chalked this up to living in a moldy city and the grass seed capital of North America, took my allergy medications, ran my neti rinses, and hoped for the best. But it was bad.

My brain slowed down. I couldn't form sentences and often misspelled words I thought I knew. *Envrionment. No, shit. E-n-v-i-r-o-n-m-e-n-t. Is it "something" or "some thing"?* I gave up on some of my favorites like *diarrhea* and *maneuver.* I started counting on my fingers because I couldn't hold simple numbers in my head. I would pick up a favorite book thinking maybe I needed some inspiration, only to have the terrible effort of climbing through the lines wipe out my energy and put me to sleep.

My brother had similar symptoms. He stopped drawing and making music because his hands hurt. I'd never seen a day in his life where he wasn't creating something. We both broke out in rashes one morning. Red dots germinated across our skin, and we couldn't stop scratching. Then we both endured forty-eight hours of fevers shifting to chills and back to fevers again as the spots spread. When the cycle stopped, we didn't want to move.

We had swollen bumps along our necks and above and below our clavicles. Touching the bumps felt like punches from a bare fist. Our noses couldn't smell. I didn't know until a decade later these were signs of a backed up lymphatic system. It was the middle of summer, the time when everyone wants to play and soak up as much vitamin D as possible in the PNW, and we wanted to avoid any sunlight. It hurt our skin. It took too much energy to stand up and walk to our back patio. Adriana begged for play time in the sun and instead we left her on the couch depressed until we took her out on two-block walks at night.

Exasperated, I traveled to the VA hospital atop the western slopes of Portland. My primary care physician took me through a short medical history and drew my blood.

"You have mononucleosis," he said flatly during the first week of August 2010. I don't remember his face. It seemed like I was wasting his time. Blood work showed high antibodies for cytomegalovirus and Epstein-Barr virus, both in the Herpesvirales order and both associated with mono.

"Like, the kissing disease that kids get?"

"Yes. It's been reactivated from a dormant state in your DNA. It'll probably take a couple months for your immune system to clear it out. Head home and rest up."

I went home, tired and unsatisfied. I didn't need bloodwork to know Mitch had the same viruses. We sat around the kitchen table figuring out what to do next. Mono? Mono is easy to test for, but "rest up and this will go away" wasn't a treatment plan with any teeth.

The doctor said the coinfection should clear up in a month or two. It didn't. Neither of us got better. We coughed every day and our throats stayed sore. While the rash disappeared and our vampire rejection of the sun lessened, a drop-dead fatigue remained. Inflammation left our joints stiff and the bumps along our necks and clavicles didn't shrink. We slept for eleven, twelve, thirteen hours at a stretch, and woke up tired and stiffer from being so bedridden. Work, school, and creativity came to a halt for the two of us as the fall of 2010 started. I dragged my body into the shower and blasted cold water over my skin every morning. The water had no effect.

18

THE TOXIC TRIANGLE OF WARFARE

L ike many veterans, Alex dealt with a lot of death during his deployment, and mourning friends lost in combat blended into grief for fellow Marines and other people who died in other ways, both during his service and afterward. Many of these deaths have been suicides. Others look accidental, but Alex sees self-destructive behavior in these deaths, too. Two-thirds of the way through sniper school, for example, Alex's first spotter, LCpl Sean Crockett, died in a single-car accident outside of Camp Pendleton. Alcohol was involved—Sean had tried to fight Alex outside of a bar earlier in the night for trying to take him home to dry out. When Alex sees the police report, he sees self-destruction, and has a hard time not labeling Sean's death a suicide. So too with the platoon mate killed in a fight with a rival biker gang. And then there are the suicides themselves, a slow and demoralizing piling on of deaths in Alex's extended Marine Corps family that make his heart skip a beat every time the phone rings.

It took me a while to realize just how much these deaths in the family motivated Alex to work with me to tell his story. I think I only really realized it when he started writing about concussions and helmets. Alex certainly had the mechanism for a head injury in his background, but despite the roof fall, he had left the service with a clean bill of head-injury health. In 2020, he even went back to Salt Lake City to reconfirm his mental faculties in a second barrage of tests, just to make sure. No issues. If Alex was looking for answers to his own health struggles, it seemed like TBI wasn't it.

And yet, traumatic brain injury shapes the veteran experience in a variety of ways. For many Marines, TBI represents the third side of the toxic triangle of modern warfare. For combat veterans in the Global War on Terror, TBI is the most common condition to show up alongside PTSD. In 2012, a Congressional Budget Office report found that 25 percent of Iraq and Afghanistan veterans treated for PTSD in 2009 also had symptomatic TBI.[1] In real numbers that's more than 26,000 cases of PTSD and TBI together in 2009 alone. Both PTSD and TBI often go unreported or underreported, so the real number is probably significantly higher. I suspect that the relative priority given to PTSD diagnoses at that time means that the percentage is low, too.

"Traumatic brain injury" is a catch-all term for physical injuries to the brain caused by sudden trauma. When I was growing up hitting my head on things (youth ski racing didn't used to require helmets), we called it a concussion. You get your bell rung and you walk it off, no big deal. You take a shot to the head and it knocks you out or you see stars or can't figure out what street you live on, your day is over. Maybe you go to the doctor or your parents keep an eye on you to make sure you don't fall asleep for fear that your brain may hemorrhage and you may not wake up. In today's medical literature, most concussions and their attendant symptoms fit into a category of mild TBI (mTBI), which can occur with or without ongoing symptoms including headache, fatigue, irritability, and sleep problems.

Severe TBI is a different kettle of fish. Symptoms of TBI often reflect a brain's attempts to heal damaged tissues, a process that creates waste products that can temporarily disrupt brain chemistry and dysregulate other brain functions. This also occurs in severe TBI, but in cases of severe TBI, structures of the brain are often permanently damaged, and the neurophysiological symptoms can be more severe and lasting, and can include spatial awareness problems and the disruption of a variety of motor skills. Particularly severe cases also impact cognition. There is also a category of medium-severity TBI somewhere between the full-on egg buster and the hard knock to the noggin, but the categories are pretty loose.

These are common neuropsychological symptoms. They also crop up in discussions about lead, mercury, pesticides, Gulf War illness, and PTSD. Mild TBI can be difficult to detect, and often just gets better on its own. Severe TBI is often much easier to diagnose, though not always. Sometimes it gets better on its own, but sometimes it doesn't. And when it doesn't, it can be very difficult to differentiate from PTSD.

PTSD and TBI play together in a variety of strange ways. For starters, a brain with TBI is like a PTSD petri dish. Among veterans and service members, TBI is the best predictor of PTSD researchers have found. Between 2008 and 2012, a team of psychiatrists based out of the VA Medical Center in San Diego tracked more than 1,600 Marines from Camp Pendleton to Iraq or Afghanistan and back again. Rates of PTSD among the Marines in this group who got their bells rung in country were double the rates of PTSD for those who kept their heads out of harm's way.[2] There is research that suggests TBI creates a physical condition that sets you up for PTSD, but it's also worth noting the common-sense position that getting knocked out in combat is probably scary and certainly stressful.

Regardless of their measured etiological relationship, the two conditions simply have a lot in common, and they are often lumped together.[3] PTSD and TBI share both many of the same acute neuropsychiatric symptoms and many of the same long-term physical and behavioral outcomes. They also share some of the same neurobiological markers—that is, at the cellular level, they do some pretty similar things to our brains. As the Congressional Budget Office noted in 2012, it's likely that a good number of Marines with TBI got diagnosed with PTSD; a good number with PTSD got diagnosed with TBI; and a good number with both either got diagnosed with only one, or fell through the cracks altogether.

Similar as their symptoms are, the one-or-both question is an important one. PTSD and TBI often compound each other in their impacts, combining to exacerbate some of the worst outcomes of each problem individually. For example, PTSD and TBI have both been associated with persistent post-concussive symptoms lasting much longer than normal symptoms of a mild concussion, a condition called "post-concussion syndrome." This is true even in PTSD patients who have no record of head trauma. But post-concussion syndrome is by far the most common in patients who have both PTSD and TBI—a situation common among combat veterans and active-duty service members.

PTSD and TBI don't just confound each other in diagnosis and compound each other in effect; they also tend to create mutually reinforcing problems in treatment. A 2017 study found that TBI significantly impaired a form of trauma recovery common in treating PTSD among veterans.[4] Meanwhile, a 2015 study of college athletes suggests that mental health issues (like PTSD) track well with slow recoveries from concussions.[5] That is: if you have a TBI, it's hard to treat you effectively for PTSD; if you have PTSD, it's hard to treat your TBI.

Perhaps more alarming still is the connection between PTSD, TBI, and suicide. Veterans' suicide rates have been a major Veterans Affairs issue for more than a decade. One oft-quoted but misleading statistic that lawmakers have glommed onto is that twenty-two veterans commit suicide every day. For veterans of Iraq and Afghanistan, the number is more like one per day. But one a day for that group is still 50 percent higher than the suicide rate among the broader American public, and it's still a major problem. In veterans with TBI, the rate goes up significantly. Add PTSD and TBI together, and it goes way up again, in ways have hit Alex's community of Marines especially hard.[6]

WHEN ALEX FIRST MENTIONED HIS BROTHER'S SUICIDE TO ME IN OUR interviews, it was almost a throwaway. It was at the end of our third marathon session, and the interview was essentially over. The camera batteries had run out, so I only have the backup audio, but I remember the way Alex turned his head to look out the window and grimaced the way you might trying to swallow a spoonful of cough syrup with a swollen sore throat. We had been talking about shooting, and about what I increasingly began to realize was a mechanism for consistent, low-level lead exposure.

"Do you still shoot?" I asked.

"Not really," he said. "I'm sure it's still there, but I would have to practice a ton. After my brother died, I sold all of my guns, so all that stopped."

He didn't invite a follow-up, but it was easy enough to find the obituary in the *Salt Lake Tribune*. Mitchell Reed Lemons, 1985–2011. "Survived by his parents and his big brother and best friend, Alexander Lemons." It is a desperate and disorganized document that reflects the depth of the family's grief. It also has Alex's fingerprints all over it. And just as Alex did when he first told me about Mitch's suicide, it only alludes to the cause of death. "In lieu of flowers," it reads, "the family wishes that you would put your arms around someone who has troubles and tell them they are of infinite worth and that no matter what, they will be loved forever and loved for always."

IN 2014, A PSYCHIATRIST AT THE BOSTON UNIVERSITY SCHOOL OF Medicine named Bessel van der Kolk published a book called *The Body Keeps the Score*. In it, van der Kolk articulated for a popular audience an understanding of the way PTSD impacts the body and mind together that he and his colleagues had explored in research and in practice for over three decades. Van der Kolk was particularly interested in the relationships between trauma and developmental stages in kids and teens, but ultimately his research helped to support connections between the emotional and physical experiences of PTSD, highlighting how post-traumatic stress causes the brain to put the body on hormonal high alert, wreaking havoc on the immune system and getting in the way of both physical and emotional healing. For van der Kolk, a memory of a traumatic event is not an artifact of the past. Rather, traumatic memories collapse time, inserting the past into the present in ways that often manifest physiologically even if the subject has no conscious memory of the original traumatic event. "Trauma" in this formulation becomes less an event than a state of physical being.

The Body Keeps the Score has been a wildly successful book, spending an improbable four and a half years on the *New York Times* bestseller list. The book has been massively influential in shaping both the popular discourse on trauma and the professional treatment of it. As a cultural phenomenon, van der Kolk's work gave voice to a growing popular embrace of trauma as an organizing concept for understanding the modern human experience, both for individuals and for whole communities. For mental health care professionals in particular, the book also reinforced and built upon many of the groundbreaking conclusions of Judith Herman's 1997 book *Trauma and Recovery*, helping to legitimate a collection of non-pharmaceutical, somatic treatments for trauma only selectively acknowledged by health care institutions taking their cues from authorities like the *DSM-5*. Though Alex's PTSD treatments predate van der Kolk's book, the specific combined emotional and body-awareness therapies that Alex received for PTSD and its attendant anorexia are in accord with many of the treatments discussed in the book.[7]

The Body Keeps the Score is about trauma; it is not, on its face, about grief. Psychologists and social workers make an important distinction between the two. All things considered, mourning a loved one is pretty normal behavior. Counselors and therapists assist people with grief all the time, but struggling with sadness, depression, and guilt in the wake of a loss doesn't necessarily land a person in the *DSM-5*, nor does it typically require the creative, long-term therapeutic interventions that van der Kolk prescribes. And yet, grief and trauma are not totally distinct. They often overlap in both their causes and their symptoms, and there are even categories of traumatic loss that acknowledge the way certain types of grief present as forms of trauma, complete with symptoms of PTSD.[8]

And grief, too, impacts the body. In particular, four decades of research suggest that grief can throw the immune system out of whack, causing systemic inflammation, fatigue, weak antibody responses, and other symptoms difficult to distinguish from both those of PTSD and those of toxic exposures. Typically, the physical symptoms of grief begin to abate in six to twelve months of the death of a loved one, but because grief, like trauma, is complicated, it is difficult to say when a person ought to return to "normal." Even more so when that person suffers from PTSD after four toxic tours in the Middle East.

Whatever the cause, it's no surprise that Alex was still sick in 2012. And it's no surprise that he is still interested in head injuries and suicide.

19

"YOU'RE PROBABLY OKAY"

My brother's head injuries didn't come from combat; they probably came from his life as a professional skier. Growing up I could turn and burn faster than him, but neither of us were cut out for the tight pants and pads of ski racing. Mitch and I turned to moguls, steep chutes, and backcountry jumps instead. I was good in the bumps, and eventually sniffed success as a competitive mogul skier before I burned out and happily threw in the towel. Mitch was better in the air, and he made it as a pro. He routinely sent it over hundred-foot gaps at Grizzly Gulch in the canyon near our house, and later booted monster tabletops at the X Games. He landed everything until he didn't. When he crashed, he crashed big, from high in the air and at high speeds. And then he would get back up and try again. On the bad days, he would have to sit through a concussion protocol first, but then he would come back to life, ready to go. Sometimes he wore a helmet and other times he didn't.

During my winter leave break before pumping out again in 2006, we piled his skis and a couple shovels into the back of his truck. We drove up into the smog and foothills above downtown Salt Lake as the sun set before finding a set of stair rails without any knobs on them.

Mitch always took me on adventures when I was home. He understood what I needed and never asked the kind of the dumb questions everyone did about the war. This wasn't, I only recognize today, just a quality of a good sibling. He was dealing with a comparable secret that he didn't believe he could talk about.

"How close do you want the kicker?" I asked him. The jump would send Mitch high enough and far enough to land sideways on the rail, with enough speed to slide the whole thing smoothly, top to bottom.

Mood swings showed up unannounced in Mitch's early twenties with regularity. He bounced between friendliness and high fives to fugue states and bar fights. His giftedness was greater than anyone I'd ever met. As a self-taught artist, he painted, threw clay, and sampled and mixed beats with joy. Then we'd break into arguments that ended in fisticuffs. It all reminded me of the light-switch mood flips of the multiple-tour vets in 1/4. His eyes looked different that winter than those of the baby brother I had helped care for years before. They were darker, moodier.

"Closer, Alex." His snowball tagged me in the back.

We threw shovelfuls of snow on the grass and pavement at the bottom of the rail. We waxed the rail and detuned his edges a bit more. His body stayed balanced and smooth as he glided along the metal and popped off the rail onto the snow mattress. The smile under his eyes flashed when he hiked back up the stairs and I watched for the cops under the bright city lights and particulate matter. He landed every slide that night and wasn't wearing a helmet.

Since 2010, medical examiners and concussion specialists have sawed open the skulls of overdosed and suicided veterans. They might want to include professional skiers like Mitch in that group. Again and again, they found scarring and neuron damage identical to the brains of chronic traumatic encephalopathy–ridden football players. Despite mounting evidence of higher g-forces in explosions, the Blast Injury Research Program and the helmet industry made little progress. While the Army gave blown-up Joes a twenty-four-hour rest and concussion protocol beginning in 2010 and the services pumped out lighter helmets like the Marines' Enhanced Combat Helmet (ECH) and the Army's 2.0 Advanced Combat Helmet (ACH), both helmets still had inferior blast protection.[1]

My Iraqi counterparts, and those in Afghanistan, have it even worse. Neither the DoD nor their own governments screened them. They ran into the same roadside bombs we did with PASGT and LWH helmets. I bet a few of them even fell through roofs.

Severe concussions cause memory loss, neuron disappearance, motor impairment, and dementia. Yet, an injured brain knows how to fix itself under the right conditions. But the repair shop only operates in our sleep when epinephrine levels, the fight or flight hormone, turn off or down. If you're sleeping deeply, the brain is squeezed like a sponge, shrinking by 20 percent, and brain waves flush proteins and other waste through the brain's lymph system and out of your skull. Standing nightly hours of fire watch or running night operations and patrols is unavoidable. You learn to sleep under the spinning blades of a Chinook or standing up. However, in a war with a constant shortage of troops going on back-to-back-to-back deployments or fifteen-month tours because there was no draft, you never rest at all. Many concussions that might've healed didn't, raising the stakes for permanent brain damage.

After my brother's death, I looked through cadaver reports and brain tissue samples of athletes and veterans of my wars to understand these sea changes in Mitch. Double dozens of Marines I served with went through similar changes. Maybe I did, too. Repeated or severe TBIs that don't heal turn the brain on itself. They may push someone avoiding their past into deeper depression or identity loss until suicide looks like the only exit. My brother matched some of these symptoms in his final months.

With our mono diagnoses in the late summer of 2010, my brother and I sat at home in Portland and rested. We rusted. Adriana looked confused and then frustrated when we couldn't do more than a two-block walk around our house. We spent the few hours awake filling skateboard orders and talking on our patio underneath a second-growth forest of Doug fir trees as the supposed end of combat operations in Iraq was announced.

Chronic illness freezes you in time and sometimes lets you consider things you've avoided by constantly being on the move or working. In Mitch's case, he was ready to talk about his sexuality. Like me, he wasn't usually needy and rarely asked for help, so the questions he asked—"Is this okay?"—sounded awkward from his mouth and underneath his shaved head. His secrets leaked out in pieces. I wanted to be helpful, caring. We were both sick, I pushed through the health problems because we had changed places. I needed to be the older brother again.

"I know I'm more attracted to men, but I'm still attracted to women." I was the only person Mitch trusted enough to talk about it.

"Roger that." I constantly mixed in big brother and platoon sergeant. This wasn't the first or the last time I would sit with someone spiraling towards their end. This wasn't another Marine, though. This was Mitch. "How long have you felt this way?"

He didn't have to wait to recall it. "Maybe since I was twelve or thirteen." He had a perfect and detailed memory for the past. His short-term memory was fried, and he couldn't remember if he had taken Adriana out right after he came back from a walk with her. But this he remembered.

Most of the time, I shut up and listened. The only constructive thing I told him was, "Keep a journal. Write it out." Then I would tell him, "You'll figure it out. Just give it some time." I gave him hugs throughout the sessions and slapped him on the back. Shame fought to control him every day. He never reached a point where he could embrace his own nature. His journal entries show a battle between two personalities and sometimes more. He chain-smoked, almost to smoke the self-hating voice out. It was a familiar voice, and not just from my own battle with anorexia. His outbursts throughout those last months, in person and on paper, echo other friends diagnosed with TBIs who went to war with themselves before ending it all.

Mitch struggled on to the first day of spring in 2011. I eventually pushed him into counseling, and he started receiving SSRI medications. But none of what I did could've stopped the forces inside his potentially damaged brain and wounded heart and unknown history of toxic exposures. When we finally found the body, in the one place where I told the search party I organized to look, I was relieved.

Mitch's death was different from the others. It was the first time I could grieve without having a mission to delay or sabotage the process. The pain blew apart my insides like a never-ending roadside bomb. My guilt cycled up and down. I tried to calculate what else I could've done every day for the next decade. I couldn't look at Adriana's face and gave her to a friend. Mitch's art went into boxes. I packed up all the music he made and mailed the hard drives to one of his friends, left Portland, and shut down the skateboard company for good. The temptation to fall back on calorie controls and forced vomit rose, but the new skills I'd learned kept me from doing the old practice. I didn't want or need anyone to have to take care of me.

Volunteering as a stream restoration tech offered the only breaks from the pain. My local Audubon chapter was transforming 128 acres of torn-up cow pasture into wild habitat for migratory songbirds, a carbon sink, and a floodplain for the increasingly violent Jordan River in Salt Lake. My college ecology professor, two coworkers, and I planted and watered willow species, Fremont cottonwoods, and Woods' roses. I picked up trash and rebuilt culverts. The movement freed up my stiffened joints and got my lymph system moving again. I didn't know why, but I started urinating every two hours and now I could piss anywhere on the preserve. Bullock's orioles called like belt-fed machine guns firing, *chuttt-chut-chut-chut-chut . . . chuttter-chut.* Neon-blue lazuli buntings streaked past me and blasted their songs.

The work let me escape the litany of questions, stupid comments, and unbearable silences that make up life after a suicide. I wanted to scream out at a society that had murdered my brother and sent my friends to their deaths with apathy. Instead, I watched the birds. I lost my sense of self, and my shouts receded into the background. The bobbing movements and head tilts of the orange-black machines and blue gleams sucked me in. When I got tired, I napped under the willows or went home. When I was bored or had no energy to get to the site, I stayed in bed. I could pay my bills and volunteer because the VA finally granted me service compensation, four years after my first application, for foot injuries, shoulder surgery, and PTSD with a 70 percent disability rating in April.

What I now call "Long Mono" worsened after Mitch's death. While I no longer tested positive for antibodies, I kept picking up colds and my body put up minimal resistance. My allergies got worse and working outside didn't help. I responded with more neti pot rinses or put lip balm on the inside of my nostrils to collect allergens. The low levels of battery power in my cells drained even lower as the summer of 2011 began. I kept wearing black, and especially black socks, not out of any mourning custom, but to keep my frigid body from dropping any colder in the summer heat. I stopped reading the news and books, thinking it was just depression when my brain didn't have the stamina to follow the lines. I started forgetting things. I missed appointments, couldn't recall if I shut off an irrigation main the night before, and misplaced my wallet or phone or keys.

When I was discharged, I punched my ticket for a disability rating for PTSD. But the real win was walking away without a TBI. It was like winning the lottery. The minor concussions I sustained in blasts, punches to my face, and the roof fall never developed into long-term brain damage. Much later, in February 2020, a more extensive, five-hour screening in the Rehabilitation Sciences Program at the University of Utah cleared me again. "Honestly, nothing registered out of the ordinary," the TBI specialist told me at the end. I didn't tip over or blank out through the dozens of physical and mental tests. "You're probably okay."

Still, I was not okay in 2011. I missed my brother. I was also sick and getting sicker, embracing all my grief and taking breaks from it with heavy doses of nature, but finding it increasingly difficult to get out of bed.

PART 4

SNAKE OIL

Navigating Exposures in the
American Medical System

20

"CORPSMAN UP!"

The shot echoed through Camp Twin Towers during the first year of occupation in the middle of July 2003. Most of First Squad, Second Platoon laid in our racks sleeping through the late afternoon with a patrol planned for the evening. Others sat awake and read letters or books. Marines talked quietly in the lighted hallways of the former Iraqi Army compound and played cards. The overhead fans that might've provided relief from the heat rarely worked. We sweated without electricity like the rest of Hashimiyah.

We got creative in our efforts to keep cool. Wearing only shorts and flip-flops if you weren't in the quick reaction force brought the temperature down a few degrees. Eating hot food became a chore. Water went in by the gallons and pissed out in empty bottles that we dumped into the shit barrels or burn pits later in the night. We wore bandannas submerged in water around our necks. We soaked OD-green shirts and draped them over our heads or put them back on wet.

Ice was the best. We bought it from local children at the front gate and the formula never changed.

"Mis-tah. Two dollars, one block." They parked donkey carts stacked with bricks of ice on the shoulder of the road behind the concertina wire and Hesco barriers. The donkeys always looked tired and frightened. They stood and swatted flies with their tails under a crisscross of old whip scars and fresh beatings.

"*Jayyid.* Okay, but I need *ithneen,*" I flashed the kid two fingers. The children enjoyed the high sales and talking with Marines.

I handed him the money. "*Shukran.*" Arabic for thank you, or I thank you a lot. He carried the blocks one by one over his shoulder on a rag and Simpson and I slung them over ours. The ice always stung through my T-shirt. Then the melting block ran down my chest and between my legs.

The more aggressive ice handlers tried to upsell us on bootleg DVDs or more expensive vices.

"Ficky-ficky?" or, more tempting, "Whiskey, Mistah? Whiskey, Mar-eeen?"

"No thanks, kid." He gave the same thumbs-up every time and returned to the cart. By the middle of the summer, no one said "Good Bush" or "Thank you America."

We brought the ice inside and chopped it with KA-BARs and hammers and filled our ice chests. We threw Kuwaiti bottled water filled with Gatorade powder into the ice baths. I picked up small pieces on the floor and rubbed my neck. We cooled in the darkness and avoided the future. General Mattis kept telling us in monthly meetings at the Pistol Factory in Hillah that we would go home in a few more days. Reality outside the wire extended the tour another month. He came back and played the same speech, the same lie, over again, "My fine young men . . . " He must have known by then that we wouldn't be going home for years.

Now we waited and cooled. We slept and daydreamed.

Pop.

We all knew the crack of a 9mm. The sound didn't come from something exploding in the burn pit. The laughter stopped and a hip-hop beat filled in behind the shot.

All we could hear was the chorus.

"Corpsmen up! Corpsmen fucking up!"

We all jumped to our feet. "Fuck!" we heard from outside. "Doc! Doc!" Sergeant Mattmiller swung in front of us and stood in the doorway.

"Stay in your fucking rooms! Stay in your fucking racks!" The corpsmen grabbed their med bags and hauled ass out of our building.

We sat inside in time-out. The buzz buzzed. Information filtered in. Someone was hit. They were working on him. We overheard a Marine get on comms and call Blue Diamond for a medevac bird from Diwaniyah. Yells outside told other Marines, "Make a fucking hole! We gotta carry him through there!"

"Wait, who shot him?" Andre asked and asked again.

My new company gunny gave me a strange reprieve. I had to unload the drop of evening hot chow from Battalion that showed up early. When I walked out, I passed Doc Newton and the other corpsmen working on Doc DJ Moreno in the bed of a Humvee. Doc Moreno, who had shot me up with a lifetime's worth of anthrax vaccine. I stared and then stopped looking. My arms took over. The cooks and supply Marines stuffed silver trays and boxes of canned peaches and plastic dinnerware into my hands. We stacked plastic tubs and steel trays on tables. McGuire, now a Gunny, stood outside the circle of corpsmen and watched in his black gloves and black boots. We both knew.

A Dustoff bird approached and landed. It carried the corpse away. Clouds of dirt and more than the usual burn pit smoke blew through the hallways and into our rooms. I can't remember anyone eating that night.

When you're in the grunts, the only thing that matters is the platoon. You acknowledge other platoons and fight for them, but they always seem like crosstown rivals. Doc Moreno, from First Platoon, and I would bump into each other on the *Dubpuke* or our shitty outposts. He was one of the old dogs, wrapped up in Nirvana and The Beastie Boys, at twenty-six. He was mild-mannered and had delivered a baby in the naval hospital in Guam. He loved taking care of us.

Petty Officer Moreno took the round into his head. I saw the clean hole, high on a cheek, as they worked on him in the back of the truck. It was his legs and not the face that told me. The legs relaxed beyond the point they could in sleep. I knew. McGuire knew. I kept unloading the chow.

I saw Doc Moreno one final time, later that year in December of 2003.

One of my dad's friends wanted to buy me dinner at the Hotel Monaco in downtown Salt Lake. I showed up and went through the motions. I sat in a chair facing Main Street and listened to everyone else talk. The food came and everyone around argued about the war. The light-rail cars plowed through falling snow and the streets became darker.

Towards the end, the voices inside the restaurant died and my own reflection caught me looking at the window. Eyes locked onto other eyes. Doc Moreno stood outside on the street and stared back at me. Doc's face was intact, neutral, but toothless. He wore his tricolor desert uniform and his baby face sat on top of narrow shoulders. I started to get up and then stopped. You can't go outside and talk to a dead man. But why is he here and what does he want? The snow fell through him and hit the cement. Cars and foot traffic passed into him. He didn't move.

We left as the snowstorm picked up. I looked for him through the car windows and found nothing.

21

HEALERS

D eep into my research with Alex, I found myself talking about mercury at dinner with an old friend of mine I'll call Jeff, a toxicologist and ER doctor who helps coordinate a major urban hospital's
disaster management plan. It was July of 2020, and we grilled elk burgers
in his backyard, staying a self-conscious minimum of six feet apart as
we moved from table to grill to outdoor beer fridge back to table. He was
thrilled to talk about anything other than Covid-19.

I did not ask Jeff about mercury because he is the world's leading
authority on the subject. He is not. Jeff does do some research, but he
is best as a front-line doctor who solves problems. Once, when we were
staying at the house of a friend in the mountains of California, someone asked Jeff if he could figure out a larger table so that we could host a
large group for dinner. Jeff thought about it briefly, and then hopped in his
rented minivan and drove off to the hardware store. About an hour later,
he came back with a van full of lumber cut to size to build a functional
tabletop, along with a sack of seventeen nails.

Why seventeen nails? we asked.

"Because I might bend one." Twenty minutes later, we had a four-
by-eight plywood table and one extra nail. That is the kind of guy Jeff is.

Jeff is exactly the kind of doctor that Alex would have encountered on his route through the mainstream American medical system. Before Jeff became a toxicologist, he did a residency in emergency medicine, where he started taking shifts at Portland's VA hospital. He still takes shifts at the VA—shifts he values highly for the sense of purpose and gratitude he feels at the end of a night. I wanted to know what he thought of mercury poisoning precisely because he is not, strictly speaking, an expert in mercury.

My dinner with Jeff came shortly after one of my early meetings with Alex in my cramped little office on the fourth floor of Eliot Hall. Alex had reached into his leather bag and handed me a clunky translucent blue bottle, clearly full of pills. I squinted at the label: "meso-2,3-dimercaptosuccinic acid." DMSA. The pills were not the kind of horse-appropriate megapills you see in high-priced vitamin bottles, but they certainly weren't small.

"Open it up and take a whiff," Alex instructed.

I unscrewed the white plastic cap and sniffed cautiously. First, a blast of sulfur, a stink-bomb grade of acrid terrible that did more than smell bad. It was a rotten-eggs-and-desert-sands smell that almost skipped my nose altogether, reaching up through my nostrils with malicious intent, grabbing hold of my mouth, my throat, my taste buds—my whole face—and turning them inside out. I jerked my head away. And then, a strange after-smell. Grapefruit. Strong grapefruit. Grapefruit for days. Totally disconnected from the sulfur, and following so closely on the heels of that sulfur, deeply unsettling.

I closed the lid and handed Alex back the bottle.

"What the hell is this stuff?" I asked.

"Nurse practitioner gave it to me," he said. "It's a chelator. For lead."

As I mentioned in our discussion of lead, a chelating agent is a chemical compound that binds with certain metal ions, making those ions unavailable to other charged compounds that occur naturally in the body. Chelation therapy is a way of mobilizing chelators to remove heavy metals from the body. Heavy metals in your body usually do their damage by impersonating other elements and binding to sulfhydryl groups called "thiols" that serve sort of like forward operating bases in the constant fight against insurgent reactive oxygen species in your cells. Reactive oxygen species break stuff down; thiols help repair the stuff that these "free radicals" damage. Chelators are essentially packs of thiols, meant not to repair cells but to catch specific heavy metals in the bloodstream before they attach to the thiol of a cell structure that's actually doing something important. Once bound to a free thiol, the metal floats around, hopefully finding its way into your urine or bile as it moves out of your body.

The primary use case for chelation is not lead; it's mercury. Though other soft metals like lead and cadmium also bind thiols, thiols are also known as "mercaptans," from the Latin *mercurio captāns*, or "mercury-capturing." (2,3-dimercapto-1-propanesulfonic acid, DMPS, and the stuff Alex had me sniff, dimercaptosuccinic acid, DMSA, both preserve the Latin description.)

As a way to treat significant known exposures to heavy metals, chelation therapy is not that controversial. It's also nothing new. In fact, its history traverses familiar terrain. Heavy metal chelation was first developed during the First World War as an antidote to a chemical weapon called lewisite. A compound of arsenic named for American chemist Winford Lewis, lewisite never saw use during the Great War, but the United States and the Axis powers stockpiled the stuff in the late 1930s, and many military commanders thought it would be the chlorine gas of the next great conflict. A number of scientists thought the same thing, and as the Germans began to bomb Britain in the early days of the Second World War, a team of British biochemists began to ramp up their work on an antidote. What they came up with was something very similar to DMPS, a substance that Americans quickly dubbed British Anti-Lewisite, or BAL.[1]

The war unfolded with very little in the way of gas, but BAL and its relatives DMPS (synthesized by the Soviets) and DMSA (a Chinese creation) soon entered into the international pharmacopeia as antidotes for acute arsenic and mercury exposure. And there the matter stood until the early 1970s, when the story moved to another familiar piece of terrain: Iraq.

By the end of the 1960s, Iraq was emerging as an important player in the politics of the Middle East, but a severe drought decimated the country's 1970 harvest, endangering the food supply for nearly half a million Iraqis. So the regime's number-two man at the time, Saddam Hussein, brokered a deal with the US to send high-yield MexiPak seed grain from the US and Mexico to help cover the shortfall. It was then the largest wheat seed deal in world history.[2] The grain—which was never meant to be eaten, but rather to be planted for the following year's crop—was dyed red to indicate that it had been treated with a then-common toxic fungicide: methylmercury.

In the late fall of 1971, 95,000 tons of red-dyed mercury-treated wheat and barley showed up in Basra, placed in sacks marked with warnings that the grain was not for consumption. But the sacks arrived after the planting season. Once word spread that the government was giving out grain, farmers across Iraq either sold or sowed their existing grain so as to avoid getting caught long on a commodity whose value was plummeting. They then replaced their winter supply of food grain with sacks of free government grain. The warnings on those sacks were written in Spanish and English. Some had skulls and crossbones on them. People washed the wheat and the red dye came off. Then they ground it into flour and made bread. And then they ate.

By December, people (mostly minority Kurds and Shiite Muslims) started showing up in hospitals in Kirkuk with symptoms of mercury poisoning. In mild cases, they complained of numbness and tingling. In more severe cases, they lost their balance, went blind, and suffered full nervous system failures. Hospitals reported more than 6,500 cases of mercury poisoning, and upwards of 450 people died.[3]

Not all the tainted grain was eaten. By January 1972, the government had begun to issue warnings against eating the MexiPak. Soon the Iraqi Army outlawed the sale of the grain, and ordered that it be disposed of. Iraqi farmers started dumping their grain wherever they could. One of the easiest places to dump it was the Tigris River, and soon the authorities had to ban the sale of local fish, too. Thirty-five years later, when Alex sat down with mullahs and local leaders to eat the fish in Iraq's national dish, *masgouf*, Tigris River sediment likely still bore mercury loads towards the upper limit of most international standards.[4]

As the grain crisis unfolded along the Tigris, the Iraqi government put out a quiet call for international help in the *British Medical Journal*. They got a response from, among others, Dow Chemical. Dow had business and legal reasons to take an interest in the Iraqi grain crisis. The company was facing a $35 million lawsuit filed in 1971 by the province of Ontario, Canada for damages from mercury, and the State of Ohio had a similar lawsuit brewing against Dow for mercury contamination in the state's waterways. The Iraqi case gave Dow an opportunity to get ahead on the emerging health impacts of methylmercury. Dow itself had developed a resin-based oral mercury chelator that it was eager to test. Its developer, University of Rochester professor Thomas Clarkson, flew to Baghdad, where Dow sent him a hundred pounds of resin after obtaining special approval from the FDA to administer the new drug to sick Iraqis. As Clarkson and his Iraqi colleagues later wrote, the resin more or less worked, but when he tried the DMPS the Soviets sent over, that worked better.[5] Chelation has been a tool in the toxicologist's kit ever since.

Chelation is an effective way to remove heavy metals from your body, but intensive chelation therapy is no walk in the park. Metals like mercury and lead are not the only things chelators bind to. They also strip your body of essential minerals like calcium, iron, and zinc. Chelation protocols tend to include a raft of supplements to replace the things that the chelators themselves make you pee out. What's more, heavy metals tend to let go of thiol groups and bind to others relatively frequently, meaning the mercury picked up by a chelator in one part of the body may bind to a functioning thiol group somewhere else in the body before it actually gets flushed out. Relocating mercury might be better if it takes it out of the control center and puts it into the waste stream, but it's not exactly good for your liver or your kidneys. And because chelators don't have guidance systems once they're in your body, it's not always likely they'll get heavy metals out of high-value areas like your brain in the first place.[6] Even so, faced with a choice between the nasty side effects of chelation and the damage from acute heavy metal poisoning, toxicologists like Jeff tend to choose chelation.

But I wanted to talk to Jeff about another side of chelation. If chelation therapy is well-established practice in cases of significant known exposure, the practice is also colored by the way some doctors at the fringes of mainstream American medicine use it in cases where exposure is less clear cut. Cases like Alex's. In 2012, Alex had a doctor of "integrative medicine" diagnose him with mercury poisoning. To make the diagnosis, the doctor relied on a "chelation challenge test," which is a way of using pills like the ones Alex had me sniff in my office to diagnose heavy metals exposure rather than to treat it. These challenge tests, according to the American College of Medical Toxicology, lack reliable standards, in part because of the nature of chelation itself.[7] Because most people have *some* amount of background lead or mercury in their bloodstream at any given time, comparing post-chelation urine to normal urine will almost always yield a positive result, even if a person's long-term heavy metal burden is low. The doctor used the questionable test to diagnose mercury, and then prescribed Alex a chelation protocol. I was dubious.

Today, Alex is also a little skeptical, if less so than I am. But for him, the reliability of the challenge test is beside the point. The 2012 mercury diagnosis stands as a turning point in his illness, the point at which he finally branched out from the VA and the narrow-minded approach to health it embodied for him and began to take control over his own recovery. Chelation therapy certainly wasn't the craziest thing he tried, and because DMSA and other chelators work as well with other heavy metals as they do with mercury, there is a non-zero probability that even a false mercury diagnosis may have provided deliverance from that more likely toxicant, lead.

To understand why the mercury diagnosis was so important to Alex—and why, given the ACMT's low opinion of challenge tests, Alex and I don't want to simply discard it out of hand—it helps to remember that before there was the mostly Healthy Alex working with me to tell his story in these pages, there was Sick Alex, trying with what he calls a "quarter brain"—a sort of foggy cognitive impairment that compromised his ability to judge cure from con—to understand the story as it unfolded. By his own standards today, the Sick Alex of old was not so clear minded, and the record of self-study I inherited from him bears many of the marks of his decade of sickness. In early drafts, Sick Alex's writing would toggle between the life-hardened skepticism of a jilted Marine and the stubborn, almost desperate credulity of the hopeful sufferer. Sick Alex was a seeker. In a system designed to match patients to diseases in neat bureaucratic boxes, Sick Alex had fallen through the cracks and into a world of insecurity, uncertainty, and frustration. He was interested in an explanation, but what he really craved was an Answer, a toehold in the world of the well that might pull him out of limbo and put him on a track—any track—that led out of the land of the sick. Mercury was that first toehold.

WHEN SICK ALEX TOOK CHARGE OF HIS HEALTH IN EARNEST IN 2012, he didn't just look for answers; he also looked for guides, individual people whose ideas and publications could illuminate a road back to health. Naturopaths, nutritionists, practitioners of "integrative medicine," and others. We can call them healers. In our early days together, Alex introduced me to many of these healers through their books, handing them over, often sheepishly, in small stacks of two or three in my office during our interviews.

There is an archetype to the authors Alex found as guides during his journey through the brain fog. Alex's guides all focused on mercury, but the archetype extends to many alternative or "integrative" healers more broadly, whatever their focus. They are by no means all the same, but they present as variations on a set of themes, sharing among them some common characteristics that make them particularly suited to guiding a sick person like Alex through a mysterious evil like that of mercury.

First, they are not stupid people. Not remotely. They are not misguided or irrational. Many of them are quite well educated, with impressive academic pedigrees and complementary life histories that inform their interest in mercury and health. A few have PhDs, and the letters shine brightly after their names in most of their publications and promotional materials. (This, by the way, is a giant red flag for me when it comes to credibility.) That these higher degrees are rarely in medicine make the healers that hold them no less intelligent. Indeed, for many, the out-of-the-box thinking derived from their nonmedical or alternative medical expertise often plays into their biography as healers.

Second, alternative health guides interested in mercury almost to a person have come to their positions as healers through hard-won experiences with their own bodies. They are, in short, active survivors. Most of them started with allopathic medicine, the term that has come to refer to the suite of modern medical techniques associated with rigorous evidence, clinical trials, surgical techniques, and heavy reliance on high-tech pharmaceuticals. (The term "allopathy" is in many ways poorly applied in a modern context. From the Greek *allos*, or different/other, and *pathos*, or suffering, "allopathy" meant to suggest the administration of medicines that treat conditions by creating other types of symptoms, and was originally used as a derogatory term for doctors who relied on bloodletting and other methods of shocking the body out of humoral imbalance. In common modern usage, much of the stigma and most of the meaning have been lost.)[8] When doctors practicing allopathic methods either failed to diagnose and ameliorate these future healers' mélange of confusing and frustrating symptoms—or, just as frequently and perhaps more troublingly, failed to take those symptoms seriously—the healer took their health into their own hands, and eventually came to the realization that they had been haunted by the mysterious and versatile supervillain of the periodic table: mercury.

And to be fair, it may take a person who has traveled the unsteady terrain of sickness to lead others through to good health. It would be easy to make the archetype a caricature, but the reality is that their experiences navigating both allopathic medical systems and the world of alternative or integrative healing give them a real knowledge of the landscape they help their charges traverse.

The healer is not just a survivor, however; they are also a self-styled guide. Through experience, intuition, compassion, and deep research, they have since teased out at least some of mercury's secrets, and stand ready to guide the deserving mercury-poisoned masses to the promised land of good health.

Perhaps "ready" is not a strong enough word. "Eager" may be a better description. Or "compelled." The final characteristic of a typical anti-mercury healer is a certain type of DIY evangelism. They put out books—more often than not self-published—typically based on extensive (if highly selective) research and often cloaked in the trappings of peer-reviewed scientific texts (whether they are peer-reviewed or not). They run websites and establish centers of healing in order to spread the gospel and heal the sick. Some have made quite a living off of their anti-mercury evangelism, and the network of consultation fees, lab tests, chelation therapy concoctions, and necessary chelation supplements offers some significant moneymaking opportunities. But even if they make money at their calling, the doctors and other healers invested in detoxifying the mercury-addled masses tend to be true believers, and the message almost universally emphasizes a story of self-empowerment.

To be clear, I don't think Sick Alex was either crazy or irrational in his approach to these people. Alex's response to an illness with no obvious explanation and a medical system that didn't take him seriously was deeply rational—maybe the only rational thing he could have done. Faced with people who couldn't help him, Alex went in search of people who could. He began to take seriously professionals whose work at the margins of mainstream allopathic medicine might hold some value for treating an illness that also seemed to exist at the margins. That VA doctors like Jeff and stodgy academics like me sometimes lump these healers in with the hucksters and snake-oil salesmen who populate the dark spaces of modern American medicine, making money on desperation and dubious promises, was simply not his problem. To continue trusting doctors and systems that wouldn't help him, even as his physical and emotional health continued to deteriorate—that would have been insane.

Alex's particular healer focused on mercury exposure from dental amalgams—as if, strangely, his wartime experience had never existed or was beside the point. If Alex had started with a different healer, he might have started with a different set of exposures. Maybe it would have been lead from shooting, to my mind still a singularly important source of heavy metals in a sniper's life. Or maybe he would have still focused on mercury, but from a different source. Methylmercury released from burn pit fires or in the fish *masgouf*. An environmental toxicologist or a rheumatologist almost surely would have found a better entry point into Alex's historical anatomy than dental amalgams. But even if there were rare doctors around in 2012 who might be willing and able to trace a decade of potential exposures through Alex's body from Recruit Depot San Diego to the Tigris River, there was no way that Alex was going to find them except through blind chance.

ALL OF THIS IS WHY I WANTED TO TALK TO JEFF ABOUT MERCURY. Even when patient histories suggest exposure, the Oregon Medical Board requires that doctors order "well-recognized diagnostic testing" to establish or rule out heavy metals toxicity. Patient histories are insufficient for diagnosis, and post-chelation challenge testing is not a "well-recognized diagnostic test." Doctors have been censured for diagnosing heavy metals this way. What, I wondered, was wrong with taking seriously patients' self-assessments? And, more importantly, what do "well-recognized diagnostic tests" look like? To put that differently, if you can't use a challenge test and you can't trust your patient, how on earth does anybody ever get diagnosed with mercury poisoning?

But that's not what I led with. I wanted an unfiltered reaction first.

"Hey," I asked, "what can you tell me about post-chelation challenge testing?"

Jeff laughed. Jeff has a deep, impulsive rumble of a laugh that sometimes seems to take him by surprise, showing his cards before he has a chance to play his hand. And he tends to laugh most quickly when he thinks something is ridiculous. I had my reaction.

"Wait," he said, "is this for the book?"

I admitted that it was.

"Alright, listen. I'm not an expert in these tests themselves, but let me give you some context for how we see them with our patients. Our

patients come to us and they say that have mercury poisoning or whatever. What they've done is gone and paid out of pocket to someone who
says 'Hey, based on your history you should get tested for mercury.' And
so they give this guy a bottle of urine to send to the lab for a test, which of
course the patient has to pay for. And then the guy shows them this sheet
of results from his lab and says, 'Here, look, you have mercury in your
system. You need to get that out.' And then the guy prescribes a therapy
and a whole pile of expensive supplements, which of course the patient
also pays this guy for. And so in the end this doctor or whatever he is gets
paid for the visits, gets paid for the lab tests, gets paid for the drugs, gets
paid for the supplements, and gets paid for the follow-up. None of them
take insurance. It's all out of pocket. It just looks like a racket, you know?
I mean, I guess some people might think of a hospital in the same way if
you look at it right. But man, it seems pretty suspicious that these tests
always seem to come up positive."

"Okay," I said, "then how *do* you make a mercury diagnosis?"

Jeff thought for a minute. "Well, it's pretty rare. I mean, with really
bad acute mercury poisoning, it's usually pretty clear from the symptoms
and the exposure history. You know, you work in a chemistry lab and you
inhaled a bunch of mercury vapor and now your feet are numb or your
skin is pink or whatever. I guess that's when maybe you use chelation if
you're going to use it. But we don't do that very often. Typically you just
remove the source, treat the symptoms, and wait for the person to get better. And usually they do."

I explained the issue with Alex's mercury diagnosis, and how it had
led me to a more general set of questions about diagnosing heavy metals exposure. If you can't use post-chelation challenge tests and you can't
trust patient self-assessments without some objective confirmation,
what do you actually do to objectively confirm that a patient has heavy
metals poisoning?

With acute exposure or occupational exposure, he explained, you
go and confirm the source. "So, you know, with your guy who works on
old houses you go to the houses and test the paint." But other than that,
Jeff said, you really don't have much. Fortunately, the bar is pretty low to

tell someone not to eat lead paint. Reducing someone's exposure is never going to hurt them. After that, you try to rule other stuff out. "But yeah," he conceded, "it's pretty rare. And with long-term or chronic exposures, geez, I don't know. In terms of *objective* verification methods? You just don't have a lot of practical options."

Jeff and I talked for a long time. About mercury. About how doctors diagnose things in different medical settings. And about Alex.

Finally, as I started to gather our small collection of beer bottles up for recycling, I asked him point-blank. "So, do you think this doctor Alex went to is a quack or what?"

Jeff is an interesting guy to ask about quacks. On one hand, he is a good, well-established ER doctor and toxicologist who takes shifts at the VA. He is the face of mainstream allopathic medicine. You get sick, call Jeff. You get hurt, go see Jeff. You need to solve a problem, talk to Jeff. On the other hand, Jeff is also pretty open-minded about medicine, and he certainly doesn't claim the kind of doctor's omnipotence that critics of mainstream medicine often ascribe to its practitioners. Jeff himself almost went to school to become an osteopath before he opted for conventional medical school. His is a pretty clear-eyed commitment to his profession, warts and all.

"Honestly, I don't know. Seems like he's using a test the medical community disapproves of, and you can't do that. There are rules. But does that make him a quack? I mean, there is a lot of mercury out there. If it's one of these moneymaking schemes, then maybe I'd think he was a quack. But maybe he's convinced that this is a real problem, and who knows, maybe there's something to it. I'm not on board, but I'm not about to sit here and say that we have all the answers. So yeah, I don't know. Maybe."

JEFF'S RESPONSE TO MY QUERIES ABOUT MERCURY POISONING LEFT me with a puzzle. Jeff and well-meaning VA doctors and toxicologists like him stand as a port of entry into the mainstream American medical system. Within that system there exist professional toxicologists—Jeff among them—with the tools and expertise to diagnose and treat both acute and chronic heavy metal exposure. According to the ACMT, these professionals can confirm exposure histories and oversee chelation protocols within a set of responsible guidelines approved by the American Medical Association. That is: mainstream medicine accepts that heavy metals toxicity is a thing, and they have the tools to address it.

And yet, the barrier to entry into the world of heavy metals treatment is quite high, defined by a narrow set of criteria that would seem to keep all but the most obvious cases out. Jeff, for example, is a trained toxicologist. But he is a toxicologist first trained as an ER doctor, and one who for good reasons is much more attuned to acute toxicity than to chronic, low-level exposures. It is unlikely that Alex would ever get to see Jeff, but even if he did, Jeff himself would have been unlikely to attribute Alex's symptoms to lead or mercury without a much more compelling and directly verifiable exposure history. Especially given Alex's PTSD diagnosis, a lesser doctor than Jeff might even be overtly dismissive of Alex's hunch that he had heavy metals poisoning. He might be condescending. And he might not even believe that Alex was sick in the first place. Even dealing with someone more like Jeff, there is essentially no chance that any but a tiny fraction of patients in Alex's position would get referred to the appropriate medical practitioners within a system that typically categorizes acute toxicity within the framework of emergency medicine and other kinds of toxicity within the framework of medical research.

And so, if you are Sick Alex, where do you go? Where *can* you go? Back to a general practitioner who diagnoses you with mono? To the overloaded VA, which has a hard time seeing past your PTSD? To a specialist of some sort? (And what kind of specialist anyway?)

If you have nowhere else to go, you go to the healers. You go to the people who inhabit the borderlands of medical respectability who, having traversed this landscape themselves, offer a solution, an answer, or at least a way to find out. Or, to the skeptical: you go to the quacks. What choice do you have?

22

"IT'S WORKING. THIS IS WORKING. IT HAS WORKED."

Doc Moreno swam through my dreams in 2012. My waking memories, too. He was the same age as my brother when he died. I had been home for over four years and there had been no transition. Every job offer felt like a prison sentence. When I forced myself to move back to Portland for the second time and take another crack at grad school, it came with the same lukewarm commitment. I was looking for a fight every day. The war was all I had, and I figured—hoped—it would eventually kill me. But here I was.

The spreading illness knocked me off my horse. Any lingering fantasy about returning to something like a Marine life disappeared. My VA primary care physician said my case of "Long Mono" should clear up in a month or two; two years later, the drop-dead fatigue and brain fog had not ended.

Old and new symptoms struck. My photophobia came back and I wore my sunglasses all the time in Portland, even after sunset. Simple, familiar tasks like driving stick shift began to fail, and I started missing gears and grinding the clutch or stalling out like a first-timer. More headaches arrived. I needed to urinate constantly. I slept for eleven, twelve, thirteen hours at a stretch, often broken up by twenty-minute breaks, wide awake, part of them spent standing over my toilet. Then I woke up tired. Caffeine, walks, and

Tai Chi did nothing. I caught colds and flus one after another. My immune system revolted and everything I did made it worse. When I forced myself to stumble through school in 2012, the only thing I seemed good at from my pre-enlistment life, my body and mind screamed. My muscles felt like frozen clay and my ligaments dried bowstrings. My brain didn't want to create or play.

The VA wasn't helpful. Neither were private doctors. Maybe I couldn't communicate what was happening; maybe they didn't have the language or interest to ask. I started asking myself what the causes were and searching for answers.

An ad on the bulletin board at my neighborhood co-op in Portland caught my eye. It was an ad for a doctor of "integrative medicine." At first, it sounded like utter new-age bullshit, familiar in a city of health shops selling Himalayan salt lamps and adults who bought crystals to balance out rotten emotions. It made diagnoses through a range of social, spiritual, environmental, physical, and emotional influences. And yet, one of those words—environment, which I still couldn't spell—pulled me in. "Environment" contained something legitimate for the naturalist in me. The doctor had been in the Navy. A Doc Moreno type. Nine times out of ten, a corpsman wouldn't lie to a Marine. I booked an appointment.

A nurse took me through vitals and left me to sit in the office. There was no window. The walls held no cheap motivational posters, no pain scales from one to ten with Lego faces, no "Understanding Diabetes" murals. Combat outposts in Iraq had more animated sick bays. The place was all business, and the business was me. I thought about getting up and leaving.

Knock-knock-knock on the door. Fuck it. I'm here.

"Tell me what's wrong." It was matter-of-fact. Doctors had blown me off or interrupted my story before. I hesitated.

"It's a lot. Or, I think it's a lot. I'm not actually sure." Another pause.

"Okay, maybe just tell as much as you can. We have to figure out the basics." I went through deployments and homecomings and illnesses. The meeting must have lasted forty-five minutes.

"Don't worry," the doctor said at the end of the appointment, "We'll figure it out."

We reduced some of my symptoms and worries with food allergy tests and a sleep study. I stopped eating gluten, garlic, dairy, almonds, pineapple, and a few spices in exchange for an hour of sleep and less congestion. The sleep study showed a nightly inability to get into REM and a borderline oxygen level, but I wasn't snoring. The doc guessed I had central sleep apnea.

I kept trying to whip myself back into school. After a sunbaked Labor Day weekend, I sat in my study reading *The Tragedy of American Diplomacy* by William Appleman Williams for one of two classes I had signed up for with Josh, long before I got to know him. I read and took notes. Rental stickers covered the book. Reading through the aged, yellowing paper, I started jumping over sentences. My eyes raced ahead to the next line or next paragraph, as my brain sat on earlier words. In class, I'd want to participate, but then I couldn't remember anything I had read the day before, despite the dated notes in front of my face. Sometimes I stared blankly—infantile, maybe even drooling—at my classmates, not sure what I was doing in the warm sunlit garden-level classroom or who they were. I tried to reassure myself that this wasn't me, that this was just the exhaustion.

My doctor had a hunch at our next appointment. "I had a manager for a Single-A team come into my office one day." It was a story about baseball. I paid close attention.

"'Doc,' he said, 'you've got to help my players.' The team doctors couldn't figure out what was wrong with two of their star relievers. They were hurling balls at the beginning of the season, ninety-six, ninety-seven miles per hour." I could hear the catcher's mitt popping. "Midway through the summer," the doctor continued, "they barely got the ball over the plate at forty miles per hour." The fatigue and aches of both players sounded like my own.

The manager was quizzed on their diet. "This was their first season of ball in the Gulf and they both loved to fish. They caught tuna and swordfish off the boat as often as they could, eating it twice a day in a protein craze."

The baseball story had a happy ending. My doctor had them stop eating fish and then put them on cycles of an antioxidant called alpha-lipoic acid. It could loosely attach to mercury atoms in the body and brain to drag them out through the urinary and digestive system. Four months later and near the end of the season, both prospects hurled balls at high nineties with a newfound energy and focus.

This was the first story I'd ever heard about mercury poisoning. Doc moved me off the chair and used a marker to sketch the structure of a mercury atom on the paper I had been sitting on and explained how fish bioaccumulate it without getting sick. Finally, the doctor explained how we could test my body for mercury through hair analysis and chelating agents. So, we tested with a DMPS challenge test. The gallon-sized jug of urine I dropped off twenty-four hours after the injection showed deposits of lead, aluminum, antimony, arsenic, cadmium, platinum, thorium, and of course, mercury.

"After you find a mercury-free dentist to remove your fillings, you'll have a long recovery ahead of you," Doc warned in our next appointment. "You'll need chemical chelators to detox."

"How long, Doc?" I asked. I wanted boot camp exactitude. The doctor couldn't estimate and advised me to drop out of grad school and minimize my responsibilities.

———

AT FIRST, THE HEAVY METALS DIAGNOSIS FELT LIKE DELIVERANCE.

"I've got mercury inside my brain," I told my mom and dad by phone, summarizing the diagnosis. "That's why I'm up and down all the time." I knew it was true, even when an autopsy of my brain was the only way to know for sure. But deliverance soon gave way to rage, and then confusion. I wanted health and sanity. If I had neither of them, then who was the man inside my body during and after the war? Wounded? Poisoned? Crazy?

Thinking about mercury brought me back to my last deployment. Every few days during my last tour we ate fish in one form or another. We dined on grass carp, common carp, and silver carp with our Iraqi Army and sketchy police counterparts, and during meetings with officials and tribal sheikhs for nearly twelve months.

We ate masgouf. Masgouf fed Iraqis as a kind de facto national dish, dating back to Sumerian and Akkadian history. Fishers caught carp swimming in the chocolate waters of the big rivers. A seller at the market bashed them with a wooden club, then gutted and partially scaled them. They dusted the skin and insides in thick salt crystals. Buyers took the fish home and jammed them on spikes where they roasted over pomegranate and citrus wood or charcoal.

Iraqi officials stamped a public advisory warning on wild fish consumption in 2003. Sanctions stripped water engineers of the parts needed in fixing sewer treatment plants. The war ruined water quality in clouds of choking sediment. Chemical and human waste filled the rivers. Then came the bodies, floating in every river and canal as Iraqis turned on each other in what they called "the troubles," "the events," or "the sectarianism." The breakdown of native fisheries pressed entrepreneurs to build canals to new fishponds. They expected to seal the farm fish from contamination, but they all grew up in the same polluted, corpse-laden water.

We ate the fish because it was a tactic in our new strategy. We continued treating the insurgency as a single enemy all the way into 2006. With no objectives, we moved behind large T-walls on big FOBs and drove around waiting to get blown up as Iraq nosedived. By 2007, David Petraeus, along with Mattis, were at least willing to roll the dice on a new plan.

The conversion Petraeus expected every American to undergo was called counterinsurgency. We focused less on whack-a-mole killing and more on security and governance, the very things we should have prepared for in Kuwait before the 2003 invasion. Petraeus sent grunts to embed with Iraqi Security Forces, to talk to the tribes, and to protect civilians. The mindfuck for many of my friends included befriending Iraqis who had tried to kill them on previous tours. My three-Marine team played our tiny part in this as we specialized in negotiations with local headmen. Petraeus wanted them to stop shooting each other and start enforcing some kind of order. They wanted us to stop shooting them and help protect them from their own enemies, which were sometimes also our enemies. We negotiated for each other's loyalty.

Eating *masgouf* or boiled goat heads always indicated the next level of tribal reconciliation. We wanted a certain sheikh, say from the Jebouri clan, to stop looking the other way as Shia fighters planted roadside bombs to kill Iraqis and coalition troops. The money he took kept his tribe from starvation. We offered to pay more than the insurgents and to rebuild schools, water treatment plants, and clinics. We wanted to trade for the names and locations of the worst ringleaders. Sometimes, and we always preferred this, a tribe would kill the fundamentalists themselves. The gambit required trust and no one trusted us. So we visited their homes to eat fish and move the relationship slowly forward, not knowing if anything we did would work.

We sat on rugs, unarmed, with a dozen other men as the women and lesser-knowns cooked. The fish arrived at our bootless feet covered in a blanket of *khubz* bread and clouds of Sumer and Miami cigarette smoke filled the room. Fish tails stuck out over silver trays. The remaining scales fell off like busted glass. Mountains of rice and veggie dishes lined the rug-table. We were told to eat first. We never ate with utensils. Washed fingers went into the roasted flesh and then into our mouths. An approving nod always came from a sheikh at this point. Then he stuffed his fingers into the carcass, ate, and laughed.

<hr />

I STARTED FULL-FLEDGED CHELATION ON MY OWN IN SALT LAKE CITY AS 2012 ENDED. I had dropped out of school and moved home to my parents' house, again. I read dental studies from Nordic countries and ex-dentists in America who stopped using mercury in fillings. I read memoirs and searched online forums of other mercury sufferers, and they all confirmed what my doctor concluded. I joined the chase.

A mercury-free dentist removed my fillings in November and replaced them with a nonreactive composite. The war in Iraq, still going strong during the "Breaking of Walls" campaign by ISIS, looked like it was in my rearview mirror. I lay in the chair for three hours with a rubber plug in my throat and suction pulling vapor out of my mouth. I breathed through a nasal canula. A gown covered my body, and I wore a wrap around my head and face. Mercury removal took place in a separate room from other dental visits. The room contained larger air filters than other rooms, safely pulling the vapor into a collector. I didn't feel worse after removal. I stopped urinating so often and my headaches receded.

Oral DMPS became my mainstay, and I got it via script through a nurse practitioner and naturopath who specialized in heavy metals detox.

I was put on 25 mg of DMPS continuously, every eight hours, for three months. Then I began the first round of 5 mg of alpha-lipoic acid, a fat- and water-soluble chelator that, unlike DMPS or DMSA, can get inside our cells and pass through the blood-brain barrier. A two-compartment plastic container kept track of the pills for me. I printed out stickers so I wouldn't forget which was which and took the alpha-lipoic acid every three hours, around the clock.

Results were mixed. I had a small migraine for an hour during the first day and twitches in my right eyebrow that flipped on and off. The second day revealed moments of mental clarity and a happy outlook. I moved through four days and completed the round by hitting the sauna at the gym. Wrapped in a towel and holding a rag cinched full of ice against my forehead, I sweated for twenty minutes to try to minimize the redistribution that happens in the intervals between rounds of chelation. The sweat went into other towels I wiped off with. Then I chomped on two capsules of activated charcoal, from advice I found in an online support group, to sweep up whatever remained in the system and jumped into a cold shower for five to ten minutes. The cycle continued with four to five days of rest until the next round began.

My NP/naturopath also wrote me a script for Valtrex, an antiviral medication, to treat my "Long Mono," along with 1,000 mg of the amino acid lysine and some oral vitamin D. In the naturopath's practice and in the literature, a less common symptom of mononucleosis was sensitivity to light. Without the body making vitamin D from the ultraviolet light I still recoiled from, I only dug a deeper hole for my health. After three months of those additions, I wore my sunglasses less often and only needed eleven hours of sleep. I no longer needed Valtrex or vitamin D by the middle of spring. This let me volunteer a few hours a week again on a restoration site owned by Great Salt Lake Audubon, where we turned part of the Sharon Steel Superfund site back into habitat for migratory songbirds.

My offensive food list got longer. I cut out coffee, sauerkraut, eggs, broccoli, and bok choi. Cutting them out seemed to reduce some of my manic episodes and longer self-discussions. My social life, already stunted, shrank to my family and online sick bodies. People with restrictive diets are terrible playmates and partygoers. Better to self-isolate instead of dragging your gluten-free, salicylate-reduced, organic non-corn corn bread to a friend's house where it always ends up in the dumpster. In the end, I divided my waking hours by escaping into Giants baseball and episodes of *Bonanza* and the Rod Serling version of *The Twilight Zone*.

Chelation. Simple. Boring. Slow. I started keeping a cumulative tally, which I wrote down as a box score.

2013 BOX SCORE

ALA: 168 days

DMSA: 5 days

Sauna: 65 days

Average Wake Up Time: 0930

Average Wake Up Temperature: 97.7 F

I kept chelating in 2014. I kept feeling bad, now battling fits of obsessive-compulsive behavior and depression. The eyelid twitch from the year before intensified. I exhibited more hypothyroid symptoms. My voice became hoarser, half of my left outer eyebrow disappeared, and I lost eyelashes. Bruises popped at the softest bump to my skin and newer, short-lived migraines flashed against the front of my skull. Strangest of all, a plate-sized discoloration grew on my sternum for two months in late winter. The rash turned from red to green, the green of a copper oxidized roof. It was copper.

On graduation from sniper school, all HOGs receive a 7.62mm × 51mm NATO round, drilled out and placed on a parachute cord, to wear as a necklace. Superstitious Marines believe a HOG's tooth was the round intended to kill you. Wearing it guaranteed immortality. In my case, it was just a reminder of pain and hard-earned wisdom.

Now the copper came back out. My skin smelled like a glass jar of coins pulled from old sofas and car floors. I began taking molybdenum to inhibit copper absorption. The bright green stain on my chest disappeared after three weeks, but suddenly my testicles began to ache. Anecdotally, other heavy metal patients claimed they hit a dump phase related to my copper battle in the first part of their recovery. Scientific literature offered no evaluations of this claim; I believed it anyway.

Tossing in DMSA to chelate lead brought another level of misery. The side effects of three days' DMSA felt different than lipoic acid and DMPS. Moving lead out once a month stirred up frozen moments where I turned into a space cadet. My hands felt detached from my wrists, and I stared blankly out the window in ten-minute stretches. When my brain came back to me, I forgot what I'd been doing. And then I might start staring again. A hangover with no nausea circled my day-to-day on those rounds. A day job was still impossible and my $1,228.00 disability checks remained my only source of income.

I went through the rounds and rode a bipolar wave for most of the year in a quarantine state where I pulled volunteer time at the Audubon property. I could listen to birds and pass out under a willow thicket. "Don't forget to water the plants on the preserve tomorrow." I sent texts to myself like that every night knowing my memory wouldn't hold it. Then I'd take 10 mg of slow-release melatonin and 5 mg of fast-release to stay asleep.

Or I would listen to any of the hundred records Mitch had left me in a dozen milk cartons. I also went to fifty home games of the Salt Lake Bees, Triple-A affiliate of the Walt Disney Angels with my mom. It was our sanctuary. We told our stories about Mitch and let the players soften the blows. My eyes could follow the ball until the seventh inning and then I'd go home exhausted but satisfied to participate in something not involving my crash test body.

I avoided most of my friends. They wouldn't believe my story and I didn't have the energy to give it. I added more supplements and bought a plastic tray with twenty-eight compartments for everything I threw down my gullet. I kept telling myself every day that this would only take one more year and then I could go back to everything I was missing.

2013-2014 BOX SCORE

ALA: 304 days

DMSA: 34 days

Sauna: 129 days

Average Wake Up Time: 0900

Average Wake Up Temperature: 97.7 F

Sick bodies fight back with distinct twenty-first-century advantages. The interweb, first off, offers workarounds to get lab work and buy supplements. Thyroid panels and hair tests don't need a doctor's authorization. I would, for example, cut hair from my head and neck every six months and send it to a lab in Chicago. The results showed heavy metals were still coming out and I needed that story. Or consider the drugs. Drugs like DMPS require a prescription in the United States. But in South Africa, anyone can buy the chelator online and have it mailed home. Second, health forums or books with the fellow sick can replace expensive or futile doctor's visits. You can crowd-source your symptoms. I did this dozens of times. One online recommendation led me to a book that told me to test our tap for uranium, which picked up the high levels of naturally occurring uranium in the water percolating through the granite mountains above my house and into the public drinking water. Finally, the digital world ends the isolation of illness. Other people believe you and offer help. Most sick people need, beyond anything else, a witness.

But I was alone. I was spending too much time alone and didn't know what other choice I had. When was the last time this Marine had a boner? Nothing stimulated my system. All the publications and books I read on mercury poisoning had an answer: the pituitary gland produces your sex hormones, everything from the cuddle drug oxytocin to follicle-stimulating and luteinizing hormones that fire up sex organs and sex hormones. Get the mercury out of the pituitary gland and the system will stop misfiring. I stayed alone and cycled through the routine of baseball, my allergen-free diet, records, binging shows like *Lost* and *Deadwood*, and taking my pills.

In January 2013, the VA set up an Airborne Hazards and Open Burn Pit Registry online and I filled out the self-assessment as I chelated. It looked more like a bipartisan can-kick than a way to legitimately help veterans, but I knew by then that paperwork was the lifeblood of the VA. The more veterans who reported places and exposures, the more the system would be forced to respond. I messaged friends and told them to register.

Mercury and lead cause defiant levels of procrastination and indecision. Or this might be the depression that inevitably arrives with chronic illness. The haircut you need gets delayed. You wait a week as more hair grows and something holds you back from the barber's chair. You agonize over decisions: Blue or yellow organic corn? Do I need a walk or a three-lap swim? Do you say hello to strangers or smile silently? My brain sat in neutral. Everyone since childhood had favorite colors and foods. I had no answers. Blue . . . no OD green . . . but . . . black, mate, black. Then I'd circle back to blue and find myself staring at rose. When I couldn't decide on something, I flipped one of my great grandfather's 1901 silver dollars. Liberty face: yellow corn. Eagle face: blue corn. Flip. Liberty face: black shirt. Eagle face: white shirt. Flip.

2013-2015 BOX SCORE

ALA: 392 days

DMSA: 75 days

Sauna: 166 days

Average Wake Up Time: 0900

Average Wake Up Temperature: 97.9 F

I moved back into the world of relationships when I probably should've stayed on the shelf in 2016. It wasn't a coin flip, but it sometimes felt like one.

I began dating a fellow traveler in the land of the sick. We both needed help and someone who wouldn't dismiss our reality. Her illness revolved around Lyme disease and her digestive tract, and she encouraged my own gut check. My microbiome had revolted throughout the war and my illness. I fought yeast infections and avoided my list of food intolerances. She convinced me to have my gut biome sequenced. I swabbed my ass and waste with several long Q-tips and placed them in printed plastic bags headed for a lab. The results displayed 145 groups living in my "Saddam's Revenge" gut: *Clostridium*—my count: 620; norm: 11995. *Streptococcus thermophilus*—my count: 2; norm: 38. *Bifidobacterium*—my count: 7; norm: 135. *Lactobacillales*—my count: 118; norm: 2282. And on and on, with all my counts below normal. The list of bad bacteria and parasites was long. If the gut operated like another brain controlling moods, the thyroid, and focus, then it looked like I was still a long way from recovery.

We went to England in September so she could get a fecal matter transplant (FMT) at the Taymount Clinic in Letchworth Garden City north of London. If probiotics and prebiotics acted as a Band-Aid, then FMT behaved like a heart transplant. The procedure entailed finding rare individuals who grew up on pesticide-free food, never took gut-killing antibiotics, and had minimal exposures to heavy metals and other chemicals. They tested candidates and then brought back frozen poop to a depository for analysis in exchange for stacks of cash. Patients with cases of *Clostridioides difficile*, ulcerative colitis, and Crohn's disease were cured after the clinic injected implants of healthy waste into their colons with a turkey baster and plastic tube.

I hadn't planned or partaken in a globe-spanning trip like this since 2008. After the third day, I knew what bus to look for and what platform to stand on at Kings Cross without referring to a timetable or my phone every minute. I looked for drivers and trees I recognized in the city and in the countryside.

Other parts of me were still stuck.

"Alex, you haven't fucked me for weeks."

I stood in our rented flat and listened. I was embarrassed, mostly in the

Mormon parts of my brain. I tried this: "I know. I've felt so blahhh for months. Maybe it's my downed hormones again."

"Not everything is mercury, Alex," and she looked right into me. "You're just fucking scared."

She was right.

We flew back from London with twenty frozen implants in our checked luggage. She felt better and could eat more food. She tolerated more stress. Eventually, I took a turn at the alien procedure. The thawed mix squirted inside me at room temperature. I held it inside my colon for forty-five minutes and then released. After doing this three times, I felt more energetic and tolerated several rounds of glutinous beer. But the implants cost of $460 a shot, sold in sets of ten. The VA wasn't about to cover that and shopping the black market for healthy fecal matter seemed less important than my love-and-hate relationship with heavy metals chelation.

In 2016, after London, exhaustion with my sick persona and boredom brought me to another coin flip: Was I ready to get back to grad school? School made more sense than a nine-to-five job where I still didn't think I had the stamina to perform. I still had no idea what I wanted to do in life, what it meant to no longer be a Marine. I signed up for my master's program—my third try—and also kicked off an associate of applied sciences in environmental restoration at Portland Community College because it ensured 100 percent of my tuition and rent would get covered.

Before we packed up for Portland, I filed a VA claim for heavy metals exposure. A collection of letters from my doctor, naturopath, and my mercury-free dentist were stacked on top of years of hair tests, other bloodwork, and the SOAP notes doctors use to assess patients' conditions and make a plan for treatment. Statements from friends and family members went into the pile. The whirlwind of other exposures delineated in these chapters wasn't yet on my radar.

The final part of the claim sent me through a three-hour VA Gulf War Registry health exam with an environmental medicine doc at a place I was growing to admire, the George E. Wahlen hospital towering over downtown Salt Lake in August.

We met in a large room empty except for a desk and two chairs. He wore brown khakis and a light blue button down with no white coat. We crawled through a rough draft of my story. He followed through his glasses and agreed at points where I argued for the connections between my health and burning cigarette warehouses and throwing batteries and CFL bulbs into the burn pits. When I mentioned toxic teeth, he looked at me like I was a Martian.

"There is some valid data here," he said after he heard my story. "You clearly had heavy metals poisoning." He looked over the challenge test again. His voice played a low octave of doubt.

"What's next?" I wanted more. The disability payment wasn't the objective, though I had sunk $15,000.00 into my recovery by this time. The rage for certainty was really what was driving me. I wanted an Answer.

"Blood work. Then we'll send you to a review with mental health. The decision board will meet later once we have all the material." We shook hands. I left with the sensation that he wanted to do more and say more.

By early December, I had a response. Denied. Denied at the beginning of October, only weeks after the submission. They had never bothered to notify me.

Issue/Contention: Residual disabilities due to heavy metal poisoning.

Explanation: There is no evidence to show a relationship between your claimed symptoms of residuals of heavy metal poisoning, which you had while in service, and your current medical condition. Therefore, service connection is denied.

I kept chelating.

2013-2016 BOX SCORE

ALA: 487 days

DMSA: 105 days

Sauna: 245 days

Average Wake Up Time: 0815

Average Wake Up Temperature: 98.2 F

———————

Dringzz . . . Dringzz . . . Dringzz . . . 0700

I stopped digging and took off my gloves. That let me halt the alarm on my phone. I took my chelators, 300 mg of alpha-lipoic acid and the sidekick DMPS, from the box and swallowed them. My eyes returned to the ground where my sustainable landscaping class jammed willow cuttings into the earth in early winter. The brown Tualatin River dragged itself past the restoration site. I felt energized and attentive, though every so often I kept hearing the lone shot from the 9mm Beretta that killed Doc Moreno.

My ability to concentrate took off in 2019. My ability to read, understand, and run calculations increased. I learned how to capture and store rainwater from residential and commercial roofs; then I designed my own systems. My body temperatures warmed up, lingering fatigue disappeared, and my mood improved.

Our war in Iraq survived. The bases were still the prize. More friends, all Iraqi, died fighting ISIS and I could do nothing. I had helped move a handful of Iraqi translators and their children stateside, and now I helped them become Americans. As I got healthier, the surviving Marines and corpsmen from my battalion began to forget more things, chased more bottles, and started losing their health in little ways.

———————

Dringzz . . . Dringzz . . . Dringzz . . . 1000

The alarm went off again. Chelators. Throat. Water. I started making chow by boiling some Yukon Gold potatoes. Spuds were at the heart of my master's thesis, and they began filling up my rental home. As my short-term memory recovered, my long-term memory also began to drip back into my life. The harder pops of boiling bubbles reminded me of a 9mm.

Dringzz . . . Dringzz . . . Dringzz . . . 1300.

Take pills.

I had weekly thesis meetings with Josh that winter and spring. Years of study bring you to the endgame. You check in and smash ideas between each other or get comments on the first trashy drafts you write. The project came together. My brain finally understood how to connect strands of my argument running through congressional records, clippings from newspapers in southern Idaho during the 1950s, and beet and spud botany. I became more thankful with this better self. I made new friends and cheered them on. Everyone around me was mired in student debt and stress while I gave imaginary high fives to the New Dealers who paid me to attend school through the GI Bill. I jumped in my car after some of those meetings and drove to Mount Hood.

I parked in the lot at Meadows ski resort and looked at the volcano powdered in snow. It looked deadly and inviting. I went through the mental checklist our parents built for us when we were kids: skis, boots, poles, gloves, goggles, helmet, pass. The seven essentials. Then boot warmers, neck gaiter, and on and on. I didn't forget anything.

I don't remember a time when I didn't know how to ski. I was on snow at three. Years of coaching engaged different parts of my brain, but I had always been buoyed by those childhood fundamentals, the same, the cliché goes, as riding a bike.

Now I had to relearn how to ski. How do you turn? My adult body didn't do it. It needed to re-create the moves step-by-step. It felt like having to learn how to eat cereal or put pants on all over again as an adult, relying only on literal instructions. Ankles roll and shins lean forward to initiate a turn. Left leg weighted to make right turn, right leg rolling harder to turn left. My hips didn't know how to stand or where to point. I stopped and put my hands on my hips, moving them manually into the right position, down the fall line. I tried again, slow turns on easy trails again and again.

Dringzz . . . Dringzz . . . Dringzz . . . 1600

The alarm on my phone made me pull off a glove while seated on the swinging chair lift and pop a pill. It's working. This is working. It has worked.

Dringzz . . . Dringzz . . . Dringzz . . . 1900

I turned over the pills in my hand. White and yellow white. I snapped them up.

My relationship ended in the spring.

"I can't do this anymore. I'm moving out."

I didn't know how to respond or what to say. The pollutants couldn't be blamed anymore. I needed training wheels and lessons for relationships as much as I needed them in relearning how to ski. I wouldn't connect with anyone, romantic or platonic, human or nonhuman, until I cried through the ocean of all the dead and gave up my fear of losing anyone again.

I kept pounding away at my thesis and squeezing in a ski day here and there, driving up to Mount Hood to get above the clouds and soak up the sun.

Dringzz . . . Dringzz . . . Dringzz . . . 2200

The alarm jumped on and vibrated. You know what happens.

Spring turned to summer in 2019. Subtle improvements turned profound. I took a class on the native plants of Oregon. We memorized one hundred plants. I knew them all by leaf, flower, and fruit.

"Nice fucking shot," I remarked on a friend's chip. Eighteen holes without mentioning sickness?

Music delivered new experiences. When I played Dick Dale records, I could hear every instrument and separate them. Subtracting a guitar riff or a saxophone line in my head showed me how the whole piece worked together.

Dringzz . . . Dringzz . . . Dringzz . . . 0100

When will this end? Take your medicine and shut up. I added more chelators from the plastic bottles into my case. I moved back to Salt Lake yet again, with another two years of GI-Bill-sponsored trade school covering my expenses. A face painted in camo or the smell of diesel spoke to me. The fuzz and sweat in a ghillie suit poked me. The memories flashed and folded. The story, if it is only one story, remained incomplete. I climbed into my wartime journals to fill in the blank spots or rummaged through official Marine Corps histories to build the timelines. I called old friends, but they often didn't remember or didn't want to remember.

Dringzz . . . Dringzz . . . Dringzz . . . 0400

I rolled over and did the thing and swallowed. Usually, I went right back to sleep, but on an early summer morning I stared at the ceiling. I regretted coming to chelation this late. The words repeated nightly, "I wish I could go back." It applied to everything: lost friendships, wrecked romances, bad career decisions, and even tiny things like missed sunsets. It became harder, not easier, to separate my entire life from environmental poisoning. The return of my long-term memory brought stories out of the leaded vault. Drip, drip, drip. I had no choice. I had to listen and watch.

Dringzz . . . Dringzz . . . Dringzz . . . 0700.

I rolled over and performed the maneuver with my eyelids closed and fell back asleep, where I dreamed in full color and deeply. Leaves traded green for smoked orange or faded yellow. I hiked nearly every day in the mountains above our house and wrote into early fall. There were some pills I didn't need any longer. Others continued. I gave up online groups and searches; I didn't need consultations with my nurse practitioner. I had more energy, maybe the most I had in ten years. Still, something sticky kept dragging me down and all the pills in the world wouldn't undo it.

Dringzz . . . Dringzz . . . Dringzzz . . . 1000

My alarm ripped me from the memory. Doc Moreno out in the street again. I sat in my basement watching the first heavy snow fall in late October. A quarter inch piled into two inches as the morning lengthened. Heavy and thick flakes stuck to scrub oak bark. Many of the trees still held orange and brown leaves. The window separated me from the ice and my body felt warm. I looked at my wall calendar: OCTOBER 2019. Seven years. Seven years of relentless climbing.

It kept snowing. White erased tree trunks, patio furniture, and even the sky. I opened the pillbox and removed the capsules.

2013-2019 BOX SCORE

ALA: 818 days

DMSA: 214 days

Sauna: 394 days

Average Wake Up Time: 0645

Average Wake Up Temperature: 98.3 F

23

COMBAT READY

Alexander Lemons's recovery did not somehow stop when he and I started working on this project. I have been watching him recover even as we have been writing about his recovery. And whatever the cause—whether Alex has recovered because of chelation and the advice of the healers or despite that advice—watching him recover from his history of exposures and trauma has been a remarkable experience. I have known Alex for a long time now, and from the beginning I have known that he is intelligent. While he was a master's student, I watched Alex turn months upon months of primary source research into a compelling argument about the role of frontier ideology in supporting a late wave of Idaho homesteaders (including his grandparents) who returned home from the Second World War and the Korean War to grow potatoes and sugar beets. The writing process was tedious. He would write and make errors. I would show him the errors and explain the cause. He would fix the errors in what he had written, but the next time he submitted text, it would contain the same errors. He was learning about history, but not much about writing.

Commas were the worst. He neither understood the rules of commas nor attained an intuitive feel for where he might pause in a sentence.

Unable to combine ideas, he exacerbated the problem by writing in paragraph-long lists, often with their component parts out of parallel. He put commas everywhere they didn't belong and nowhere they did. He would make the changes I suggested, but no exhortation from Strunk and White, no online tutorial from *Grammar Girl*, and certainly no marginal rule of thumb from me could get him to see the patterns he was missing. Plenty of people struggle with commas, but in retrospect his inability to learn, to reprogram his brain to write in a different way, might have been a red flag.

That's not to say he didn't generally improve as a student. Over four semesters, I saw his writing process speed up, and he began to polish material more effectively. In class, his commentary picked up and his analysis became more professional. He was able to provide constructive feedback for his fellow students, and got as well as he gave. In short, he did the things you hope for and expect from a good student.

What I did not expect was what happened in the last few months of his time at Reed. As he wrote his thesis, Alex got better at being a student, but he also got just plain *smarter*. Typically a slow talker in class, his speech began to smooth out and speed up. His vocabulary expanded, and his word recall began to improve dramatically. He began to read faster and more accurately. In my office, he toggled between different and only partially related ideas without the typical stuttering blink and painful silence. His sense of humor began to change. Always a one-liner guy at best, he began to banter, to use sarcasm, to play with language. These are the types of things you expect from the plastic brains of college-aged kids as they change over the course of four years, but Alex is my age, and in a matter of three or four months, I watched him begin to switch on parts of his brain that I had never seen. His affect changed. Once flatly analytical, he now expresses ideas creatively and passionately. His writing became crisper, punchier. It now contains fewer errors. He still doesn't know how to use a comma, but he is learning intuitively with practice, and the practice is clearly doing him good.

It's weird working with a coauthor who is so clearly getting better, getting smarter. I knew that Alex was a smart guy, but I didn't know him before he was a Marine, before his tours in Iraq and his exposures and his PTSD and his injuries. I met Alex in 2012, near the bottom of the spiral of sickness, and only met him again in 2018 when he reappeared rather suddenly in one of my courses. I have no idea how smart he was at Westminster College in the early 2000s, and I only know in the vaguest sense how smart and talented Alex had to be to make it through the Marine Scout Sniper Course to become one of the most elite shooters in the entire US military.

More importantly, I have no idea where his ceiling is, how smart a detoxified and recovering Alexander Lemons can be. When we started this book project, Alex was still living the life of a sick person, and he turned to me to help him cut through the brain fog and ask questions that his brain wouldn't yet let him ask. By the time we arrived at the final chapters of this book, Alex had become the primary investigator, leaning on me mostly as a fact-checker and editor. By the time this book goes to print, I suspect that he won't need me at all. Maybe he already doesn't.

And yet, with all of that, there is something unsettlingly incomplete about Alex's recovery. Working on this book with Alex, I have discovered that this is not only a book about Alex's body. It is also a book about Alex's identity. The two are inseparable. Perhaps that should have been obvious to me from the beginning. But they are inseparable in ways that I couldn't have understood when I first started working with Alex in 2019. Every body—every Warbody—is also a person, and when you set out to study that body, you inevitably learn things about the person who inhabits it that you can't ignore. Good doctors know this intuitively. So should good historians. If you want to write a historical anatomy, you don't get to ignore Alex's anorexia. You don't ignore his unflinching loyalty, nor do you ignore his disillusion with the military and Western medicine and civilian society in Salt Lake City. And you don't ignore Mitch.

The other thing that you don't ignore is what Alex thinks it means to be healthy. It took me too long to realize as we wrote this book that Alex has—or had, until quite recently—a vision of health that is fixed in time and space. "Healthy" refers to the peak physical and mental condition he achieved at the end of boot camp, and it is defined in terms that resonate with his Marine identity. Combat ready. That is the military's standard of health, and it is also Alex's standard of health.

And yet, Alex's physical body has not been fixed in time and space during his illness. Rather, he has aged—more than twenty years since boot camp—and he now inhabits a world, both physical and social, in which "combat readiness" ought to have little relevance. For most of us, the gradual shift in identity that accompanies the physical, intellectual, and emotional processes of aging go mostly unnoticed. Birthdays and pulled muscles serve as waypoints in this evolution, as do the emotional traumas—heartbreaks, lost loved ones, and personal failures—that accompany the advance of years. For a sick person, however, that evolution gets put on hold. The brain fog, the poor performance, the fatigue— these are artifacts of illness rather than aging, and it is all too easy to ignore that the aging process continues apace regardless. For Alex, the benchmarks and baselines of "health" have changed over time, but they have done so behind the curtain of more pressing health concerns, and on the back side of his journey through sickness, he has had to grapple with all that has changed, all at once.

There is a parallel to this disconnect between Alex's image of physical health in the way Alex's sickness has delayed his transition to a civilian life. Combat readiness has not been solely a physical standard. It is a standard for a whole person. As far as I can tell, until recently on most days Alex continued to view his work as a HOG as the highest and best use of his talents. His postwar sickness seems to have stripped him of an opportunity to achieve similar successes in other pursuits, and his return to health, now a decade on, carries with it a bitter and often confused confrontation between Alex as a healthy fortysomething civilian and Alex as a healthy twenty-three-year-old Marine. The very things that mark Alex's recovery—his success as a student of history and conservation science, his skills as a researcher, his competence managing riparian restoration projects—create tension between a Marine's vision of health and Alex's new, healthy fortysomething reality.

This has been, in our project together, the final and perhaps most intractable impediment to Alex's recovery. But it is not an insurmountable challenge, and it is one that Alex has been chipping away at with a brain and a body that are finally, after more than a decade, up for the job. The story of how Alex has gotten here—the story of his service, his sickness, and his health—is one that I have been lucky enough to have a hand in telling. And as we have told it together, I have watched him get smarter, healthier, livelier, and more reflective. Whether or to what extent he is returning to health and recovering his old personality or finding a new and previously untested way of being in the world is a mystery to me, however. It may be a mystery to him. In any case, where he goes from here—including how he ultimately defines what "healthy" looks like, and what to do with that good health—lies outside of the scope of any amount of research I can help with. The future is a story for Alex alone to write.

24

"PICTURES AND FLAVORS AND SOUNDS"

watched snowflakes land on other snowflakes through the office window near the corrals. They parachuted down in big, one-inch forms and tackled sagebrush limbs and made them sag. The flakes kept falling and stayed big as more of the corrals and the sageland turned into white waves crossed out with fence posts. The flakes spelled the beginning of the end to Utah's twenty-two-year drought and marked the beginning of my relationship with horses.

I opened my eyes and looked through the glass after going through a guided meditation with two horse trainers. The VA shrink and one of the trainers in charge of this experiment, Bill, explained what the next twelve sessions would look like. He moved his glasses to his face and then flipped through a couple of pages in the lesson plan.

"What we're all trying to learn here is mindfulness and self-compassion. But we won't be doing it alone or in words. This isn't really talk therapy, which is something you've already told me you don't need or want." He looked at the other trainer, Amy, and then back at me. "We'll be learning how to listen to ourselves and exercise better compassion through a bond with the horse."

He took us as far back as paleontology allowed and described the herd lives of horses and then walked through the long and dependent history horses and humans created together. Other lessons would build on our first. But I needed to learn the anatomy and psychology of horses, in the same way I learned the anatomy and physiology of my own body and mind, so I wouldn't be startled by the industrial set of emotional and physical antennae they possess.

"They don't trust humans, especially when they're standing on two legs. They're prey animals and that means someone, or something, has always wanted to eat them or abuse them on every continent," Bill said. "They are always being hunted." He called the whole outlook a "horse-anality."

Amy nodded. "This is why horses evolved sensitive systems and body parts. They've learned to identify sketchy people and things. They just want to protect themselves."

I wasn't going to get it until I saw it and did it. Amy acknowledged this with one last thing from her side of the table.

"If we're not okay, then the horse will not be okay. Think of it like this: they'll sense our chaos, and we won't get any work done."

Bill closed his binder and we headed towards the stables. We walked through the building in silence and into a covered arena. The wind slapped the aluminum panels and they groaned. I was excited and ready for a surprise. I needed something new and that's what I told Bill when the Salt Lake VA sent me a notification of the pilot program.

My body passed all measurements for wellness as 2022 ended. Consistent core temps, above average male hormones, and deep, REM sleep. My pineal gland finally made enough melatonin on its own that I never supplemented it again. I remembered my dreams, embracing every nightmare, and used them to crawl deeper into myself.

Old complaints disappeared. I could eat and drink wheat. Dairy allergies were gone. I got Covid twice and recovered. The first time, I had a three-hour migraine and nothing else. It was the first and only migraine I had since 2019. The second time, I had brain fog and fatigue consistent with long COVID for seven months. I lost my sense of smell, again. My joints felt like a blowtorch had been sprayed on every sheet of fascia and I had swollen lymph nodes in my neck and along my clavicles again. Brain fog stopped me from painting and writing and I felt a depression starting to chain my body back to my bed. It brought back the fear of losing my health and, in turn, my liberty.

I know this body and its physical memories. This wasn't merely Covid. But it didn't feel like an exposure, either. This felt like "Long Mono" all over again. I called my primary care doc at the VA and asked to get a workup for Epstein-Barr virus.

A week later a nurse called me, "Your kidney, liver, and thyroid function are all normal. But your viral level shows that you're likely closer to the end of an acute mono infection. Covid reactivated it. Best thing you can do is rest as best as you are able to."

I took matters into my own hands and carried out the same treatment plan from ten years before: I took Valtrex, 1,000 mg of lysine, and walked outside with my shirt off when the sun came out, this time surrounded by snowdrifts and melting icicles. I slapped on three milligram patches of nicotine. I got massages or massaged myself to move my rusty fascia and pump my lymphatic system. This time my body smashed "Long Covid/Mono" in one month.

I stacked up a list of accomplishments that my sick body could never have performed. Five-mile hikes and daylong fly-fishing trips. I worked eight-hour workdays as a restoration tech on 1,200 acres of streams and wetlands with my teammates. My seasonal allergies disappeared. I collected fisheries data and taught ecology classes to Girl Scouts and retired schoolteachers. I swung a machete against weeds and rebuilt fences. I worked with beavers, trapping and releasing them, or building hundreds of starter beaver dams. I didn't forget things.

I earned my record, but something didn't click looking at my stats or hearing compliments by friends or doctors about how much better I looked and sounded. When you live the sick life long enough, you can't remember the feeling of health. What was the power that let me run down a beach and throw myself into the waves? My mitochondria? The endocrine system keeping my thermostat warm enough to know that the sea temps wouldn't freeze me? Or my choice-making frontal lobe?

I expected chelation and detox would reset a breaker and give me something back that had been lost so long I couldn't describe it. But there was no mystery. I found the same old brain and body, reassembled cell-by-cell and cleaned out. It worked better than ever and now that I was taking care of my platoon of one, I could finally climb into the bottom of my past and see all of it.

Amy brought out a brown quarter horse, with a black mane and tail. He had a white splash on his snout and a winter coat thick enough for a bathroom rug. He clipped his feet against the cement, passed the barn cat, and crunched into the ring.

"We won't do any leading today. You'll just meet the horse, and we'll do some grooming," Bill said from inside the ring and against the rails. "This is Sonny. Why don't you try saying hello with that brush," Amy pointed me a couple feet towards the side of his left eye.

I had a red curry brush in one hand and walked towards him. His eyes kept scanning me. Top to bottom, seeing my hands, and then back into my face. I made one stroke down his back. A pile of snow skated off the roof above us and crashed. I watched Sonny's ears track the slide and rotate towards the pileup. Then he jumped.

"Woah," I bossed and looked at his black eyes and put one of my hands on his back. His eyes watched mine. His nose followed mine and sniffed. Horses can't lie. I was unnerved and he was nervous. I was looking into one hairy-ass mirror.

"Focus on your task," Bill stepped forward and spoke and then stepped back to the fence. I moved my brush back to the big neck and pulled it down like I was squeegeeing a windshield at a gas station. After several pulls, he shifted his feet and lifted his tail. *Plop. Plop.* Then a paper-bag-sized shit hit the floor. *Ploppppp.*

Once you play the game long enough, you learn that combat is easy and teaching it is hard. I knew the only way to measure someone's readiness and give them enough confidence to get through the real thing were stress tests of the mind and body that never came out of an approved Marine Corps manual. As a Marine, I became a trainer, partly because that is who I am. I train myself and I train others, and I needed both. Picking up a guitar or a new language wasn't going to help me move on from the exposures in my past. The training I could throw myself at, training that would give me confidence in a health that felt foreign or weird, was horses.

I didn't and couldn't keep track of time or the snowstorm. Sonny couldn't groom himself the way I did, and I proved that to him with each brush stroke. His bottom lip jiggled with each stroke, and his goatee hair straightened and curled. Enough saliva drained out his mouth to fill a 40.

"Let's clean out his hooves. Grab that pick and I'll show you," and Amy pointed to a blue bucket of tools hanging on the fence. She took me through the steps and then let me work. I cleaned the next three and let his body lean onto my shoulder with each leg lift. When I got to the last hoof, his eyelids flapped, and his head bobbed like a Marine dying for sleep. I waited for Sonny to start snoring.

WE HEADED THROUGH THE TUNNEL AND DOWN THE CANYON TOWARDS THE COP-per pit. It was our longest ride of the year, eight miles, and the late fall weather excited all four of us. My riding buddy, Lisa, edged her horse, Fire, to the tunnel's exit. I squeezed my right leg to guide my horse, Hank, away from the wall so I wouldn't bang my knee up again after crashing into a post on his back in midsummer.

Hank is a quarter horse who turned twenty this year. He's nearly the same age as my war. Hank has had his own record of ups and mostly downs since birth. When Lisa introduced me to him in the spring, she said, "He's sweet, but he's been through a lot . . . He's a trainwreck." It sounded like an old description of me.

Lisa pushed Fire through the end of the tunnel. Fire has a body built for speed and barrel races. He also doesn't like being whipped or screamed at. When I found out he killed his last owner, I gave Fire a hug. We marched down a switchback and then dismounted to water the horses in the creek.

"Do you want one of my apples?" Lisa tossed me one and I took a bite. The trees grow wild in the park, and we grabbed some earlier in the ride. Hank dove his face into a pool and started sucking. I held one end of the unclipped rein in my hand and stretched my calves. I traded in my hiking boots for cowboy boots and bought a bunch of dead men's Wrangler wear from the 1970s on eBay. I snagged an American Hat Company straw cover

over the summer and that was all the gear I needed. I looked identical to photographs of myself at the age of three.

"Let's ride over the bridge and race around," Lisa said after Hank sucked in the last gallon. I flung my core into the trees and then checked my straps and cinches in the same order I always do. Consistency is still accuracy. I checked in with Hank and wiped the crusties out of his eye corners. He gave a comfy snort and I climbed on his back.

We trotted across the bridge and then into a sage patch surrounded by big Fremont cottonwoods, the ones that used to make my sinuses explode, along the stream. We kept building the trot up.

"Lope! Come on Hank, lope!" I pushed down on my heels and tapped him in the ribs. I looked down the washboard trail and saw it was clear. His lungs blew out and his legs pulled us forward. Twenty, twenty-five, and thirty miles an hour. It felt like we were one blob of cells following the trail and the copper mine getting bigger with each hoof pull. My bones and my broken in dead man's Wranglers. The saddle and the pad. The sweat and hair on Hank's mane and my neck. All the same and separate.

We picked up more speed and I felt new.

I TAKE FEWER SUPPLEMENTS AND STILL GET PERIODIC SALIVA AND BLOOD TESTS. Chelation is a monthly, four-day workout and I've racked up over 2,000 days of it. Instead of salvation, it's a protective habit, like changing the air cabin filter in your car. I'll keep avoiding the places and things that could make me sick again and trying treatments in my ongoing experiment as long as I understand how they work. I don't care what anyone thinks about my choices or how I turned out.

Some things didn't improve. I discovered I'm slightly dyslexic. I can't spell. *E-n-v-r-i-i-o-n-m-e-n-t* and *d-i-e-o-r-e-h-a* look and sound right. If you asked me to diagram a sentence, I could barely fudge my way through it. My fingers are my calculator and algebra remains as foreign a language as Arabic. What can I say? I'm a visual spatial learner, from a long line of right-brained ancestors. I don't think in words, just pictures and flavors and sounds.

HANK AND I WANTED SPEED. THE SUNLIGHT AND THE LEAVES HALF BROWN-GREEN and half missing asked us for one end-of-the-year run. I squeezed the side of his ribs and more power churned beneath me. My legs held me up in perfect balance in what felt like forty miles an hour. Nothing could knock me off as I turned around to check for Lisa and pull my hat down tighter. My arms stayed heavy and relaxed. I wasn't afraid to crash or of sudden turns. I paid attention and felt every bump in the road, watched for low tree limbs, and checked on every possible mountain lion den.

We slowed and stopped under a pedestrian bridge we marked as the turnaround point. We let the horses and ourselves catch a breath. Then, we raced back. The horses played as they necked ahead of each other and breathed. We synced up and tuned in. I had a better sense of my own strength and intelligence in the saddle. I knew where we were going on the ride and that I could have the same strength when I got off Hank.

"We should head home. You want to try a new trail and cross a busy intersection?" I nodded and leaned forward to put my hand on Hank's chest, between his front legs. It wasn't too warm or wet.

"Hank's cool, Lisa. Let's ride."

We climbed the hill out of the canyon and walked towards the mountains. All 11,260 feet of Lone Peak leaned over us as we climbed. I squeezed Hank between my legs, and he trotted around a rabbit brush, following Fire and Lisa. We trotted upwards and then slowed again to a walk. Hank snorted at everyone, letting us know he liked the hill climb, and I was smiling.

EPILOGUE

lex has always been good-natured about my skepticism of his healers, and laughs when I joke that he is one of the rubes who has been
conned by the quacks. We both know it's a poor characterization
of his journey—of anybody's journey, really. Sick Alex was in many ways
just like anybody else who goes to healers, and those people are not rubes.
They're sick people, and typically what differentiates them from sick people who go to mainstream doctors and hospitals is that something has
driven them away from the mainstream medical system. Increasingly in
the United States, as health care costs continue to rise, that something is
financial. But more often it is something intangible. The system has failed
them by dismissing them. By telling them that they're stupid or they're
crazy. Or by failing to tell them much of anything at all.

Maybe he laughs because it comes, of all people, from me. I'm not
exactly a paragon of Western medical practice. I follow the mainstream
medical community in my skepticism of the healers who diagnosed Alex
with mercury poisoning, but I am more than willing to triangulate probable lead exposures to suggest how that same medical community may
be missing cases of lead poisoning. I have run no tests on Alex, nor do
I have the training to do so. (What would I do, anyway, break dozens of

fluorescent light bulbs around him in an unventilated room and then take blood samples? Fire up a burn pit and dump three months of batteries and LCD screens on some school playground while he stood over it and inhaled?) I am certainly not a medical doctor myself. I wear scrubs as pajamas, but that's it. My training as a historian gives me tools to evaluate and corroborate evidence, but my methods couldn't be farther from those of a rigorous clinical trial.

Alex palliates my insecurities when I bring it up. He reminds me that I have no tinctures to sell, and that I don't pretend to be a healer. That was never the point, at least not from my perspective. Alex and I came together on this project to try to figure out how to tell his story—the story of his service, his sickness, and his quest for health. For me, the goal is to tell the story in a way that expands our understanding of the violence of war to include the slow violence of exposure. For Alex, that goal blends into a desire to tell a story that encourages a more holistic vision of recovery from that violence. In both cases, the stories we tell rely on our best efforts to interpret the best evidence we have.

Even so, there is something unsettling about our conclusions. Books like this—heavily researched nonfiction books—are supposed to have answers. In the beginning, you start with a question: Why did Alex get sick? And at the end, you want to say: "It was heavy metals poisoning from bullets and fish." Or "It was mainly PTSD." Or "Probably the burn pits." None of these answers are easily disprovable; in fact, one may be right, or one may be partially right, or they all may be right. But none of them are the answer we have in mind. The answer that we have in mind is still "We don't know." In fact, we don't think the answer is strictly knowable. We have no definitive answer for Alex's long, slow descent into illness. Nor for his success, after all these years, in getting control of his health. Yes, Alex has made remarkable steps towards recovery since he began chelating in 2014. But was chelation the "cure"? Or saunas? Or clean living? Or was it just time? We can't know. In exploring Alex's personal history of exposure, trauma, and recovery, we have probably generated more questions than answers. We certainly aren't ready to tell some other veteran with any kind of specificity what to do about their failing health.

What we do know is that Alexander Lemons's wartime experience exposed him to a crazy cocktail of potentially toxic substances, stressors, and physical and emotional traumas. We know that any one of these exposures might have yielded some or all the symptoms he reported, though none of these exposures yielded a reliable diagnosis for those symptoms. We know that many of his exposures, taken together, work synergistically, compounding each other's physiological impacts and confounding causal relationships between exposures, experiences, and illness. And we know that thinking narrowly or reductively about these exposures, as some of Alex's doctors have, can leave Marines like Alex out in the cold as they try to figure out how to recover their health in their postwar lives.

What do you do with uncertain information like that?

For Alex, it is tempting to write a how-to guide. *How I Cured Myself from a Mysterious Wartime Illness by Fighting the Man and Thinking Outside the Box and How You Can Too*, by Alexander Lemons and Joshua P. Howe, PhD. I understand the temptation, and I don't blame him for it. Alex is not the only Marine in his community who has suffered. Inexplicable autoimmune diseases. Brain fog. Fatigue. Depression. Persistent symptoms of TBI and PTSD. More and more, suicide. Whether because of or despite his forays into chelation, his flirtations with quack doctors, and his saunas and supplements, Alex has managed to break a long-term cycle of illness and climb a steady, upward trajectory of recovery. It is no surprise to me that a man who enlisted out of a sense of duty and became a sniper primarily to protect other Marines would want to write a survival manual for veterans of the Global War on Terror.

But we both know that we don't have the evidence to write that kind of nuts-and-bolts survival manual. Just as we don't know for sure what made Alex sick, we don't know for sure how Alex has managed to get on the path to recovery. We have at least partially reconstructed his (and other Marines') exposures, and we have recounted and investigated his efforts to solve the riddle of his illness, but specific prescriptions based on the evidence we have would amount to little more than a testimonial for one treatment plan or another. There are certainly clues here, but there is no one-size-fits-all solution.

If our deep dive into Alex's exposures haven't revealed concrete answers to the questions we asked about Alex as an individual, however, they have yielded some more systemic take-homes for the way we think about war and the health of the people who are exposed to it.

Consider what we have argued. We have argued throughout this book that Alex's history of trauma and exposure highlights forms of wartime violence that we don't typically associate with war. At any given moment, Marines and military planners are, perhaps rightly, more concerned about bullets than the lead they contain, more interested in avoiding IEDs than in grappling with the novel types of inhaled dust they create when they explode. Over the long term, however, Alex's story suggests that the lead and the dust matter. And so too do the pesticides, the burn pits, the fire retardants, and the myriad other substances that do their violence over months and years rather than in the protracted and chaotic seconds of battle.

We still don't know exactly what made Alex sick, nor do we know precisely how he was able to regain his health after a decade and a half of struggle. But our exploration of Alex's service, sickness, and quest for health does point up larger, systemic pathologies that, in light of the evidence here, have commonsense solutions.

First and foremost, as we rethink what constitutes the violence of war, we also need to rethink how we define the human and financial costs of war. Taking the slow violence of war seriously alongside the acute injuries associated with the traditional violence of war requires a new type of defense accounting that includes both the resources to mitigate exposures on the front end and the money to underwrite long-term health benefits for veterans on the back end. This new accounting will require substantial financial commitments to veterans in order to avoid the kind of narrow-minded nickel-and-diming that exposed veterans face today. For every dollar we as a society spend on technology and matériel to exercise acute violence on an enemy, we must also set aside a significant sum for the long-term care of both the service personnel who train for and deliver or support that violence *and* the people living in the regions at the wrong end of that violence.

To some extent, we already do this through the VA. In 2021, the White House asked for $270 million for the department—a 10 percent increase from 2020—next to $720 million for the Department of Defense. In 2022, Congress passed the Honoring our Promise to Address Comprehensive Toxics (PACT) Act, which created mechanisms for studying, treating, and compensating a variety of illnesses stemming from service-related toxic exposures. It remains to be seen, however, whether Congress can appropriate sufficient funds for an aggressive and truly comprehensive implementation of PACT Act programs. Alex, perhaps ironically, is now too healthy to qualify for PACT Act disability. Alex's particular case aside, $270 million may not be enough to take veterans' exposures as seriously and holistically as the act appears to mandate. If the price tag of appropriate treatment is too high, perhaps a more honest accounting that includes the slow violence of war will cause us to consider the costs and benefits of going to war in the first place differently in the future.

Taking exposures seriously goes beyond increasing the VA budget. There are also systemic problems in the way we allocate VA dollars for health care and disability compensation. Establishing "presumption" for conditions associated with exposures to things like burn pits is a much thornier problem when presumption impacts both health care and disability compensation. It is not the same kind of problem when you are just talking about health care. Both are important, but in order to get any traction on the health issues facing veterans with histories of multiple exposures, we need to decouple health care from disability compensation claims. The bureaucratic structures of the VA privilege single, easy-to-measure pathologies that conform to recognizable categories of injury and exposure. So, too, do most civilian hospitals and health insurance companies. But the slow violence of war gives the lie to bureaucratic checklists, and if we can decouple health care delivery from the financial incentives built into checklists that also impact disability compensation, we can free VA doctors to pursue veterans' exposures more completely and holistically. Alex's frustrating encounter with the one VA doctor who recognized his likely heavy metals exposures during a disabilities claim interview—way too late, and in the wrong context—underscores the point. Compensation will continue to be its own problem, but it is unconscionable to let concerns over compensation prevent veterans from getting the good health care that we *can* as a society afford to provide them.

That care needs to have a both/and approach. Bureaucracies tend to engage in a practice called "satisficing"—that is, rather than looking for the answer that best addresses a question, they gravitate towards the first answer that will do. A physician might see a series of symptoms that fit the *DSM-5* description of PTSD and chalk those symptoms up to PTSD without also screening for TBI or lead. Satisficing serves the needs of the bureaucracy; it does not serve the needs of the individual veteran. We need a structure that incentivizes creative, holistic thinking about the health of veterans—one that takes into account a broad view of veterans' exposure histories to inform the processes of assessment, diagnosis, and recovery from start to finish. Historical anatomy, practiced by medical doctors. Again, the PACT Act is a hopeful starting point, but it is only a beginning.

Finally, we need to take steps to mitigate the exposures Marines and other service personnel face in the field in the first place. War has always been bad for people's health. Since the First World War, however, the technology of warfare has dramatically increased the scale and severity of war's violence. In that period, the violence of war has also changed in kind, introducing novel types of slow violence to war's landscapes in the form of heavy metals like lead, mercury, and arsenic; synthetic chemical fire retardants, pesticides, herbicides, and weapons; plastics; and depleted uranium—all of which have been made more bioavailable as they have been aerosolized or turned to dust by newly powerful explosives, or set on fire in massive burn pits on forward operating bases. Military landscapes, including battlefields and bases and barracks back home, are remarkably toxic places. Marine bodies moving within and between these landscapes absorb the toxicants of war in uneven and unpredictable ways. So too do the regular people who live in war zones like those in Iraq and Afghanistan.

The most obvious way to mitigate the exposures of modern warfare is to avoid the wars. But that is perhaps too pithy and pat an answer, and one that critical political realists and defense planners would feast upon as unfeasible idealism. So long as militarized landscapes like MCRD San Diego and other bases and training camps continue to exist as service personnel train for war, it also doesn't really solve the problem.

If Americans are going to have to train for and go to war, we need to do a better job monitoring their exposures to things like lead, mercury, pesticides, and traumatic exposures while they do so. To some extent this is already happening. Alex was never tested for lead, but an active-duty SEAL I spoke to for this project tells me that this has changed, at least for most special forces. SEALs are tested for lead frequently, especially during training, though my contact has never seen the results of those tests. Special Forces are a start, but ultimately they should be testing *everyone*— down to the company cook—and monitoring both the spaces they train and live in and the burden of toxicants in their blood frequently enough to identify short and long-term exposure risks. Impersonal PDHA forms are not enough. We need to do better. In the event that monitoring doesn't help mitigate exposure in the first place, better testing and monitoring will at least facilitate better holistic care assessments on the back end of a service member's career.

Beyond not going to war and actually testing our military for toxic things, mitigating exposures for both Marines and civilians also requires new forms of strategic thinking about warfare itself that take relationships and ecosystems seriously as important components of military analysis. To put that more directly: if we're going to go to war, we need top military planners to think about environments and exposures. We need to consider what it is going to be like to live in the place we are fighting not just during the first months of a conflict, but for two, five, ten years down the road, even if we're actively trying to avoid being there ourselves.

To Thomas E. Ricks, strategy is about who we are and what we are trying to accomplish.[1] Ideally, a strategy that accounts for ecosystems and exposures also privileges the kinds of human relationships that underwrite the infrastructure of civil society. Moreover, in creating a strategy that accounts for ecosystems and exposures, we need to take tactical decisions about toxicity and trade-offs between acute risk and long-term exposure risk out of the hands of Marines on the ground.

At its most basic, military strategy needs to account for the old saying, "Don't shit where you eat." That sentiment needs to guide our sense of who we are as a country when we send troops abroad and what we hope to accomplish while we are there.

We might start by not burning our trash.

ACKNOWLEDGMENTS

Writing books always involves racking up debts, and even the best books can do only partial justice to the many forms of support that nurture them. For this book, our debts our legion, both as individuals and as co-authors. I'll tip my hat to a few of my own and our collective debts first; Alex will have the last word.

First and foremost, I owe an immeasurable debt to my co-author Alex Lemons himself, without whom this book literally could not have happened. I have deeply appreciated your trust, patience, and forbearance over the past five years. The faith that you have placed in me to help tell your story is not something I take for granted. Thank you.

Reed College has provided tremendous support for this project from its earliest stages. The interest and unflinching encouragement we have received from faculty members and students in the Masters of Liberal Studies Program, the History Department, the Environmental Studies Program, the American Studies Program, and elsewhere at the college reflect the best traditions of the institution. Natalie Murphy provided valuable research assistance and offered even more valuable commentary on very early drafts of the manuscript. Alice Harra and Dennis Fernandes helped us navigate toward our editor Matt Weiland, who saw our vision for the book from the beginning and provided the steady critical hand to help us achieve it. Thanks, too, to our agent Howard Yoon, for helping us articulate that vision more clearly as the project took shape, and for making sure it landed in the right place back at Norton when it was ready. And to Kate Woodrow for the sound industry advice along the way. Michelle Nijhuis, Jess Thomson, Chris Koski, Allison Howe, Tina Pohlman, and a handful of Marines all read and generously provided useful feedback on some or all of the manuscript at various stages. Matt Noble, Pamela Rosenthal, Paul Sutter, Michael Reidy, Neil Maher, Cindy Ott, Bob Wilson, Bartow Elmore, Catherine McNeur, Lynne Gratz, Aaron Ramirez, Ethan McDonald, Joe Yalowitz, and countless other friends, colleagues, students, and Marines have helped us think through the thorny problems of military exposures informally at conferences, on chairlifts, over beers, and in classes over the last five years. The book remains imperfect because of the limitations of its authors; it is nevertheless far better for all of your help.

In all things, I am forever guided by loving, curious parents and flanked by two smart and talented sisters. I also couldn't ask for a better partner. Ann, you have put up with both me and this project for a long time, providing love, encouragement, and insightful feedback in just the right proportions and at just the right times. You and Gertie make the world go round.

Joshua P. Howe

I f you're doing anything right in a memoir, then the writing gets lonelier as the sentences pile up. No one else could bring these memories out of my head and onto the paper. So, I built these stories a day at a time through fear, confusion, and pain and kept going. But my discipline and tenacity were things I was taught before they became my own. My parents deserve most of the credit. Thank you for giving me a house mover and farmer work ethic. Dad, you were the first one to teach me how to write and that writing is nothing but bench presses. Mom, thanks for giving me a Swiss Army knife as a kid and sending me to your parent's homestead all those peaceful summers ago. We've been through enough.

I owe a lot more than 25-and-5 to my instructors and classmates in Scout Sniper Basic Course 3-04. When I crossed the finish line during Hell Week, Sergeant Slafsky told me to get my ass back to the barracks to clean up and rest. The first steps ended with my face crashing into the edge of Basilone Road. Dehydrated and sleepless, I barely remember the corpsman missing a vein three times before Slafsky grabbed the catheter and hit me on the first shot before I blacked out again. I woke up the next day in the schoolhouse, covered in a wool blanket looking at a sticky pool of blood and an empty IV bag. I knew I could get through anything after that.

My only writing instructor, Andrew Cohen at Portland Community College, read the first chapter I wrote in the spring of 2019 and told me to keep going and keep lifting.

Josh Howe, I don't know what to say. We knew this gamble was worth the dice roll. Thanks for your patience and consistency.

Ingrid, thank you for your friendship and love, babe. We know each other's stories. Let's make new ones.

Stay frosty,
Alex

NOTES

INTRODUCTION

1. Michelle Murphy, *Sick Building Syndrome and the Problem of Uncertainty: Environmental Politics, Technoscience, and Women Workers* (Durham, NC: Duke University Press, 2006). As an approach, "historical anatomy" also takes cues from Nancy Langston, Linda Nash, Gregg Mittman, Kate Brown, Harriett Washington, Christopher Sellers, Brett Walker, and others who have worked hard to demonstrate how simple epidemiological narratives often fail to account for social, economic, and environmental factors that help determine who gets exposed to toxicants, how sick they get, and what recourse they have when they do. See Gregg Mitman, Michelle Murphy, and Christopher Sellers, eds., *Landscapes of Exposure: Knowledge and Illness in Modern Environments*, Osiris, [2. Ser.] 19.2004 (Chicago: University of Chicago Press, 2004); Nancy Langston, *Toxic Bodies: Hormone Disruptors and the Legacy of DES* (New Haven, CT; London: Yale University Press, 2011); Linda Lorraine Nash, *Inescapable Ecologies: A History of Environment, Disease, and Knowledge* (Berkeley: University of California Press, 2006); Kate Brown, *Plutopia: Nuclear Families, Atomic Cities, and the Great Soviet and American Plutonium Disasters* (Oxford: Oxford University Press, 2015); Harriet A. Washington, *A Terrible Thing to Waste* (New York: Little, Brown Spark, 2020); Christopher Sellers, *Hazards of the Job: From Industrial Disease to Environmental Health Sciences* (Chapel Hill: University of North Carolina Press, 1999); Brett Walker, *Toxic Archipelago: A History of Industrial Disease in Japan* (Seattle: University of Washington Press, 2011).
2. Rob Nixon, *Slow Violence and the Environmentalism of the Poor* (Cambridge, MA: Harvard University Press, 2011), 2.

1: "WHAT THE FUCK, RECRUIT?"

1. Department of Defense, "Marine Corps by Gender, Race and Ethnicity," Personnel and Readiness (Office of Diversity Management and Equal Opportunity, 2017.

2. Jasenka V. Zbozinek et al., "Initial Assessment Study: Naval Training Center, Marine Corps Recruit Depot, and Fleet Anti-Submarine Warfare Training Center" (Stearns, Conrad, and Schmidt Consulting Engineers Inc., February 1986): 5-6–5.11.

3. Jerald F. Bailey, "CTO-0093: Community Relations Support at Naval Training Center (NTC) Submittal of Third Revision of Fact Sheet Text" (Bechtel, March 4, 1997): 2–4.

2: THE VIOLENCE OF EXPOSURE

1. Bradley Snow, "The Useful Metal: A Brief History of Lead," in Living with Lead: An Environmental History of Idaho's Couer D'Alenes, 1885–2011. Snow is conservative on the dates of early smelting compared to Noel H. Gale and Zofia Stos-Gale, "Lead and Silver in the Ancient Aegean," Scientific American 244, no. 6 (1981): 176–93. On the history of lead-acid batteries, see James Morton Turner, Charged: A History of Batteries and Lessons for a Clean Future (Seattle: University of Washington Press, 2022).

2. There is a bit of an antiquarian cottage industry of monocausal explanations of the fall of the Roman Empire, lead being only one of many. For example, see Hugo Delile, Janne Blichert-Toft, Jean-Philippe Goiran, Simon Keay, and Francis Albarède, "Lead in Ancient Rome's City Waters," Proceedings of the National Academy of Sciences 111:18 (April 21, 2014): 6594–6599.

3. David E. Guberman, "Lead," in U.S. Geological Survey Minerals Yearbook 2–14, USGS (November 2017).

4. "ACMT Recommends Against Use of Post-Chelator Challenge Urinary Metal Testing," Journal of Medical Toxicology 13, no. 4 (December 2017): 352–54. For a more sympathetic review of the debate about the validity of urine testing and "challenge testing" for heavy metals from the integrative medicine side, see Pizzorno, Joseph: "Is Challenge Testing Valid for Assessing Body Metal Burden?" Integrative Medicine 14, 4 (2015): 8–14.

5. Actually measuring the amount of lead in whole blood requires some creativity and skill in the laboratory. Among the main techniques for assessing BLL, most involve passing either light, heat, or electric current through a blood sample and looking for telltale signs of lead atoms. In the case of light or heat (spectroscopy), lead atoms in blood have to be atomized through heat, either by flame or electrothermal sources like a graphite furnace, in order to be measured. Anodic stripping voltammetry (ASV)—the electric option—measures current across a blood sample in order to assess free lead ions. The technique is cheaper and easier, and a portable ASV machine is now often used at the point of care for lead exposure, but the results

are sensitive to the presence of other elements, and require calibration. *Brief Guide to Analytical Methods for Measuring Lead in Blood, Second Edition* (Geneva: World Health Organization, 2020).

6. Fortunately, not every microgram of the 85,000 metric tons of lead per year in US munitions finds its way into human bodies, either as blunt projectiles or diffuse atoms. In fact, the BLL of the average American has been steadily declining since the 1970s, largely because of bans on lead in paint and gasoline. WHO, *Brief Guide, First Edition* (2011), 2.

7. If there is a hero in the story of childhood lead poisoning, it was a University of Pittsburgh pediatrician named Herb Needleman. Needleman used data from discarded baby teeth to establish a link between elevated bone lead levels and low IQ, as well as elevated lead and delinquent behavior in teenagers. His methods of collecting teeth also made it possible to map lead exposure geographically, revealing disproportionate lead exposures in predominantly poor minority neighborhoods in Philadelphia and elsewhere. See Herbert L. Needleman et al., "Bone Lead Levels and Delinquent Behavior," *JAMA* 275, no. 5 (February 7, 1996): 363–69; Carrie Arnold, "The Man Who Warned the World About Lead," PBS, May 31, 2017; Lydia Denworth, *Toxic Truth: A Scientist, a Doctor, and the Battle Over Lead* (Boston: Beacon Press, 2009)

8. National Research Council (US) and Bruce A. Fowler, eds., *Measuring Lead Exposure in Infants, Children, and Other Sensitive Populations* (Washington, DC: National Academy Press, 1993); Mark Payne et al., "Bone Lead Measurement," *Canadian Family Physician* 56, no. 11 (November 1, 2010): 1110–11.

9. "Substance Data Sheet for Occupational Exposure to Lead," Occupational Safety and Health Administration, 1910.1025 App. A. See also the comprehensive "Toxicological Profile for Lead," Agency for Toxic Substances and Disease Registry, US Department of Health and Human Services (August 2020).

10. Michael E. Barsan and Aubrey Miller, "Health Hazard Evaluation Report: HETA: 91-0346-2572, FBI Academy, Quantico, Virginia" (Quantico, VA: National Institute for Occupational Safety and Health, April 1996).

4: LEAD POISONING

1. Mark A. S. Laidlaw et al., "Lead Exposure at Firing Ranges—a *Review,*" *Environmental Health* 16, no. 1 (December 2017): 9.

2. Laidlaw et al. (2017), 2.

3. R. M. Semlali et al., "Modeling Lead Input and Output in Soils Using Lead Isotopic Geochemistry," *Environmental Science & Technology* 38, no. 5 (March 1, 2004): 1513–21.

4. As late as 2014, the Department of Defense was still using OSHA's most liberal BLL guidelines from 1978 (60 µg/dL) for military personnel. In 2018, DOD lowered the threshold for removing employees from work to 20 µg/dL, and in 2022 OSHA announced that it was considering a rule that would lower its BLL

thresholds to align more closely with CDC, NIOSH, DoD, and various state practices. "Advance Notice of Proposed Rule Making (ANPRM)-Blood Lead Level for Medical Removal," *Federal Register*, June 28, 2022. The 2013 NAS study is National Research Council, *Potential Health Risks to DoD Firing-Range Personnel from Recurrent Lead Exposure* (Washington, DC: National Academies Press, 2013). For the older DoD guidelines, see Desmond I. Bannon, Carol I. Tobias, and Alice K. Weber, "Provisional Blood Lead Guidelines for Occupational Monitoring of Lead Exposure in the DoD," Office of the Deputy Under Secretary of Defense, Installations and Environment, Environment, Safety, and Occupational Health (June 1, 2014), 4–5.

5. In Israel, the actionable level of airborne lead is 25 $\mu g/m^3$. Nili Greenberg et al., "Lead Exposure in Military Outdoor Firing Ranges," *Military Medicine* 181, no. 9 (September 2016): 1121.

6. Greenberg et al., 1121.

7. IDF trainees shot non-jacketed bullets. The FBI study I referred to earlier suggested that jacketed bullets—lead wrapped in other metal, often copper—help to mitigate some of the lead exposure risk at firing ranges. Barsan and Miller, 17.

8. It rose from 6.0 $\mu g/dL$ on the first day of training to 15 $\mu g/dL$ on day 15 of the two-week training course. On day 69 of the study—almost two months after the end of the training course—the mean BLL of cadets was still 9.0 $\mu g/dL$. R. K. Tripathi et al., "Overexposures to Lead at a Covered Outdoor Firing Range," *Journal of the American College of Toxicology* 8, no. 6 (November 1, 1989): 1189–95.

9. James D. Mancuso et al., "The Challenge of Controlling Lead and Silica Exposures from Firing Ranges in a Special Operations Force," *Military Medicine* 173, no. 2 (February 1, 2008): 182–86, cited in Laidlaw 2017. The study had 255 participants, and yielded a mean BLL of 13.9 $\mu g/dL$.

10. 70 percent of the participants measured between 25 and 39 $\mu g/dL$, with 20 percent clocking in from 40 to 59 and a full 6 percent registering more than 60 $\mu g/dL$ of lead. Kitty H. Gelberg and Ronald Depersis, "Lead Exposure among Target Shooters," *Archives of Environmental & Occupational Health* 64, no. 2 (2009): 115–20.

11. Patricia Kime, *New York Times Magazine*, April 3, 2019.

12. Louis S. Goodman, Alfred Gilman, and Laurence L. Brunton, eds., *Goodman & Gilman's Manual of Pharmacology and Therapeutics* (New York: McGraw-Hill Medical, 2008).

13. Regina A. Shih et al., "Cumulative Lead Dose and Cognitive Function in Adults: A Review of Studies That Measured Both Blood Lead and Bone Lead," *Environmental Health Perspectives* 115, no. 3 (March 2007): 483–92.

14. Ab Latif Wani, Anjum Ara, and Jawed Ahmad Usmani, "Lead Toxicity: A Review," *Interdisciplinary Toxicology* 8, no. 2 (June 2015): 55–64.

15. Wani, Ara, and Usmani, "Lead Toxicity," 60.

16. Daniel Coyle, *The Talent Code: Greatness Isn't Born: It's Grown, Here's How* (New York: Bantam Books, 2009)

17. Both of these things—tired muscles and reduced cognitive function—tend to

worsen in most adults with age, and it is telling that some researchers equate the cognitive effects of lead exposure to the cognitive effects of aging. R. A. Shih et al., "Environmental Lead Exposure and Cognitive Function in Community-Dwelling Older Adults," *Neurology* 67, no. 9 (November 1, 2006): 1556–62; Timothy V. P. Bliss and Sam F. Cooke, "Long-Term Potentiation and Long-Term Depression: A Clinical Perspective," *Clinics* 66, no. Suppl 1 (June 2011): 3–17.

5: "*GAS! GAS! GAS!*"

1. Carrie Johnson, Mary Beth Sheridan, and William Branigin, "Officials Say Scientist Was Solely Responsible for Anthrax *Attacks*," *Washing*ton Post, August 6, 2008.

6: CHEMICAL WEAPONS

1. For a compelling contextualization of the Gulf War and the later Iraq War in terms of United States involvement in military conflict in the Middle East more broadly, see Andrew J. Bacevich, *America's War for the Greater Middle East: A Military History* (New York: Random House, 2015).
2. W. Seth Carus, "Defining 'Weapons of Mass Destruction,'" *Center for the Study of Weapons of Mass Destruction, Occasional Paper No. 8* (Washington, DC: National Defense University Press, 2012).
3. Daniel Immerwahr, *How to Hide an Empire: A History of the Greater United States*, 1st ed. (New York: Farrar, Straus and Giroux, 2019).
4. Immerwahr; Dietrich Stoltzenberg, *Fritz Haber: Chemist, Nobel Laureate, German, Jew* (Philadelphia: Chemical Heritage Press, 2004).
5. L. Karalliedde et al., "Possible Immediate and Long-Term Health Effects Following Exposure to Chemical Warfare Agents," *Public Health* 114, no. 4 (July 2000): 238–48.
6. On Schrader and his work for the German War Ministry at IG Farben, see Jonathan Tucker, *War of Nerves: Chemical Warfare from World War I to Al-Qaeda* (New York: Random House, 2006), 24–41.
7. Tucker, *War of Nerves*, 158–89. See also Jacob Hamblin, "Part One: Pathways of Nature," in *Arming Mother Nature: The Birth of Catastrophic Environmentalism* (Oxford: Oxford University Press, 2013). (Hereafter "Duelfer Report.")
8. United States: Central Intelligence Agency, Charles Duelfer, and United States: Central Intelligence Agency, "Comprehensive Report of the Special Advisor to the DCI on Iraq's WMD, with Addendums (Duelfer Report)" (Central Intelligence Agency, April 25, 2005).
9. US Congress, Senate, Committee on Armed Services, *Efforts to Determine the Status of Iraqi Weapons of Mass Destruction and Related Programs*," 108th Congress, 2nd Session, January 28, 2004: 7.
10. John Schwarz, "Twelve Years Later, The Media Still Can't Get Iraq WMD Story Right," *The Intercept*, April 10, 2015. The Deulfer Report equivocates on who

exactly within the regime had what information on WMDs and when, but confirms that there was uncertainty about the weapons and their whereabouts among top Iraqi officials up to the beginning of the invasion. Deulfer Report, 65.

7: "ECCENTRIC"

1. US Department of Veterans Affairs Administration Veterans Health, "Mefloquine (Lariam®)—Public Health," General Information.

8: GULF WAR REDUX

1. Carolyn E. Fulco, Catharyn T. Liverman, and Harold C. Sox, eds., "Illnesses in Gulf War Veterans," in Depleted Uranium, Sarin, Pyridostigimine Bromide, Vaccines, vol. 1, Gulf War and Health (Washington, DC: National Academies Press, 2000).
2. See Seymour M. Hersh, Against All Enemies: The Gulf War Syndrome: The War Between America's Ailing Veterans and Their Government (New York: Library of Contemporary Thought, 1998).
3. Senator Riegle, speaking on Arming Iraq: The Export of Biological Materials and the Health of our Gulf War Veterans, 103rd Congress, 2nd Session, Congressional Record 140 (February 9, 1994): 1196.
4. Donald W. Riegle Jr. and Alfonse M. D'Amato, "U.S. Chemical and Biological Warfare-Related Dual Use Exports to Iraq and Their Possible Impact on the Health Consequences of the Gulf War: A Report of Chairman Donald W. Riegle, Jr. and Ranking Member Alfonse M. D'Amato of the Committee on Banking, Housing and Urban Affairs with Respect to Export Administration," Senate Report (103rd Congress, 2nd Session, May 25, 1994), 132.
5. Research Advisory Committee on Gulf War Veterans' Illnesses, Gulf War Illness and the Health of Gulf War Veterans: Scientific Findings and Recommendations (Washington, DC: US Government Printing Office, November 2008), 134. Hereafter RAC 2008.
6. Khamisiya is discussed throughout RAC 2008, appearing on forty-four different pages. The clearest account of the DoD's response to exposure concern comes on pp. 53 and 135. See also US Congress, Senate, Committee on Veteran's Affairs, Report of the Special Investigation Unit on Gulf War Illnesses, 105th Congress, 1998, S. PRT. 105–39, Part 1, pp. 21–32; US Congress, House, Committee on Government Reform and Oversight, Gulf War Veterans' Illnesses: VA, DoD Continue to Resist Strong Evidence Linking Toxic Causes to Chronic Health Effects (Second Report), 105th Congress, 1st Session, November 7, 1997. HR 105–38.
7. National Research Council, "History of the Edgewood Testing Program," in Possible Long-Term Health Effects of Short-Term Exposure to Chemical Agents: Volume 1 (Washington, DC: National Academies Press, 1982).
8. Carolyn E. Fulco, Catharyn T. Liverman, and Harold C. Sox, "Research

Recommendations," in *Depleted Uranium, Sarin, Pyridostigmine Bromide, Vaccines, Volume 1, GulfWar and Health* (Washington, DC: National Academies Press, 2000).

9. RAC 2008, 178.

10. Fulco, Liverman, and Sox, "Illnesses in Gulf War Veterans."

11. For a recent confirmation, see Robert W. Haley et al., "Evaluation of a Gene–Environment Interaction of PON1 and Low-Level Nerve Agent Exposure with Gulf War Illness: A Prevalence Case–Control Study Drawn from the U.S. Military Health Survey's National Population Sample," *Environmental Health Perspectives* 130, no. 5 (May 2022): 057001.

12. RAC 2008, 132.

13. RAC 2008, 180.

14. World Health Organization Model List of Essential Medicines, 23rd List (Geneva: World Health Organization, 2023), 45.

15. RAC 2008, 172.

16. RAC 2008, 173; see also RAC footnote 948.

17. James M. Madsen, Charles G. Hurst, Roger MacIntosh, and James A. Romano, Jr., *Clinical Considerations in the Use of Pyridostigmine Bromide as Pretreatment for Nerve-agent Exposure.* (Aberdeen Proving Ground, MD: US Army Medical Research Institute of Chemical Defense; January 2003), USAMRICD-SP-03-01, p. 32.

9: *"SPEED, SPEED, SPEED"*

1. Thomas E. Ricks, *Fiasco: The American Military Adventure in Iraq* (New York: Penguin Books, 2007), 127.

2. Bing West and Ray L. Smith, *The March Up: Taking Baghdad with 1st Marine Division* (New York: Bantam, 2003), 5.

10: HUGGING THE DUST

1. Samuel Noah Kramer, *The Sumerians: Their History, Culture, and Character* (Chicago: University of Chicago Press, 1963), 221.

2. Moutaz A. Al-Dabbas, Mohammed Ayad Abbas, and Raad M. Al-Khafaji, "Dust Storms Loads Analyses—Iraq," *Arabian Journal of Geosciences* 5, no. 1 (January 2012): 121–31.

3. Benjamin Bowe et al., "The 2016 Global and National Burden of Diabetes Mellitus Attributable to PM2.5 Air Pollution," *Lancet Planetary Health* 2, no. 7 (July 1, 2018): 301–12.

4. Ole Raaschou-Nielsen et al., "Air Pollution and Lung Cancer Incidence in 17 European Cohorts: Prospective Analyses from the European Study of Cohorts for Air Pollution Effects (ESCAPE)," *Lancet Oncology* 14, no. 9 (August 2013): 813–22.

5. "Iraq—PM2.5 Air Pollution, Mean Annual Exposure (Micrograms per Cubic Meter)," *Index Mundi*. Data compiled from Institute for Health Metrics and

Evaluation (IHME) *Global Burden of Disease Study*, 2017. See also Aaron van Donkelaar et al., "Global Estimates of Fine Particulate Matter Using a Combined Geophysical-Statistical Method with Information from Satellites, Models, and Monitors," *Environmental Science & Technology* 50, no. 7 (April 5, 2016): 3762–72.

6. Sheila F. Castañeda et al., "Cohort Profile Update: The US Millennium Cohort Study—Evaluating the Impact of Military Experiences on Service Members and Veteran Health," *International Journal of Epidemiology* 52, no. 4 (August 1, 2023): 222–31. See also Sheila Castañeda, et al., "Millennium Cohort Study: 20 Years of Research," Naval Health Research Center, San Diego, CA, 2021.

7. Anthony M. Szema et al., "Respiratory Symptoms Necessitating Spirometry among Soldiers with Iraq/Afghanistan War Lung Injury," *Journal of Occupational and Environmental Medicine* 53, no. 9 (September 2011): 961–65.

8. RAC 2008, 75. For more on the human and environmental impacts of the Kuwaiti oil fires, see Peter Hobbes and Lawrence Radke, "Airborne Studies of Smoke from the Kuwait Oil Fires," *Science* 256, no 5059 (May 1992): 987–91.

9. David Evans, "Burning Oil Wells Could Darken U.S. Skies," *Wilmington Morning Star*, January 21, 1991. Would-be Nobel Prize–winning chemist Paul Crutzen even ran model calculations to create a rough estimate of the cooling the fires might produce, though he hedged considerably in talking about them. Peter Aldhous, "Oil-Well Climate Catastrophe?" *Nature* 349, no. 6305 (January 1, 1991): 96–96.

10. Anthony M. Szema et al., "Iraq Dust Is Respirable, Sharp, and Metal-Laden and Induces Lung Inflammation with Fibrosis in Mice via IL-2 Upregulation and Depletion of Regulatory T Cells," *Journal of Occupational and Environmental Medicine* 56, no. 3 (March 2014): 243–51.

11. G. Fernandes et al., "Impact of Military JP-8 Fuel on Heavy-Duty Diesel Engine Performance and Emissions," *Proceedings of the Institution of Mechanical Engineers, Part D. Journal of Automobile Engineering* 221, no. 8 (August 1, 2007): 957–70; Michael Smith et al., "Effect of High Sulfur Military JP-8 Fuel on Heavy Duty Diesel Engine Emissions and EGR Cooler Condensate" (ASME 2010 Internal Combustion Engine Division Fall Technical Conference, American Society of Mechanical Engineers Digital Collection, 2011), 99–110.

12. Omar Al-Dewachi, *Ungovernable Life: Mandatory Medicine and Statecraft in Iraq* (Stanford, CA: Stanford University Press, 2017), 24.

13. Tara Rava Zolnikov, "The Maladies of Water and War: Addressing Poor Water Quality in Iraq," *American Journal of Public Health* 103, no. 6 (June 2013): 980–87.

14. Moutaz A. Al-Dabbas, Mohammed Ayad Abbas, and Raad M. Al-Khafaji, "Dust Storms Loads Analyses—Iraq," *Arabian Journal of Geosciences* 5, no. 1 (January 2012): 2.

15. M. Savabieasfahani et al., "Prenatal Metal Exposure in the Middle East: Imprint of War in Deciduous Teeth of Children," *Environmental Monitoring and Assessment* 188, no. 9 (September 2016): 505; M. Savabieasfahani et al., "Elevated Titanium

Levels in Iraqi Children with Neurodevelopmental Disorders Echo Findings in Occupation Soldiers," *Environmental Monitoring and Assessment* 187, no. 1 (January 2015): 4127.

16. Murtaza Hussain, "Iraqi Children Born Near U.S. Military Base Show Elevated Rates of 'Serious Congenital Deformities,' Study Finds," *The Intercept*, November 25, 2019. M. Al-Sabbak et al., "Metal Contamination and the Epidemic of Congenital Birth Defects in Iraqi Cities," *Bulletin of Environmental Contamination and Toxicology* 89, no. 5 (November 2012): 937–44. There was originally some controversy over a 2013 study conducted by the WHO and the Iraqi Ministry of Health that cast doubt on prevalence of congenital birth defects in Iraq, but subsequent studies seem to have ignored the WHO report. See Paul C. Webster, "Questions Raised over Iraq Congenital Birth Defects Study," *The Lancet* 382, no. 9899 (October 5, 2013): 1165–66; Tariq S. Al-Hadithi et al., "Birth Defects in Iraq and the Plausibility of Environmental Exposure: A Review," *Conflict and Health* 6 (July 28, 2012): 3; Ahmed Majeed Al-Shammari, "Environmental Pollutions Associated to Conflicts in Iraq and Related Health Problems," *Reviews on Environmental Health* 31, no. 2 (June 1, 2016): 245–50; Mozhgan Savabieasfahani, "Iraqi Birth Defects and the WHO Report," *Class, Race and Corporate Power* 1, no. 1 (2013): 1–3.

17. D. P. Arfsten, K. R. Still, and G. D. Ritchie, "A Review of the Effects of Uranium and Depleted Uranium Exposure on Reproduction and Fetal Development," *Toxicology and Industrial Health* 17, no. 5–10 (June 1, 2001): 180–91.

18. "Q's and A's—New Information Regarding Birth Defects," *Gulf War Review: Information for Veterans Who Served in Desert Storm*, 12:1 (November 2003): 10.

19. Ashraf M. A. Hussain and Riyadh K. Lafta, "Cancer Trends in Iraq 2000–2016," *Oman Medical Journal* 36, no. 1 (January 31, 2021): 219.

20. Mona Chalabi, "Iraq War Leukemia Rates Worse than after Hiroshima Bombing," *The Guardian*, April 3, 2023. See also Chris Busby, Malak Hamdan, and Entesar Ariabi, "Cancer, Infant Mortality and Birth Sex-Ratio in Fallujah, Iraq 2005–2009," *International Journal of Environmental Research and Public Health* 7, no. 7 (July 2010): 2828–37; Amy Hagopian et al., "Trends in Childhood Leukemia in Basrah, Iraq, 1993–2007," *American Journal of Public Health* 100, no. 6 (June 2010): 1081–87.

21. Ross Caputi, "The Victims of Fallujah's Health Crisis Are Stifled by Western Science," *The Guardian*, October 25, 2012.

11: "YOU JUST DIDN'T THINK ABOUT ANYTHING YOU WERE DOING"

1. Scott A. Thornton et al., "Gastroenteritis in US Marines during Operation Iraqi Freedom," *Clinical Infectious Diseases* 40, no. 4 (February 15, 2005): 519–25.

2. "Burning Trash and Factories Belching Smoke Choke Iraqis," *Voice of America*, June 5, 2019.

12: BURN PITS

3. "Dumpster *fire*," *Merriam-Webster's Collegiate* Dictionary, Merriam-Webster.

1. Jennifer Percy, "The Things They Burned," *The New Republic*, November 22, 2016.

2. *Long-Term Health Consequences of Exposure to Burn Pits in Iraq and Afghanistan* (Washington, DC: National Academies Press, 2011), 5.

3. John Esterbrook, "Rumsfeld: It Would Be A Short War," CBS News, November 13, 2002.

4. *Long-Term Health Consequences of Exposure to Burn Pits in Iraq and Afghanistan*.

5. Jeremy A. MacMahon, Donald A. Bruun, and Pamela Lein, "Military Burn Pits: A Toxic Legacy of War," *Open Access Government*, January 4, 2023; Meghann Myers, "Why DoD Is Still Using Burn Pits, Even While Now Acknowledging Their Danger," *Military Times*, July 12, 2019; Department of Defense, *Open Burn Pit Report to Congress*, April 2019.

6. Coalition Provisional Authority, *Coalition Provisional Authority Order Number 17: Status of the Coalition, Foreign Liaison Missions, Their Personnel and Contractors (revised)* (Coalition Provisional Authority, 2004); see also Michael Hirsh, "Blackwater and the Bush Legacy," *Newsweek*, October 1, 2007.

7. Jane Corbin, "BBC Uncovers Lost Iraq Billions," BBC News, June 10, 2008.

8. James Risen, "Army Overseer Tells of Ouster Over KBR Stir," *New York Times*, June 17, 2008; "Top Iraq Contractor Skirts U.S. Taxes Offshore: Shell Companies in Cayman Islands Allow KBR to avoid Medicare, Social Security deductions," *Boston Globe*, March 6, 2008; Office of Public Affairs, US Department of Justice, "Kellogg Brown & Root LLC Pleads Guilty to Foreign Bribery Charges and Agrees to Pay $402 Million Criminal Fine," Press Release, February 11, 2009; Statement of Rep. Henry A. Waxman, "Contracting Abuses in Iraq," House Committee on Government Reform, October 15, 2003; "Investigator: Soldier's electrocution 'negligent homicide,'" CNN, January 22, 2009; *Jones et al v. Halliburton*, US District Court for the Eastern District of Texas, May 16, 2007, case no 1:2007cv00295; "Nepalese Sue U.S. Company over Iraq," BBC News, August 28, 2008. More recently, KBR paid out more than $13 million for a settlement to resolve a case involving kickbacks and false claims involving contracts in Iraq and Kuwait. Office of Public Affairs, US Department of Justice, "KBR Defendants Agree to Settle Kickback and False Claims Allegations," Press Release, June 14, 2022.

9. The class action suit ultimately consolidated hundreds of individual claims and more than sixty distinct lawsuits against KBR involving burn pits, and wound its way through the court system for a decade before the US Supreme Court decided not to hear it in 2019. The original case was filed in the District of Maryland, and eventually went through the Fourth District Court on its way to the Supreme Court. See *In re KBR, Inc., Burn Pit Litig.*, 893 F.3d 241 (4th Cir. 2018), *cert. denied* 139 S. Ct. 916 (2019). See also Lawrence Quil, "Veterans Claiming Illness From Burn Pits Lose Court Fight," *Morning Edition*, National Public Radio, January 16,

2019; Todd South, "Supreme Court Rejects Appeal from Veterans in Burn Pit Lawsuit against KBR, Halliburton," *Military Times,* January 14, 2019.

10. Quil, "Veterans Claiming Illness From Burn Pits Lose Court Fight."

11. See Deborah D. Avant and Renée de Nevers, "Military Contractors & the American Way of War," *Daedalus* 140, no. 3 (July 1, 2011): 88–99.

12. David N. Pellow, *Resisting Global Toxics: Transnational Movements for Environmental Justice,* Urban and Industrial Environments (Cambridge, MA: MIT Press, 2007).

13. Agency for Toxic Substances and Disease Registry (ATSDR), "Toxicological Profile for Chlorinated Dibenzo-*p*-Dioxins," US Department of Health and Human Services (Atlanta, GA, 1998).

14. *Long-Term Health Consequences of Exposure to Burn Pits in Iraq and Afghanistan,* 5.

15. See Edwin A. Martini, *Agent Orange: History, Science, and the Politics of Uncertainty* (Amherst: University of Massachusetts Press, 2012).

16. David E. Mosher et al., "Green Warriors: Army Environmental Considerations for Contingency Operations from Planning Through Post-Conflict" (Santa Monica, CA: RAND Corporation, 2008).

17. For more on what the VA does well and the neoliberal attack on the VA, see Suzanne Gordon, *The Battle for Veterans' Healthcare: Dispatches from the Frontlines of Policy Making and Patient Care* (Ithaca, NY: Cornell Publishing, 2017).

18. For example, see box 7-1 on the limitations and uncertainties of burn pit information in *Long-Term Health Consequences of Exposure to Burn Pits in Iraq and Afghanistan,* 113.

14: A WAR OF NERVES

19. Allan *Horwitz, PTSD: A Short* History (Baltimore: Johns Hopkins University Press, 2018).

1. Ben Shephard, *A War of Nerves: Soldiers and Psychiatrists in the Twentieth Century* (London: Jonathan Cape, 2000); Jonathan B. Tucker, *War of Nerves: Chemical Warfare from World War I to Al-Qaeda* (New York: Random House, 2006).

2. For detailed statistics on both wars, see Michael Codfelter, *Warfare and Armed Conflicts: A Statistical Encyclopedia of Casualty and Other Figures, 1492–2015 (Fourth Edition)* (Jefferson, NC: McFarland and Co., 2017), 387–534.

3. See Claire Langhamer, Lucy Noakes, and Claudia Siebrecht, *Total War: An Emotional History* (Cambridge: Oxford University Press, 2020).

4. See Edmund Russell, *War and Nature: Fighting Humans and Insects with Chemicals from World War I to Silent Spring,* Studies in Environment and History (New York: Cambridge University Press, 2001).

5. Eef Meerschman et al., "Geostatistical Assessment of the Impact of World War I on the Spatial Occurrence of Soil Heavy Metals," *AMBIO* 40, no. 4 (June 2011): 417–24.

6. Great Britain and War Office, *Statistics of the Military Effort of the British Empire*

during the Great War 1914 Jefferson, NC1920, 2015, 479; Raviel Netz, *Barbed Wire: An Ecology of Modernity* (Middletown, CT: Wesleyan University Press, 2004), 108.

7. Greg Allwood, "What Were the Actual Odds of Dying in WWI?" *Forces.net*, March 4, 2020.

8. See Meerschman et al., "Geostatistical Assessment"; M. Van Meirvenne et al., "Could Shelling in the First World War Have Increased Copper Concentrations in the Soil around Ypres?," *European Journal of Soil Science* 59, no. 2 (April 2008): 372–79; T. Bausinger and J. Preuß, "Environmental Remnants of the First World War: Soil Contamination of a Burning Ground for Arsenical Ammunition," *Bulletin of Environmental Contamination and Toxicology* 74, no. 6 (June 2005): 1045–53.

9. H. Cushing, *The Life of Sir William Osler* (Oxford, 1925), 2, 484, as quoted in Shephard, *War of Nerves*, 2.

10. Shephard, *War of Nerves*, 44.

11. Ben Shephard, "Risk Factors and PTSD: A Historian's Perspective," in *Posttraumatic Stress Disorder*, ed. Gerald M. Rosen (Chichester, UK: John Wiley & Sons Ltd, 2004), 42.

15: "FIRST CIV DIV"

12. Siegfried Sasson, "Repression of War Experi*ence," in Counter-Attack, and O*ther Poems (New York: E.P. Dutton, 1918).

16: BOTH/AND

1. For a concise history of PTSD, see Allan V. *Horwitz, PTSD: A Sho*rt History, Johns Hopkins Biographies of Disease (Baltimore: Johns Hopkins University Press, 2018); See also Ben Shephard, "From Post-Vietnam Syndrome to Post-Traumatic Stress Dis*order, in A War of Nerves: Soldiers and Psychiatrists in the Twentie*th Century (London: Jonathan Cape, 2000), 355–68.

2. American Psychiatric Association, *Diagnostic and Statistical Manual of Mental Disorders DSM-III.* (Washington, DC: American Psychiatric Association, 1980), 238.

3. Richard McNally, "Conceptual Problems with the DSM-IV Criteria for Posttraumatic Stress Disorder, in Gerald Rosen, ed., *Posttraumatic Stress Disorder: Issues and Controversies* (Hoboken, NJ: J. Wiley, 2004), 1 pg. 14; American Psychiatric Association, *Diagnostic and Statistical Manual of Mental Disorders: DSM-IV* (Washington, DC: American Psychiatric Association, 1994).

4. Carol S. North et al., "The Evolution of PTSD Criteria across Editions of DSM," *Annals of Clinical Psychiatry: Official Journal of the American Academy of Clinical Psychiatrists* 28, no. 3 (August 2016): 197–208.

5. Naomi Breslau et al., "Trauma Exposure and Posttraumatic Stress Disorder: A Study of Youths in Urban America," *Journal of Urban Health: Bulletin of the New York Academy of Medicine* 81, no. 4 (December 2004): 530–44.

6. Marilyn L. Bowman and Rachel Yehuda, "Risk Factors and the Adversity-Stress

Model," in *Posttraumatic Stress Disorder*, ed. Gerald M. Rosen (Chichester, UK: John Wiley & Sons Ltd, 2004), 16.

7. American Psychiatric Association, *Diagnostic and Statistical Manual of Mental Disorders: DSM-5*, Fifth Edition (Washington, DC: American Psychiatric Association, 2013), 272.

8. Bookwalter et al., "Posttraumatic Stress Disorder and Risk of Selected Autoimmune Disease among Military Personnel," *BMC Psychiatry* 20:23 (2020).

9. Geir Bjørklund et al., "Metals, Autoimmunity, and Neuroendocrinology: Is There a Connection?," *Environmental Research* 187 (August 2020).

10. See Allan Young, "When Traumatic Memory Was a Problem: On the Historical Antecedents of PTSD," in Rosen (ed.), *Posttraumatic Stress Disorder*, 139.

11. Linda Nash provides useful ideas for thinking about the nature of toxicity and how we measure it in "Purity and Danger: Historical Reflections of the Regulation of Environmental Pollutants," *Environmental History* 13: 4 (October 2008): 651–58. See also Nash, "The Fruits of Ill-Health: Pesticides and Workers' Bodies in Post-World War II California," *Osiris*, Second Series, Landscapes of Exposure: Knowledge and Illness in Modern Environments, 19 (2004): 203–19.

12. Ian Hacking, "Madness: Biological or Constructed," in *The Social Construction of What?* (Cambridge, MA: Harvard University Press, 1999); Young, "When Traumatic Memory Was a Problem," 141.

13. Brooke A. Bartlett and Karen S. Mitchell, "Eating Disorders in Military and Veteran Men and Women: A Systematic Review," *International Journal of Eating Disorders* 48, no. 8 (December 2015): 1057–69.

14. Bartlett and Mitchell, "Eating Disorders," 1065–66.

15. The VA combines incidents of harassment and assault into the category of "Military Sexual Trauma," and notes that one in three female veterans screened by VA medical providers reported some form of MST. The number was one in fifty for men. US Department of Veterans Affairs, "Military Sexual Trauma Factsheet," May 2021.

16. Kimberly A. Arditte Hall et al., "Military-Related Trauma Is Associated with Eating Disorder Symptoms in Male Veterans," *International Journal of Eating Disorders* 50, no. 11 (November 2017): 1328–31.

17: *"HELMETS ARE EVERYTHING"*

1. Terri Tanielian and Lisa H. *Jaycox, Invisible Wounds of War: Psychological and Cognitive Injuries, Their Consequences, and Services to Assist* Recovery (Rand Corporation, 2008), 50, 52–53, 126, and 305; Bauman an*d Rasor, Shattered Minds: How the Pentagon Fails Our Troops with Faulty Helmets* (Lincoln, NB: Potomac Books, 2019), 236–43.

2. Bauman and Rasor, 51–52 and 54–55.

3. Bauman and Rasor, 54–56; Elizabeth Sandel, *Shaken Brain: The Science, Care, and Treatment of Concussion* (Cambridge, MA: Harvard University Press, 2020), 16–17. Steven P Broglio, et al., "The Biochemical Properties of Concussions in High

School Football," *Medicine Science Sports Exercise* 42.11 (2010): 2. It's easier to optimize for a fall than it is for an IED blast, but helmet researchers use essentially the same method for both. The process involves dropping an inverted helmet from three meters onto a hemispherical anvil, creating a known initial g-force. Sensors inside the helmet measure the effective g-forces inside the helmet on impact. It sounds counterintuitive, but when a helmet absorbs and tolerates more g-forces when striking the anvil, it means those forces are going into the brain and causing more damage. The g-force ratings of helmets reflect the leftover g-forces that get translated to the sensors. Pickled brains in glass jars say that lower is better. The stock MICH had a rating of 150 g. Still enough to cause a concussion, but not bad if you consider that we're talking about explosions and projectiles. Special Operations confirmed the benefits of the MICH two years into the Afghanistan adventure: their shooters reported few brain injuries in the MICH versus ten per day among Marines in the wretched PASGT.

4. Marine Corps, "Marine Corps Helmets, MICH (TC-2000), Lightweight Helmet (LWH), PASGT," Natick. Soldier Center, Natick MA 01760, August 1, 2003; US Congress, House Committee on Armed Services, *H.A.S.C. No. 109-122: Update on the Use of Combat Helmets, Vehicle Armor, and Body Armor by Ground Forces in Operation Iraqi Freedom and Operation Enduring Freedom*, 109 Congress, Second Session, June 15, 2006. Not every Marine received the LWH until deep into 2004. It weighed less and had greater ballistic impact than the PASGT. In designing it, the Corps ignored comfort, visibility, and non-ballistic impact despite their own 2003 study showing the superiority of MICH with padding suspension. The LWH with stock padding made it to 158 g on the anvil in a lab. You could replace the pads and buy your own Ballistic Liner and Suspension System (BLSS) from Oregon Aero. The pads were key. Completely unbeknownst to any of us, they even reduced blunt force impact to 79 g in the old PASGT.

5. "Army Considers Using German-Type Helmet," *New York Times*, April 20, 1941; "Shell Removes General's Star," *New York Times*, November 22, 1944; Charles W. Houff and Joseph P. Delaney, *Historical Documentation of the Infantry Helmet— Research and Development*, US Army, Human Engineering Laboratory, Aberdeen Proving Ground, February 1973, 5–7, 15–16, 26, and 36–37.

6. Bauman and Rasor, 98. Bob Meaders, "Statement Before the Armed Services Committee, Subcommittee on Tcatical Air and Land Forces Concerning the Use of Combat Helments, Vehicle Armor, and Body Armor by Ground Forces in OIF and OEF," *Update on the Use of Combat Helmets*, June 15, 2006, 7.

18: THE TOXIC TRIANGLE OF WARFARE

1. US Congressional Budget *Office, The Veterans Health Administration's Treatment of PTSD and Traumatic Brain Injury Among Recent Combat Veterans* (February 2012), viii.

2. Kate A. Yurgil et al., "Association Between Traumatic Brain Injury and Risk of

Posttraumatic Stress Disorder in Active-Duty Marines," *JAMA Psychiatry* 71, no. 2 (February 1, 2014): 149.

3. Jasmeet P. Hayes, "PTSD and TBI Comorbidity," *PTSD Research Quarterly* 30, no. 2 (2019): 1–4.

4. Daniel E. Glenn et al., "Fear Learning Alterations after Traumatic Brain Injury and Their Role in Development of Posttraumatic Stress Symptoms," *Depression and Anxiety* 34, no. 8 (August 2017): 723–33, as cited in Hayes, 2.

5. Gray Vargas et al., "Predictors and Prevalence of Postconcussion Depression Symptoms in Collegiate Athletes," *Journal of Athletic Training* 50, no. 3 (March 2015): 250–55.

6. Stacy Bare, "The Truth About 22 Veteran Suicides A Day—Task & Purpose," *Task and Purpose*, June 2, 2015; Hayes, "PTSD and TBI Comorbidity," 1, 3; Jennifer R. Fonda et al., "Traumatic Brain Injury and Attempted Suicide Among Veterans of the Wars in Iraq and Afghanistan," *American Journal of Epidemiology* 186, no. 2 (July 15, 2017): 220–26.

7. Bessel van der Kolk, *The Body Keeps the Score: Brain, Mind, and Body in the Healing of Trauma* (New York: Penguin Books, 2015); Judith Herman, *Trauma and Recovery: The Aftermath of Violence—From Domestic Abuse to Political Terror* (New York: Basic Books, 1997).

8. Lindsey Philips, "Untangling Trauma and Grief after Loss," *Counseling Today*, May 4, 2021. See also A. Bifulco, "Loss Trauma," in *Encyclopedia of Stress (Second Edition)*, ed. George Fink (New York: Academic Press, 2007), 612–15.

19: "YOU'RE PROBABLY OKAY"

1. Sharon Baughman Shively, et al., "Characterization of Interface Astroglial Scarring in the Human Brain After Blast Exposure: A Post-Mortem Case *Series*," *Lancet Neurology* 15 (2016): 3, 4–5, and 7–8; Bennet Omalu, "Chronic Traumatic Encephalopathy in an Iraqi War Veteran with Posttraumatic Stress Disorder Who Committed *Suicide*," *Neurosurgical Focus*, vol. 31 (November 2011): 2–5; "Army Takes New Approach on Troops' Brain *Injuries*," *Dallas Morning News*, July 18, 2011; Helene Cooper and Eric Schmitt, "Trump Dismisses Troops' Possible Brain Injuries as 'Head*aches*,'" *New York Times*, January 29, 2020.

21: HEALERS

2. Michael J. Kosnett, "The Role of Chelation in the Treatment of Arsenic and Mercury Poisoning," *Journal of Medical Toxicology* 9 (2013): 348.

1. Jane M Hightower, *Diagnosis: Mercury: Money, Politics, and Poison* (Washington, DC: Island Press, 2011), 139.

2. Hightower, *Diagnosis Mercury*, 141.

3. Very few recent studies of Tigris River mercury loads exist, and none were conducted during the war. Reyam Ajmi, "Investigating Mercury Existence in Some

Stations in Tigris River in Iraq," *Journal of Environmental Science and Engineering A* 2 (April 20, 2013), 6. A more general review of global environmental mercury processes is Daniel Obrist et al., "A Review of Global Environmental Mercury Processes in Response to Human and Natural Perturbations: Changes of Emissions, Climate, and Land Use," *Ambio* 47, no. 2 (March 2018): 116–40.

4. T. W. Clarkson, L. Magos, C. Cox, M. R. Greenwood, L. Amin-Zaki, M. A. Majeed, and S. F. Al-Damluji, "Tests of Efficacy of Antidotes for Removal of Methylmercury in Human Poisoning during the Iraq Outbreak," *Journal of Pharmacology and Experimental Therapeutics* 218:1 (1981): 74–83. See also Hightower, *Diagnosis Mercury*, 144–45.

5. Kosnett, "The Role of Chelation," 352.

6. "ACMT Recommends Against Use of Post-Chelator Challenge Urinary Metal Testing," *Journal of Medical Toxicology* 13, no. 4 (December 2017): 352–54

7. Mark Weatherall, "Making Medicine Scientific: Empiricism, Rationality, and Quackery in Mid-Victorian Britain," *Social History of Medicine* 9, no. 2 (August 1, 1996): 175–94, 182. See also James C. Whorton, *Nature Cures: The History of Alternative Medicine in America* (Oxford: Oxford University Press, 2002), 8, 52.

EPILOGUE

8. Thomas E. Ricks, *Fiasco: The American Military Adventure in Iraq* (New York: Penguin Books, 2007), 127.

INDEX